LIBERAL PROTECTIONISM

STUDIES IN INTERNATIONAL POLITICAL ECONOMY

Edited by Stephen D. Krasner
Department of Political Science
Stanford University

Albert O. Hirschman, *National Power and the Structure of Foreign Trade*

Robert A. Pastor, *Congress and the Politics of U.S. Foreign Economic Policy 1929-1976*

Oran R. Young, *Natural Resources and the State: The Political Economy of Resource Management*

Oran R. Young, *Resource Regimes: Natural Resources and Social Institutions*

Stephen J. Kobrin, *Managing Political Risk Assessment: Strategic Response to Environmental Change*

Charles Lipson, *Standing Guard: Protecting Foreign Capital in the Nineteenth and Twentieth Centuries*

Stephen D. Krasner, *Structural Conflict: The Third World Against Global Liberalism*

Vinod K. Aggarwal, *Liberal Protectionism: The International Politics of Organized Textile Trade*

LIBERAL PROTECTIONISM

The International Politics of
Organized Textile Trade

VINOD K. AGGARWAL

UNIVERSITY OF CALIFORNIA PRESS
Berkeley   Los Angeles   London

University of California Press
Berkeley and Los Angeles, California

University of California Press, Ltd.
London, England

Copyright © 1985 by The Regents of the University of California

Library of Congress Cataloging in Publication Data

Aggarwal, Vinod K.
  Liberal protectionism.

  (Studies in international political economy)
  Bibliography, p.
  Includes index.
  1. Textile industry—Government policy. 2. Clothing
trade—Government policy. 3. Free trade and protection.
4. International Economic Relations 5. Textile industry—
Government policy—United States. 6. Clothing Trade—
Government policy—United States.
I. Title.   II. Series.
HD9850.6.A35 1985   382′.45677′00973   84-16460
ISBN 0-520-05396-6

Printed In the United States of America

1 2 3 4 5 6 7 8 9

TO MY PARENTS

Contents

Preface

When I first decided to find an area where I could apply my ideas on international cooperation and conflict, I did not realize that textile trade would prove to be such a rich laboratory. Many of the issues in international politics and economics which concern scholars and policymakers can be seen here. The development of less developed countries, adjustment by the industrialized countries, cooperation among northern countries, cooperation among southern countries, and the prospects for organized trade are just a few of the issues that are raised in textile trade negotiations. I hope that applying a theoretical perspective to examine conflict and cooperation in this area will provide insight into and help to cope with some of the current crises in the world political economy.

In researching and writing this book, I have accumulated many debts and acquired many friends. Robert Keohane inspired me to work on problems in international political economy. As an adviser and friend, he has encouraged me to develop my ideas in a systematic manner. Without him, this book would not have been possible. Stephen Krasner first suggested that I examine international textile trade to test my theoretical ideas. As editor of the series in which this book appears, he has further ensured that my ideas are presented clearly. Alexander George and Robert North provided numerous insights that have stimulated my own thinking. Their willingness to discuss ideas has proved invaluable.

A. F. K. Organski first introduced me to the systematic investigation of world politics. These early impressions from my freshman days were nurtured by Daniel Levine and J. David Singer.

Many friends and colleagues have helped to make this study possible. For their assistance and support, I would like to thank Pierre Allan, Lynn Alvarez, Michael Barzelay, Linda Cahn, Stuart Chemtob, Albert Fishlow, Ernst Haas, Stephan Haggard, David Hudnut, Anthony Jurich,

Peter Katzenstein, Edward Kim, Gregory Luebbert, Elizabeth Norville, Kenneth Oye, Ronald Purver, Marilyn Skiles, Lucia Skwarek, Philip Trezise, Shu Urata, Mike Van Waas, Kenneth Waltz, Kent Weaver, Mark Zacher, and John Zysman. Ronald Gutfleish's research assistance and editorial help have proved critical in completing the book.

Numerous individuals willingly gave their time to discuss the intricacies of textile trade and politics. In various interviews, they gave me a feel for this subject which cannot be obtained from books or documents.

A number of institutions provided financial support and assistance. My field research in Europe was funded by the Center for Research in International Studies at Stanford University and an SSRC-Fulbright grant. My research in Washington, D.C., was made possible by a fellowship from the Brookings Institution. The libraries and staffs of the Brookings Institution, EEC, FAO, GATT, Stanford University, and the University of California, Berkeley, greatly aided my research.

I would especially like to thank my family for their encouragement and support. Inevitably, they became involved in one facet or another of my research. My father read and commented on parts of the manuscript and my mother helped with my research. The theoretical framework I use in this study owes much to conversations with my brother, Sudhir Aggarwal. My sister, Bina Murarka, contributed valuable comments.

I am grateful to all of the individuals, universities, and other organizations that made my work possible. The responsibility for errors and interpretations of events is, of course, mine.

Abbreviations

ACMI	American Cotton Manufacturers Institute
ATMI	American Textile Manufacturers Institute
BTC	British Textile Confederation
DC	Developed Country
DNR	*Daily News Record*
EC	European Community
EEC	European Economic Community
FEER	*Far Eastern Economic Review*
GATT	General Agreement on Tariffs and Trade
GSP	General System of Preferences
ICA	International Cooperation Administration
ITC	International Trade Commission
LDC	Less Developed Country
LTA	Long-Term Arrangement on Cotton Textiles
MFA	Multi-Fiber Arrangement
MITI	Ministry for International Trade and Industry
MMF	Man-Made Fiber
MTN	Multilateral Trade Negotiations
MVP	Minimum Viable Production
NIC	Newly Industrializing Country
NYT	*New York Times*
OECD	Organization for Economic Cooperation and Development
OMA	Orderly Marketing Agreement
PRC	People's Republic of China
STA	Short-Term Arrangement on Cotton Textiles
sye	square yard equivalent
TSB	Textiles Surveillance Body
UNCTAD	United Nations Conference on Trade and Development
VER	Voluntary Export Restraint

PART I
THE THEORY

At a time when International Relations in general, and their economic aspects in particular, are increasingly recognized as of growing complexity and significance, it is important to undertake their study, not simply on the one hand as a series of isolated political, diplomatic, and historical incidents nor on the other hand solely as matters of international trade, shipping, and finance, but rather by analysis of the fundamental politico-economic structure which so largely determines, directly or indirectly, their public policies.

—John Donaldson, International
Economic Relations: A Treatise on
World Economy and World Politics, 1928

1

The Growth of Protection and International Regimes

The fabric of international rules in trade is unraveling. Increasingly restrictive policies pursued by developed countries obstruct trade in an ever-growing number of products and challenge the liberal conception of a smooth transformation of the international order based on a growing division of labor. American automakers, French winegrowers, and British steelworkers, among many others, all deluge their governments with complaints about "unfair foreign competition." While the woes of the steel and auto industries may dominate the headlines today, twenty-five years ago the loudest complaints were from the textile and apparel producers. In only a few more years we may be hearing the cries of the personal computer industry. How might these issues be resolved? A look at the textile and apparel trade, an area that has had the longest experience with international bargaining over market shares, may prove useful in enabling us to predict what the future might bring for autos, wine, steel, and computers.

The evolution of international bargaining over the arrangements developed in textile and apparel trade illustrates the competing forces of liberalism and protectionism at work. While full-blown protectionism has been restrained through the development of an international regime regulating intervention in textile trade,[1] the progressive weakening and increasingly protectionist orientation of a regime forced to cope with a growing array of products now casts doubt on the prospects for "organized" world trade. Trade in textile and apparel products is particularly important to the less developed countries (LDCs), comprising up to three-quarters of their manufactured exports. Growing protection in textiles and other products impedes the developing countries' efforts to industrialize and finance their debts through the development and export of manufactures. And protectionist policies, aside from causing economic inefficiencies, have high political costs. Disputes have arisen between the North and South, among the northern countries, and among southern countries in negotiations over textile market shares.

This study examines the evolution of international regimes in textile trade with the objective of furthering our understanding of the process of regime transformation. I address three key questions: Why are regimes developed? What accounts for the strength, nature, and scope of regimes? And finally, what effect do regimes have on national behaviors and transactions? The answers to these questions shed light on the future prospects for textile and apparel trade and suggest ways to control the seemingly inexorable movement toward increasing world protection in other sectors as well. By more fully understanding the evolution of the textile regime from the 1950s to the present, we may gain insight into the future of the General Agreement on Tariffs and Trade (GATT) and learn if it is possible to slow the growing slide toward protectionism.

I argue that international regime development and change can best be understood from an international systemic perspective. Although I incorporate domestic political factors and the beliefs and behavior of decision makers as part of my analysis of regime change, they are used only for supplementary explanation. The core of the argument concentrates on utilizing the characteristics of the textile subsystem and its relationship to the overall trading and international systems to explain and predict how decision makers respond in international negotiations to the constraints and inducements of these systems.

Briefly, I argue that international regimes are desired by actors for three reasons. First, they may prevent broader international arrangements (such as the GATT) from being undermined, a constraint I label "nesting." Second, regimes provide a way to control the behavior of other countries through a system of rules.[2] Third, regimes minimize the organizational costs of conducting multiple negotiations and provide participants with information about the market and interventionist actions.

I contend that the theory of hegemonic stability (which predicts strong regimes when a single power is dominant) provides an accurate explanation of regime strength, particularly if one focuses on issue-specific capabilities and if capabilities are correctly operationalized in terms of oligopsony power. The nature of the regime depends on the degree and direction of trade flows among producers, and on the degree of cognitive consensus on principles and norms (what I term the "meta-regime") over how the regime should operate. The scope of the regime is affected, in turn, by the need to control intervention in an increasing number of sectors and by cognitive consensus on what particular products comprise a coherent issue area to be regulated. Finally, this work argues that the effect of regimes on national behavior and transactions must be understood in light of domestic political structures and changes in technology and tastes.

The issue-specific systemic approach followed here contrasts sharply with most work on protection in trade. Scholars investigating trade issues have generally paid much more attention to the domestic politics of protection or to the role of decision makers in international bargaining than to systemic level characteristics. Some who have considered systemic level explanations have focused on the overall trading system rather than on specific issue-areas within trade. These studies tend to be cast at an excessively high level of abstraction and often obscure important shifts within various sectors of trade. Others looking at trade protection have simply missed the importance of international collaborative efforts in the form of international regimes, arguing instead that all deviations from liberal trade can be lumped together as irrational measures that hinder efficiency and growth. By examining international bargaining over regime transformation from 1950 to 1982 from an issue-specific systemic perspective, I hope to contribute to our understanding of conflict and collaboration in trade.

THE NEW PROTECTIONISM

Drawing on lessons learned from the disastrous effects of competitive protectionist trade policies in the 1930s, the United States set out to form a new, more open international trading order after World War II. To this end, it led the negotiations in developing the Havana Charter, which called for the formation of the trade counterpart to the International Monetary Fund—the International Trade Organization (ITO). But the comprehensiveness of the Havana Charter led to its demise: protectionists complained that it was too liberal; liberals claimed that it was too protectionist. These strange bedfellows joined hands in lobbying the U.S. Congress to reject the Charter—and with it, the ITO. By default, the GATT, originally designed to be a temporary treaty to establish guidelines for tariff negotiations, was left as the code governing international trade. Under U.S. prodding and support, this temporary treaty blossomed into a small but highly influential international organization to act as the conscience (some would hope, policeman) to promote free trade.

Although the GATT has survived as an institution, its authority has diminished in the face of increasing efforts to circumvent its proscriptions.[3] Its rules, while applying primarily to trade in manufactures rather than in agriculture, quite clearly prohibit the use of quotas to restrain trade except in carefully specified cases.[4] The initial violations of the GATT principles came in the case of textile and apparel trade in the 1950s as Japan and others were asked to "voluntarily" restrain their exports. But this was only the beginning. Since that time, voluntary export restraints (VERs) and orderly marketing agreements (OMAs) have cropped up in a variety of industrial sectors. Among the most significant, the Japanese agreed to VERs to restrict their exports to the United States of steel in 1968, color televisions in 1977, and autos in 1981. Similar restraints to the European Economic Community (EEC) by Japan and other countries exist in sectors such as autos, steel, machine tools, and videotape recorders. As Robert Reich has noted,

As the free trade ideal has become hopelessly inadequate to guide these shifts, international economic agencies and formal trade processes sponsored by the U.S. have been gradually bypassed and enfeebled. Only the easiest of disputes are settled within the GATT system; most major issues of global economic change are dealt with outside it.[5]

The increasing pressures for protectionist actions appear to have at least two sources. First, in a number of industries, developed countries (DCs) have had their markets for exports closed off because of import substitution policies by the LDCs. The United Kingdom experienced the loss of many of its textile markets after World War II: its exports were down to 40,000 tons of fabrics in the 1960s, in contrast to 700,000 tons in 1913 and 140,000 tons in 1948.[6] With the spread of LDC domestic production, exports of cotton fabrics as a percentage of total world production declined from 29 percent in 1913 to 12 percent in 1964.[7] This gradual replacement of DC export markets (which started in the 1930s with the growth of protectionism and the worldwide depression) left Europe with approximately 40 to 50 percent surplus production capacity in textiles; some countries, such as the United Kingdom, were left with over 75 percent excess capacity.[8]

This effect has been seen in other sectors as well. For instance, steel production in the LDCs increased by 50 percent from 1974 to 1977 while that of the United States fell by 6 percent. Their share of world steel production has risen from 2 percent in 1950 to an estimated 11 percent in 1977. Japan's share went from 3 percent to 15 percent during the same time.[9] Conversely, the U.S. share decreased from 39 percent to 15 percent from 1955 to 1981.[10]

A second factor encouraging the growth of protection is the rapid rise in manufactured exports from the LDCs and Japan to the United States and Europe. In the initial stages, the turn away from import-substituting industrialization toward an export-oriented strategy—most prominently by the newly industrializing countries (NICs)—proved to be highly successful. Their manufactured exports grew at an annual rate of 12.2 percent from 1963 to 1973, and 20 percent from 1973 to 1976, two-thirds of which reached DC markets in the 1970s. South Korea's manufactured exports to the United States increased at a real rate per annum of 36.6 percent from 1965 to 1975. The corresponding figures for Taiwan, Brazil, and Mexico are 28.8, 25.4, and 21.2 percent, respectively. While these imports from the LDCs as a percentage of the industrialized countries' consumption has only increased from 0.4 percent in 1960 to 1.2 percent in 1975,[11] particular sectors have sought protection as competition from exports has contributed to surplus capacity. The fact that the major proportion of these increased imports originates from only a few countries makes protection even easier.

The competition over markets for manufactures which once was just "North-North" (a three-way battle between Western Europe, the United States, and Japan) has now become "North-South" as well with the rapid growth of manufactures from the NICs. The North-South problem, which from the southern perspective is one of trying to increase export shares, in turn leads to a North-North problem of minimizing *import* shares. The last problem becomes particularly acute as exports blocked by one country find their way to less protected markets. Escalating retaliation could well become the norm—with obvious consequences for the heavily indebted NICs.

By taking advantage of their low-cost labor, firms from Japan and the NICs have entered world markets and successfully competed against firms in Europe and the United States. The "lesson" for other developing countries seemed to be that import substitution policies could be supplemented or even replaced by export promotion; in some cases "infant industries" could grow up and succeed in the "adult" world. For instance, Japan's share of world auto production increased from 2.9 percent in 1960 to 28.4 percent in 1980, and by 1981 accounted for 80 percent of all U.S. auto imports. Imports have increasingly taken over the U.S. auto market, rising from under 15 percent in 1970 to almost 30 percent in 1981, while U.S. capacity utilization decreased from almost 80 percent in 1967 to just under 60 percent in 1981.[12] In steel, imports captured over 20 percent of the market for the first time in 1982. Combined with declining demand for steel, U.S. mills were running at only 30 percent capacity at year's end.[13]

The problem of industrial overcapacity is not novel, nor are industrial demands for government protection. In the past (e.g., in various countries from 1600 to 1750, in the United Kingdom in the 1870s, and throughout the industrialized world during the depression of the 1930s), excess capacity problems existed and were "cured" by the idling of production as governments refused to bail out industries in trouble. In some cases, however, governments did respond and sought to procure markets through the use of force. In the post-World War II era, however, governments are not allowed to stand idle while production is rationalized through the competitive pressures of supply and demand. The new role of the government as the caretaker of society prevents free capital and labor mobility across sectors. Rather than allowing private losses resulting from the need to adapt to a changing division of labor, governments have been called upon to intervene on behalf of particular industries to prevent their demise.

Though effective policies of industrial adjustment could potentially facilitate the adjustment process, few developed countries have been able to pursue forward-looking adjustment policies.[14] Instead, governments have often simply responded to the loudest cries for restrictions by instituting controls on imports of one sort or another. If this phenomenon takes place in a number of countries, goods are diverted from one country to another in response to the closing off of markets. The result is growing international economic conflict and increasing political tension.

International regimes, and, in particular, the textile regime, have been seen by some as a way of moderating international conflict over market shares. For instance, one analyst has argued in responding to expressed fears of trade wars: "The alternative is not jingoistic protectionism. It is managed trade, on the model of the Multi-Fiber Arrangement [MFA]."[15] The construction of rules and procedures specifying the conditions under which countries may intervene in the market may well permit compromise and offer a mechanism for the equitable sharing of adjustment costs. But can trade be successfully organized? And is the regime in textile trade worthy of emulation? This study argues that hegemony in trade and international regimes can have its dark side as well. International regimes designed by a hegemon with a liberal orientation to restrict protection and facilitate trade can be twisted to facilitate competitive protection and restrict trade. The liberal protectionist arrangements of the 1960s have been distorted from a positive force for moderate protection to a negative force that facilitates it. What was originally hoped to be a stable equilibrium between liberalism and protectionism now appears to be a way station on the road from one point to the other.

THE IMPORTANCE OF TEXTILE AND APPAREL TRADE

Textile and apparel trade has long involved international conflict and intrigue. This is not entirely unexpected since the textile and apparel industries were at the vanguard of industrialization. Indeed, British Commercial Attaché William Gastrell reported in 1897 that "Great Britain has, amongst all her gigantic industries no more important branch than this one, so renowned throughout the world over."[16] They continue to be significant for developed countries in terms of employment and manufacturing output. In 1980 the U.S. International Trade Commission (ITC) estimated that 14 percent of manufacturing employment in developed countries and 30 percent in developing countries was in the textile and apparel industries.[17] Most important, these were the first major manufacturing industries in the newly developing countries because of the relatively simple technology required for their production and because of their labor-intensive nature. As a result, these products are key components of LDC exports (see table 1).

Conflict among countries over trade in textile and apparel products began in the 1300s (and possibly even earlier).[18] In medieval England, the import of woolen cloth was banned by a statute issued by King Edward

TABLE 1

PERCENTAGE SHARE OF TEXTILE AND APPAREL PRODUCTS
IN THE TOTAL MANUFACTURED AND OVERALL EXPORTS OF SELECTED COUNTRIES,
1970 AND 1980

Country	Textiles and apparel as percent of total manufactured exports		Textiles and apparel as percent of all exports	
	1970	1980	1970	1980
Pakistan	77.6	78.0	45.0	37.4
Egypt	76.0	83.1	19.1	9.2
Portugal	56.5	41.3	25.4	26.7
India	48.7	33.0	24.5	19.6
South Korea	47.0	34.5	35.7	30.0
Hong Kong	43.5	38.6	38.7	34.1
Colombia	25.6	37.0	1.9	6.4
Singapore	21.8	9.9	5.5	4.1
Greece	21.6	38.9	7.3	17.0
Israel	18.9	10.6	11.8	7.1
Tunisia	16.6	75.7	2.1	17.6
Spain	11.4	7.2	5.7	4.8
Brazil	10.7	11.5	1.3	3.9
Mexico	9.5	12.6	3.0	1.1
Philippines	7.8	27.9	0.6	6.2
Kenya	3.4	6.7	2.3	0.6

SOURCE: United Nations Statistical Office, *Yearbook of International Trade Statistics* (various years); *U.N. Commodity Trade Statistics* (various years).

NOTE: 1980 figures for India and Israel are 1978 and 1979 respectively.

III in 1337. One study criticizing the notion that the development of protection was due to pressure groups and organized activities by producers carefully notes that the textile industries were an exception.[19]

In the late 1600s, the textile industry in England successfully prevented an influx of inexpensive handcrafted textiles from India and China.[20] Behind the trade barriers imposed by the British Crown, English textile manufacturers were able to bring their infant industry to maturity.[21] As is well known, England was subsequently able to export large quantities of cotton textiles to India, thereby destroying India's indigenous industry. As a result of England's increasing control over its fragmented princely states, India became a key importer of mechanically produced goods in the 1800s.[22]

Textiles came to play a somewhat different role in England in the 1800s when the textile industry became associated with the movement toward economic liberalism. Adam Smith's ideology of laissez-faire fit hand in glove with the desire of the Manchester cotton textile manufacturers for an open world market. Although the extent to which British power was used to secure an open trading system that proved highly beneficial to the textile and other manufacturing industries remains open to debate,[23] the rapid growth of the English textile industry resulting from open trade and its key role in English exports is undeniable. As late as 1895 textile exports accounted for over one-third of the total value of British exports, despite a decline in their prices (attributed to the effects of foreign competition).[24]

Important changes which radically affected the textile and apparel industries in the United Kingdom and other developed countries took place in the twentieth century. Britain entered the century accounting for 70 percent of the world's trade textile trade.[25] Yet after the world depression began in 1929, the position of the industrialized countries in the textile and apparel industries was vigorously challenged. Foremost among the aspirants for domination in textile trade was Japan.[26] In 1933 it had become the premier exporter of cotton textile products in the world.[27] The less developed countries soon followed the Japanese example. Through import substitution, and as a consequence of their very low labor costs, these countries made inroads into the markets of the developed countries. Especially after World War II, Hong Kong, South Korea, India, Pakistan, and Japan began to export cotton textile products in larger and larger quantities. Although total imports were still a relatively minor fraction of the domestic market of many countries (less than 2 percent of the American market in 1955), this growing export drive was attacked by textile and apparel producers in the developed countries.[28]

The textile and apparel industries were experiencing numerous problems unrelated to imports.[29] In the United States, for example, there was a major movement under way by northern textile and apparel producers to relocate to the South as increasing unionization of labor in the North led businesses to seek cheaper wages. In other countries, growing intraindustry competition was taking place as a result of the development of synthetic fibers. Integrated producers using synthetic fibers or blends drove out more traditional manufacturers of cotton and/or wool-based products. Contributing to their lack of competitiveness was the failure of many manufacturers to keep up with style changes in the market. Furthermore, other materials such as plastics or paper products often substituted for textile products. The implication of these changes is quite clear: even without imports many mills in developed countries would have closed.

Though these factors were affecting the textile and apparel industries, manufacturers were most concerned with restricting imports. The character of the domestic coalition-building process and the relative strength of business vis-à-vis labor provided the motive forces for this import focus. Imports could serve as scapegoats for domestic problems and allow manufacturers to seek restrictions preserving their market—without direct intervention by the government in the production process. And for domestic coalition purposes, manufacturers of different fibers were more willing to go along with import restrictions than to pursue aid for specific manufacturers. In country after country, manufacturers banded together with labor to seek the protection of their respective governments.

In the United States, the movement to restrict imports in the post-World War II period began as early as 1953 when the American Cotton Manufacturers Institute (ACMI), the most important cotton textile producers peak organization, was moving to "combat the deluge of free trade propaganda flooding the country."[30] Through skillful coalition building and effective lobbying, the ACMI threatened to block trade bills if they did not obtain restrictions on the imports of textile and apparel products from Japan. The Japanese realized that prospects for increasing exports in light of ACMI's efforts were bleak, and "voluntarily" restrained their exports of a number of cotton-based products in 1955. Mounting pressure from the U.S. government to restrict their exports for a longer period led to further restraints. In 1956, the Japanese voluntarily restricted their exports for a period of five years.

Other developing countries soon jumped into the vacuum created by restraints on Japanese exports to the United States with exports of their own. Among the LDCs, Hong Kong quickly increased its market share. While Japan's share of total U.S. cotton imports declined from 54.5 percent in 1956 to 34.1 percent in 1961, Hong Kong's share rose from less than 0.5 percent to over 23 percent during the same period.[31] While domestic producers pushed for a global quota to control imports of textile and apparel products from all sources, the U.S. government first sought to conclude a bilateral agreement with Hong Kong. This effort failed when Hong Kong resisted American pressure. In response, Douglas Dillon, the under secretary of state, asked the GATT participants to develop a program to cope with low-priced imports.[32] The 1959 agreement on "market disruption" from low-priced imports served as an important element of the Short-Term Arrangement on Cotton Textiles (STA) developed in 1961.

The problems facing the American textile and apparel industries were not unique. In the United Kingdom, not only were imports from the LDCs increasing but in addition its textile exports had been falling almost continuously since the early 1900s. The value of British textile exports (in constant prices) fell by over 70 percent from 1913 to 1955.[33] In fact, the United Kingdom—the country that had initiated the industrial revolution with textiles—by 1958 imported more cotton cloth than it exported, in part because cotton textiles from India, Pakistan, and Hong Kong could be imported duty-free under the Imperial Preference System.[34] To cope with the resulting surplus industrial capacity the British sought to have these countries "voluntarily" restrict imports in the late 1950s. As a result, these Commonwealth countries, in an agreement known as the Lancashire Pact, agreed to restrain their exports of cotton textiles on an interindustry basis.

The European countries used Article XII of the GATT, which allowed restraints on imports for balance of payments reasons, to restrict imports of textile and apparel products from LDCs. Yet, after these LDCs had improved their economic position and returned to currency convertibility in 1958, they still did not liberalize their import restrictions. Instead, they maintained their restrictions in violation of the GATT. As discussed in Part II, the perpetuation of these restraints proved to be an important reason for the American attempt to develop a textile and apparel international regime.

In 1961, as part of a seven-point plan to aid the American cotton textile and apparel industries, President Kennedy instructed the under secretary of state, George Ball, to work toward an international agreement on textile trade. A temporary one-year agreement (the STA) was reached, effective October 1, 1961. The STA was followed by the Long-Term Arrangement on Cotton Textiles (LTA),[35] which was effective for a period of five years.

Both the STA and the LTA contained procedures for governments to follow if they claimed market disruption or the threat of market disruption from imports.[36] In such an event, importing countries were allowed to conclude bilateral agreements with exporting countries, or impose unilateral restraints if they could not secure agreement with the exporters. Unilateral measures had to adhere to the regime's provisions mandating growth in quotas and other provisions. Under the LTA, most importing countries chose to conclude bilateral agreements with exporters; for example, by 1966 the United States concluded eighteen bilateral agreements.

Although the LTA partially satisfied cotton textile and apparel manufacturers in DCs and permitted LDCs to increase their exports (within limits), it failed to address trade in man-made fiber and wool-based goods. The LTA encouraged the development of various blends to enable exporting countries to circumvent the restrictions on cotton products (the arrangement specified that cotton products would be defined as having over 50 percent cotton content). Pressure to restrict man-made fiber and wool-based products soon increased. In the mid-1960s, European countries began to restrain unilaterally and bilaterally the imports of LDC wool and man-made fiber textile and apparel products—without abiding by GATT or any other international rules. Domestic groups in the United States sought similar restraints, but the American government (as well as the LDCs) resisted this effort. Yet the EEC's restrictions on LDC and Japanese wool and man-made fiber-based products put pressure on the United States, since imports were being diverted to the American market. It soon became clear to these exporters and to the United States that an international regime would be a better device than such unregulated bilateral restraints. At a minimum, a regime would provide some constraints on the actions of importing countries.

The United States had tried to develop a multifiber regime as early as 1969, but the Europeans strongly resisted this effort. They saw the American desire for a regime as a ploy to restrain their own exports to the United States. Moreover, they were quite happy to restrict the exports of less developed countries and Japan on a bilateral and unilateral basis. In 1971, following difficult and protracted negotiations, the United States concluded bilateral agreements with Japan and other Far Eastern exporters. By comparison, the development of the MFA[37] was easy. It was signed on 20 December 1973, and took effect on January 1974 for a period of four years. Although similar to the LTA in its basic conception, the rules of the MFA were more specific and comprehensive, and a body to monitor the actions of importing and exporting countries was set up. This group, the Textiles Surveillance Body (TSB), consisted of members of various importing and exporting countries. The delegates to the TSB were to serve as technical experts in monitoring agreements, although, in practice, political criteria have often determined their actions.

The first renewal of the MFA took place in 1977. In contrast to previous negotiations, the EEC took a very active role in defining the nature of the arrangement. Due to long delays in concluding bilateral agreements with exporting countries (which resulted from EEC's complex internal bargaining process), imports into the Community rose rapidly. The EEC asked for a number of major changes in the MFA but met with resistance from both the LDCs and the United States. After protracted bargaining, the MFA was renewed in December 1977 but was considerably weakened by an "escape clause."[38]

The latest renewal of the MFA, in 1981, has further undermined the regime's influence over national restrictive actions. Both the United States and the EEC pressed for inclusion of clauses in the MFA which would essentially serve as a legal and political cover for sharply protectionist actions. The regime now allows cutbacks in trade levels for major suppliers and potentially removes what little flexibility the exporters had in shifting their export composition within the textile and apparel area. The character of the MFA has fundamentally shifted, to the point where the regime may actually *encourage* restrictive actions by providing a simple mechanism that facilitates the "negotiation" of restrictive accords.

ORGANIZATION OF THE STUDY

This study consists of three parts. In the remainder of this part, I develop the theoretical approach that guides the investigation of regime transformation in textile trade from 1950 to 1982. Chapter 2 differentiates the dependent variable of regime transformation into a number of dimensions and places international regimes in a broader theoretical context. Based on the dimensions of strength, nature, and scope, I characterize the changes that we have seen over the last thirty years in textile trade. To explain these changes, I then present my systemic argument on the evolution of regimes and examine system characteristics over the time period in question. The systemic level theory is supplemented by a consideration of domestic politics, transnational coalitions, and bureaucratic struggles. I also focus on the learning process and misperceptions that decision makers may experience. Finally, this chapter describes the method of "process-tracing"—an approach that traces the reactions of decision makers to systemic factors through an intensive analysis of the decision making process.

Based on the theoretical approach outlined in chapter 2, Part II presents a detailed investigation of bargaining in textile trade. Each of four chapters—nonexistence, creation, maintenance, and destruction of regimes—analyzes bargaining in similar fashion. I first examine the degree to which the various international structures constrain both the behavior of decision makers and the outcomes that we see. Put succinctly, are the factors here claimed to be important both necessary and sufficient in determining the outcomes? Second, I consider the extent to which international structural factors may have been misperceived by decision makers. Third, I evaluate the extent to which domestic and individual level factors were decisive in producing the observed outcome. Fourth, I look at the behavior of countries once the regime has been implemented and also consider the changes in trade flows feeding back onto the basic international structural factors used to account for regime change.

In Part III, I review my findings and examine the utility of an international systemic approach for illuminating the process of regime transformation. I consider the extent to which such a model might be usefully supplemented by other factors and consider its relevance to the examination of other issue-areas. Finally, I assess the prospects for the arrangements in the textile and apparel issue-area as well as the role of international regimes in managing growing protectionism in other sectors of the world economy.

2

The Process of International Regime Transformation

The transformation of international regimes can be understood from an international systemic perspective. While factors such as domestic politics and the characteristics of decision-makers are undoubtedly important, a full understanding of regime transformation requires an examination of the impact of international structure. The relevant international structure, however, is not simply that of the overall international system: the structure of issue-specific systems, such as the trading and textile trade system, must be analyzed together to yield an adequate explanation of regime change.

A convincing demonstration of the influence of international structure on the outcomes of international negotiations could proceed in two ways. One method would be to muster a sufficient number of cases with a high degree of variation in outcomes so that the influence of international structure on decision makers' perceptions could be established. Given the absence of a large number of cases of regime transformation in textile trade, however, I argue that a second approach, known as "process-tracing," is an effective and even potentially superior substitute. In process-tracing, the decision-making procedure in a negotiation is systematically analyzed with an eye to identifying the degree to which participants appear to respond to international systemic or other constraints.

THE OBJECTIVE: INTERNATIONAL REGIMES

I argue here that international regimes should be defined as rules and procedures that regulate national actions. Moreover, I place the concept of a regime within a broader theoretical framework of meta-regimes (principles and norms), international regimes, national actions, and international transactions. This simplifies the task of theory construction: it permits a precise focus for analysis and facilitates the task of categorizing the changes that have taken place in efforts to regulate textile trade since 1950.

As with most concepts in political science, international regimes have been imprecisely defined and applied. Definitions range from a narrow conception as modes of institutionalized organization to very broad definitions indistinguishable from all of international politics. An excessively narrow definition may make the concept of regimes redundant and simply relabel an existing phenomenon; an excessively broad definition is virtually useless as an analytical concept. The definition used here is in part a response to previous uses of the regime concept.

The concept of regime derives from the Latin word *regimen,* a form of the word *regere,* which means "to rule" in English. In international law, regimes are seen as mechanisms regulating the behavior of countries in a manner similar to the regulation of individuals in nation-states.[1] The analogy to the domestic arena must not be taken too literally, however. In an overall anarchic world system, international regimes do not take on the role of governments. Instead, they are closer to "quasi-agreements,"[2] that is, agreements among sovereign entities. Enforcement of regulations to ensure behavior consistent with the regime is usually done with the consent of all parties to the accord.

The term "international regime" became popular following Keohane and Nye's usage in *Power and Interdependence.* Yet their use of that term was not totally clear. They argue that

by creating or accepting procedures, rules, or institutions for certain kinds of activity, governments regulate and control transnational and interstate relations. We refer to these governing arrangements as *international regimes.*[3]

They continue by arguing that regimes which are "the sets of governing arrangements that affect relationships of interdependence" are international regimes.[4] This usage is potentially confusing. It fails to distinguish between the control of transactions by countries and the control of national behavior by regimes. Such a distinction is important because the effect of regimes on actual flows such as trade, monetary transactions, and the like, are mediated by national choices. Of course, countries do not always abide by regimes, and regimes do not always fully specify the requisite action.

More recently, in a collection of articles on international regimes, Krasner defines international regimes as follows:

Regimes can be defined as sets of implicit or explicit principles, norms, rules, and decision-making procedures around which actors' expectations converge in a given area of international relations. Principles are beliefs of fact, causation, and rectitude. Norms are standards of behavior defined in terms of rights and obligations. Rules are specific prescriptions or proscriptions for action. Decision-making procedures are prevailing practices for making and implementing collective choice.[5]

Although in many ways this is an improvement on previous definitions of international regimes, it suffers from excessive complexity and fails to distinguish among different phenomena. As I will argue, the theories that might explain principles and norms, on the one hand, and rules and procedures, on the other, are quite distinct. It is analytically misleading, therefore, to merge all these terms into a single dependent variable.

In my view, there is a need to specify four different terms. At the most basic level, one can conceive of various transactions. These can be monetary, trade, information, and other such flows. Transactions are then partially influenced at the next level by national actions consisting of unilateral controls and bilateral accords. International regimes in turn guide the imposition of national controls and accords. They are a multilateral system of rules and procedures to *regulate* national actions.[6] We will consider a number of different characteristics of regimes such as their strength, nature, and scope. Finally, the principles and norms underlying the development of regimes can be termed a "meta-regime." By distinguishing between rules and procedures, on the one hand, and norms and principles, on the other, we can proceed to systematically analyze changes that take place in both of these areas.

Using four distinct terms has three advantages. First, it brings theoretical usage in line with more traditional terminology, and it also clarifies the notion of what regimes do. Rather than speaking of regimes as controlling "behavior"—a notoriously imprecise term—we can distinguish between the regulation of national actions and the regulation of transactions. As I have noted above, the first constitutes regime while the latter consists of controls and bilateral accords.

Second, the term "meta-regime" avoids the need for distinguishing change within regimes from a change in regimes. An example of this confusion serves as an illustration. Krasner states that "if the aspects of a regime become less coherent or if actual practice is increasingly inconsistent with principles, norms, rules, and procedures then a regime has weakened."[7] But the notion of "less coherent" and "inconsistent" with respect to so many terms (principles, norms, rules, and procedures) makes it difficult to work with the concept of a regime. Krasner notes earlier that "there may be many rules and decision making procedures that are consistent with the same norms and principles."[8] It is much better to think of such instances as situations with different regimes even though the meta-regime is the same. In trade, for example, the meta-regime has persisted while numerous significant changes have taken place in the GATT regime. That is, liberalism is still seen as being a principle that most countries can agree on, but there is much less agreement on rules and procedures.

Third, and most important, the distinction between regime and meta-regime helps us in synthesizing recent work on regime change. Two contending approaches to regime change, structural analysis and cognitive analysis, have been the subject of recent debates.[9] But these modes of analysis should not be seen as being mutually exclusive, competing models to explain the transformation of international regimes: cognitive theories more successfully explain the development of principles and norms (meta-regime), while structural theories more successfully explain the development of rules and procedures.

In examining regimes, I am looking not only at characteristics of these accords but also at *why* a regime is used or not used as a method of regulating national controls. An important clarification introduced by Keohane is helpful in sorting out these issues. He argues that one should distinguish between the "supply" of regimes and the "demand" for regimes. In this connection, he asserts that "hegemonic stability theory" (the argument that the presence of a single major power in a system leads to the construction of a regime) is inadequate. While a power approach suggests when a regime can, or is likely to be created, it gives little insight into why countries would wish to develop a regime rather than simply choose to conclude a "large number of separate *ad hoc* agreements on matters of substantive importance."[10] In his analysis of the demand for regimes, Keohane argues that international regimes serve to facilitate the conclusion of agreements among countries by overcoming problems of transaction costs and imperfect information.

A similar analysis of supply and demand can be used for explaining the origin of principles and norms. The supply of meta-regimes is influenced by the development of consensual knowledge about the functioning of different systems and the interaction among various issues. The greater the number of areas on which there is consensual knowledge, the greater the supply of meta-regimes. The analogue to the demand for regimes in the meta-regime case is the development of goals by decision makers in various countries. As the number of goals they wish to pursue expands, the demand for collaboration increases.[11]

As stated earlier, the cognitive approach explains the development of norms and principles and the structural approach explains the development of rules and procedures. This helps us to understand regimes imposed by one country and grudgingly accepted by others. These regimes lack a meta-regime: there is no agreement on knowledge, and the goals that actors pursue are different. The anomaly of the GATT's persistence, even though the United States had declined in capabilities relative to the Europeans, is now explained. As long as the meta-regime persists, the regime will undergo numerous changes, but a certain amount of order in the trading system will continue.

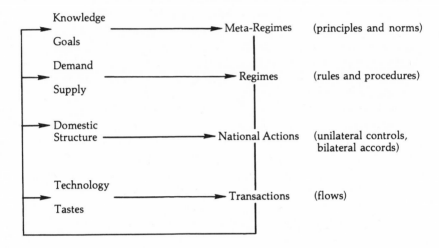

Figure 1. A Framework for Analysis

As is illustrated in figure 1, meta-regimes are here considered to be a result of knowledge and goals. International regimes can be explained by changing demand for regimes because of informational and organizational costs, and other factors on the demand side which will be discussed below. The supply of regimes is affected by the presence or absence of a hegemonic state. In addition to these basic factors, regimes are influenced by the characteristics of the meta-regime (assuming for the moment that one exists). National actions are influenced by domestic structure and other internal factors as well as by the existing international regime. Finally, transactions are a function of evolving technology, changes in tastes, and national actions to regulate transaction.

This study focuses on two questions: Why are regimes formed? And what accounts for the strength, nature, and scope of regimes? "Strength" refers to the stringency with which rules regulate the behavior of countries. "Nature" refers to the objects promoted by the regime rules and procedures. "Scope" is the range of issues or products regulated by a regime. Against this formal prescription we can observe the actual behavior of countries. In the case of textile trade "nature" refers to the openness promoted by a regime. If the regime attempts to prevent the imposition of controls, I refer to it as a regime that is "liberal" in nature. Conversely, if the regime promotes the use of national controls in an issue-area, then I refer to it as an "interventionist" regime (in the case of trade, this would imply protectionism).

It is important to note that a strong regime can be liberal or interventionist in nature. An illustration of the concepts of strength and nature in the context of the overall trade regime may help clarify this terminology. Intervention by countries in international trade is currently regulated by an international regime, the GATT, which has regulated the imposition of trade controls by signatory countries since 1947. The meta-regime consists in part of beliefs in multilateralism, nondiscrimination, and liberalism. The regime specifies the conditions under which countries can use quantitative restrictions and countervailing duties, and the types of customs fees that may be charged on imports. Strength in the case of the trade regime refers to the leeway countries have in imposing controls on trade. The recent conclusion of the Tokyo Round has weakened GATT rules by permitting greater leeway in what countries may do. Nature in the case of the GATT refers to the degree of protectionism or liberalism of the regime.

The clear difference between the strength and nature of regimes is revealed most clearly in the GATT by Article XIX (dealing with safeguards). According to GATT rules, if a nation wishes to restrict the imports of another country's products because its market is being "disrupted," it must (1) do so across the board and restrict imports from all countries that export the product in question; and (2) provide compensation to other countries or be subjected to retaliation. Although the regime is clearly strong (with strict rules on the conditions under which controls can be imposed) as I have defined the term, the strength of the regime may in fact *promote* a greater degree of protectionism. As some have argued,[12] since Article XIX does not allow selective safeguards, there has been greater intervention in trade than would otherwise be the case.[13] Countries using Article XIX do so on a most-favored-nation basis and reduce imports from all countries exporting the product in question. Selectivity, by contrast, would allow countries to restrict products only from what they perceive to be the "offending" country. For example, if imports from Hong Kong are the only problem, only exports from Hong

Kong would be restricted. The trade-off here is between nondiscrimination and liberalism. The Europeans espoused selective safeguards in the Tokyo Round negotiations but were rebuffed by the LDCs, who felt (quite rightly) they would be the object of selectivity. In summary, then, the concepts of strength and nature are distinct—even though in practice they may tend to covary.

Given the above classification system, what changes have taken place over the last thirty years in the arrangements in textile and apparel trade? The dimensions of strength, nature, and scope are presented in figures 2, 3, and 4, respectively. The period from 1950 to 1982 can be divided into four parts: the nonexistence of a textile regime (1950-1960); the origins of a regime (1961-62); the maintenance of a regime and its further expansion (1963-1976); and the severe weakening and near demise of the regime (1977-1982). While a history of arrangements in textile trade was presented in chapter 1, a brief summary of the salient changes in the governing mechanisms illustrated in these three figures is presented below.

From 1950 to 1960 there was no distinct textile regime. Initially, national controls on textile and apparel imports were justified under the GATT. For example, a number of key European states had quota restrictions that were justified under the GATT for balance of payments reasons. In 1955 trade controls were first instituted in textiles and apparel in violation of the GATT (at least implicitly). Under pressure from the United States, the Japanese unilaterally restrained their exports of a variety of cotton products. This did not prove entirely satisfactory to domestic U.S. producers, and their further efforts led the Japanese to collaborate on measures to restrict their cotton textile and apparel products for a period of five years—effective January 16, 1957. Meanwhile, the United Kingdom began conducting negotiations with the governments of Hong Kong, India, and Pakistan in an attempt to have them voluntarily restrict the export of their cotton textile and apparel goods. In 1959, in the Lancashire Pact, these three governments agreed to restrain their exports.

In 1961 the first regime in textile and apparel trade was negotiated. The resulting Short-Term Arrangement on Cotton Textiles was succeeded in 1962 by the Long-Term Arrangement, which covered a five-year period. Rules and procedures were laid down specifying the conditions under which countries could conclude bilateral agreements and/or invoke unilateral restraints. The agreement was moderately liberal, in that it allowed for a minimum growth rate of 5 percent and mandated a determination of injury before restrictions could be imposed. Yet the agree-

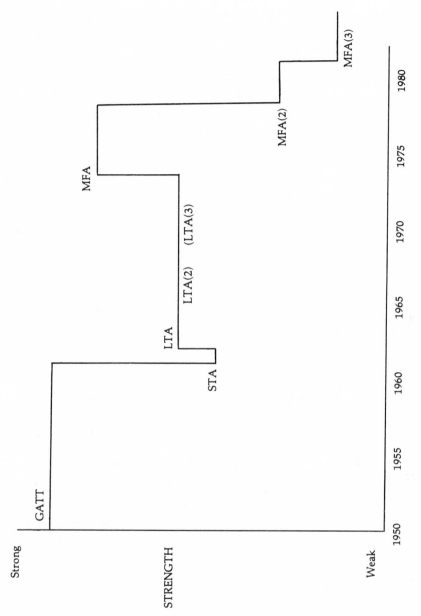

Figure 2. Strength of Regimes in Textile Trade

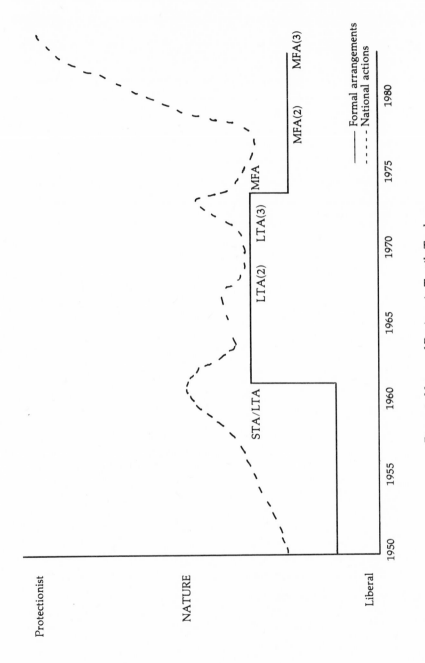

Figure 3. Nature of Regimes in Textile Trade

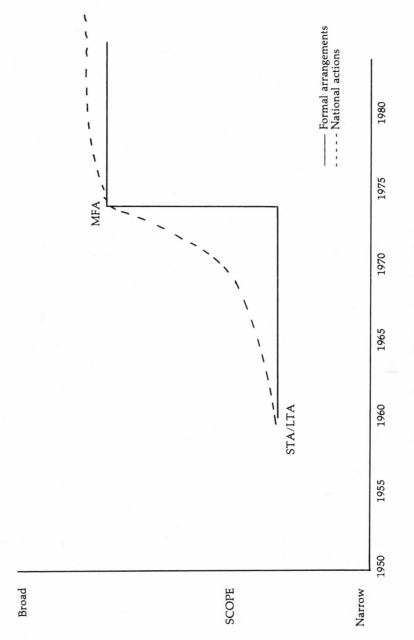

Figure 4. Scope of Regimes in Textile Trade

ment also permitted the negotiation of "mutually acceptable arrangements on other terms not inconsistent with the basic objectives of th[e] Arrangement."[14] Over the next two years, the United States and other countries concluded numerous bilateral agreements without demonstrating market disruption. The scope of the agreement was restricted to cotton textile and apparel products, although there was some talk of including wool and man-made fiber products as well.

From 1963 to 1976 the LTA was renewed twice (1967 and 1970). These renewals did not change the strength, nature, or scope of the regime. Problems cropped up in the area of man-made fiber products in the late 1960s. Domestic groups asked the U.S. government to impose restrictions on imports of man-made fiber and wool products from a number of Far Eastern suppliers. American negotiations with these exporters did not prove successful until 1971 when the United States threatened to unilaterally restrict imports from Japan. In 1973, in response to a proliferation of bilateral accords and unilateral restraints, developed and less developed countries agreed to conclude a regime covering multifiber products. The resulting accord (MFA) was stronger than the LTA since it created the Textiles Surveillance Body to monitor bilateral agreements. This group was supposed to ensure that any actions taken by states would be consistent with the provisions of the MFA. In addition, a more precise definition of market disruption was developed to further moderate restrictive actions by countries. The nature of the regime became more liberal as the minimum growth rate was increased to 6 percent and more liberal swing and flexibility provisions were introduced in the agreement. The scope of the agreement was enlarged to encompass wool and man-made fiber products in addition to cotton-based goods.

The regime has begun to unravel in the late 1970s and early 1980s. In the 1977 renewal, a statement allowing "jointly agreed reasonable departures from particular elements in particular cases"[15] left the agreement much weaker than it was previously. Countries were allowed to negotiate bilateral agreements without having to worry about satisfying the various provisions on growth, flexibility, and so on. The weakening of the regime permitted a growth in protectionism. The scope of the agreement remained the same, although major efforts to expand the agreement to include flax and ramie and handloom products were made.[16]

The most recent renewal of the MFA, in 1981, has further contributed to its deterioration as a constraint on national actions. Both the United States and the EEC pressed for the inclusion of various paragraphs in the regime which allowed them to cut quotas. While the EEC made an effort to develop a strong, protectionist regime, American pressure resulted in a weak regime that now serves as a minimal constraint on national actions.

AN INTERNATIONAL SYSTEM THEORY OF REGIME TRANSFORMATION

WHY A REGIME?

International systemic theory provides us with a parsimonious method to explain why countries develop an international regime when unilateral controls or bilateral accords would suffice to regulate transactions.[17] Three factors at the international level appear to be important: the influence of "nesting"; a desire to control the behavior of other countries; and information and organization costs.

The concept of nesting can be understood from the perspective of a hierarchy of systems. The textile system is nested within the overall trading system, and the trading system, in turn, is nested within the overall international strategic system (concerning security matters). Actions countries take in these other systems influence behavior in the textile subsystem.[18] For example, strategic confrontation between the United States and the USSR in the overall international system affects the conduct of trade. Similarly, the development of the GATT in the overall trade system influences state actions in textile trade. Theoretically, one would expect problems in the "higher-level" system to evoke greater concern than problems in subsystems, and that countries would therefore endeavor to bring subsystem behavior into line with objectives of the higher-level system.

Applying this nesting argument to textiles, we can consider the importance of the overall trading and international strategic systems. Since the GATT regime in the overall trading system regulates the imposition of trade controls in manufacturing trade generally, countries supporting the broader regime should avoid undermining the norms on which it is based—reciprocity, nondiscrimination, multilateralism, and so on[19]—as long as they can meet their objectives in textile trade. For example, since bilateral restrictive accords not meeting the GATT's specific criteria would violate its norm of multilateralism, countries supporting the GATT might endeavor to institute a multilateral accord such as the MFA. The overall trading system, which is increasingly multipolar in its distribution of capabilities, might also be expected to influence textile negotiations through competition of the key "poles"—the United States, EEC, and Japan—for the economic allegiance of the LDCs (i.e., North-South relations). The overall strategic East-West conflict might also constrain decision makers in developed countries if they feared that LDCs might turn to the East in the event they were not given sufficient Western market access. Considered over time, we might expect this to have been a greater constraint in the "tight" bipolar system of the 1950s than it is in the 1980s.

A second reason that countries might prefer regimes over bilateral arrangements is their potential for exerting indirect control over other countries' actions. If a country finds it costly to use power directly, it might prefer a rule-based arrangement to control their behavior. A country that cannot directly influence the imposition of national controls by other countries may choose to tie its own hands—as long as it is able to tie the hands of others as well. The concept of nesting is relevant here: a country may be dominant in the overall trading system, but if higher-level concerns such as international strategic considerations are important, then the direct use of force to influence others may be out of the question. Another advantage of regimes is that they serve to control large countries' behavior toward small countries. We would expect small countries to be the strongest advocates of rule systems as they might prevent the use of overt power. Therefore, the demand for regimes will be particularly high in systems characterized by many small actors and a few very large ones.

A third factor influencing the choice of a regime relates to organization and information costs.[20] Construction of a multilateral mechanism is organizationally less expensive than is the development of many bilateral contracts. Although this problem can be surmounted by the use of a "standard" negotiating form, setting up the apparatus to conduct different negotiations and organizational mechanisms to monitor them can be an expensive proposition if countries do not agree on norms.

Regimes also reduce search costs and improve the quality of information—a factor of major importance if many issues are under consideration. This aspect of regimes will be of particular interest to smaller countries with limited personnel and expertise since they will find it costly to monitor the international market and actions of others; international regimes are a mechanism for sharing costs. In addition, if there is some central monitoring facility or organization, a regime will provide "transparency" to all participants. Countries wishing to control the actions of others will be able to gather information on violations with greater ease and to compare their negotiating and trading performance with other nations. The type of actors in the system and the number of issues being considered will influence the preference for regimes or bilateral contracts.[21] The presence of small actors and multiple issues should encourage the development of regimes.

In the early 1950s few LDCs were involved in textile trade. This situation soon changed. By the late 1950s a number of newly emerging exporters had increased their exports to both the United States and the EEC countries, and by the mid-1960s both the number of issues in textile trade and the number of participants had begun to increase.[22] In the 1970s the number of issues of politico-economic importance escalated sharply. Actors were concerned with products of a wide variety of fibers (cotton, wool, man-made, flax, and jute) and a bewildering array of goods (both fabric types and apparel items). Issues included modes of control (unilateral, bilateral, or multilateral), quota regulation (flexibility and swing), and circumvention of controls (transhipping, cheating, and outward processing). One would expect that since there are many small nations involved in textile trade and since potential costs of unregulated bilateral agreements are quite high, the prospects for regime formation would be encouraging. While large countries might try to manipulate one another through a rule system, small countries would like a textile regime to provide some degree of constraint on protectionist actions by importing countries.

CHARACTERISTICS OF REGIMES: STRENGTH, NATURE, AND SCOPE

Strength. Of all the theories relating international structure to regime characteristics, the one receiving most attention involves prediction of the strength of regimes.[23] Hegemonic stability theory argues that concentration of capabilities (i.e., a single major power) in an anarchic system leads to stability and strong international regimes. When the concentration of capabilities begins to diffuse, regimes will tend to break down. Earlier formulations of this theory focused on stability in a variety of different issue-areas, but did not really provide a theoretical rationale for the existence of stability.[24] Drawing on collective goods theory, analysts have recently argued that stability can be considered a public or collective good. They thus assert that dominant countries will be willing to act as leaders in international regime formation, absorbing a disproportionate share of the costs associated with their creation and maintenance, since they will reap benefits from stability and will be able to obtain a regime with characteristics they favor.

Aside from the collective goods argument, which suggests that dominant countries will provide inducements for other countries to cooperate in maintaining a regime, the issue of externalities is important. Uncoordinated national action may harm the interests of other countries. If one country closes its market to imports, exporters may divert their goods to another country. In such a situation, the dominant country or hegemon may use positive inducements in the form of side payments and negative inducements in the form of sanctions against uncooperative countries. For instance, a hegemon in the overall strategic system can threaten violence against smaller nations. More subtly, with a threat to bar others from its market, a hegemon with monopsonistic power (i.e., a degree of monopoly buying power) may encourage "bandwagoning" behavior among countries since possibilities for "balancing" are eliminated—countries barred from the monopsonist's markets do not have the option of seeking cooperation from a competitor to the hegemon.[25] Where power is based on demand rather than on supply, the hegemon's threat to bar the entry of goods into its markets will also convince small buyers (other importing countries) to join the regime for fear of having goods diverted to their markets from the hegemon's. Thus, a unipolar system encourages stable and strong international regimes.

Measuring the distribution of capabilities in a particular system is not a simple task. Analysts continue to debate the issue of what elements provide one state with an ability to influence the behavior of other countries. Debating this in the abstract is futile; attention must be focused on the particular issue in which we are trying to explain behavior. Numerous scholars have argued that the overall international system is best seen as being bipolar after 1945, with the United States and the Soviet Union as the two poles.[26]

While there is a relatively high degree of unanimity among analysts in describing the distribution of capabilities in the overall system based primarily on military capabilities, there is less agreement on how to measure power in trade. To some extent, the ability to influence outcomes in trade is a function of the possession of tangible physical resources allowing states to produce goods. As in the oil market of the 1970s, the ability to influence the behavior of other countries in the trading area lies with the country that can produce goods needed by others—especially if the demand for these goods in consuming countries is inelastic.

But the ability to produce and export to other states is not the only source of power in this issue-area: it can also be derived from the role of countries as consumers.[27] Of course, the availability of substitutes and barriers to entry influence the ability of oligopolists or oligopsonists to exert their power in the market.[28] Since the demand for textile and apparel products tends to be more elastic than that for other goods, a threat to restrict exports would not be a source of power. Moreover, since the production of most such products is relatively easy (with some exceptions, such as man-made fiber-based products) and the degree of capital intensity tends to be relatively low for apparel production, barriers to entry are not significant. This further reduces exporters' bargaining power in textile trade.

Following this logic, I operationalize overall trade power based on both exports and imports of countries, while textile power is measured simply as consumer power. As a rough indicator of the distribution of capabilities of countries in the capitalist trading subsystem, data on the ratio of major industrialized country exports plus imports over total world trade are presented in table 2. I have also computed the U.S. share of world trade of the top three capitalist countries. This indicator shows that in the 1950s the system was dominated by the United States. By 1960, after the formation of the EEC, the U.S. share declined dramatically. Since the measure I am using does not reflect the composition of trade, this indicator should be viewed with caution. As a rough measure, however, it gives us some idea as to the changes in potential trading power.[29] In summary, the structure of the trading subsystem should be viewed as being unipolar in the 1950s, with a shift to bipolarity in the 1960s and 1970s. More recently, the system might properly be considered multipolar as Japan's share of world trade has continued to increase over time.

In textile trade, power has increasingly shifted in favor of the EEC and away from the United States. This change is clear in table 3. As in overall trade, the United States was clearly dominant in the international textile system in the 1950s and 1960s. By 1973 the American share had sharply diminished. However, the approximately 60:40 ratio of U.S. to EEC imports between 1960 and 1970 is misleading. Prior to 1973, and especially before 1970, the EEC did not have a unified policy on textile and apparel products, and the United States in fact had greater market power than the ratio suggests since the next largest importer, West Germany,

TABLE 2

POWER IN OVERALL TRADE EXPORTS PLUS IMPORTS OF SELECTED COUNTRIES AS A PERCENTAGE OF WORLD TRADE AND U.S. SHARE OF TOP THREE

			Country			
Year	U.S.	Japan	EEC	West Germany	France	U.S./ Top three
1950	15.7	1.5		3.9	5.0	64
1955	15.8	2.3		6.5	5.3	56
1960	15.1	3.4	15.9			44
1965	14.2	4.6	16.0			41
1970	15.5	6.4	16.2			41
1975	13.7	7.3	20.0			33
1980	13.8	7.7	19.9			33

SOURCE: Constructed from GATT, *International Trade*, various issues. U.N., 1982 for 1950; U.S. Department of Commerce Exports and Imports data, 1955, 1960.

NOTE: EEC imports plus exports exclude intra-EEC trade. All data based on F.O.B. exports and imports, except data for West Germany and France which are based on C.I.F. imports.

had far less than a 40 percent import share. The first significant coordinated policymaking in textile and apparel trade by the EEC was in 1977 when members worked out a single position in advance of the first MFA renewal. These various developments constituted a major change in the distribution of capabilities in textile trade.

Nature. The nature of a particular regime results in part from the metaregime underlying a particular international regime. Thus, as decision makers question the benefits of open systems, one might expect a movement toward protectionism.[30] In addition, at the process level, world prosperity or depression tends to be associated with liberalness and protectionism, respectively.[31]

A hypothesis based on the structure of the international system can account for variation in the nature of regimes. As developed countries face competition from countries producing similar products in a given industry with very different factor proportions (in this case, low labor costs), international regimes should become more protectionist.[32] However, one would expect some variation among countries and in sectors within countries based on industry and labor organizational strength and the power of the state to counteract their efforts. Nesting, a systemic-level factor discussed above, might also affect the nature of a regime: higher-level interests (such as a desire to maintain the principles and norms of the GATT) could affect the type of regime developed in textile and apparel trade.

TABLE 3

POWER IN TEXTILE TRADE.
IMPORTS OF TEXTILES AND CLOTHING,
SHARE OF COMBINED U.S. AND EEC IMPORTS, 1960-1980

| | *From Japan and LDCs* |
Year	U.S. share—%
1960	59.7
1965	58.5
1970	59.6
1973	42.8
1975	37.2
1977	39.0
1980	35.8

SOURCE: For 1960-1970, GATT Document, L/3797, 1972. For 1973-1977, GATT Document, Com/Tex/W/63, 9 October 1979. For 1980, Com/Tex/W/83. Percentages calculated from import data.

NOTE: EEC for 1960-1970 includes United Kingdom and Denmark's imports (data for Ireland not available but insignificant) to provide comparability after 1973.

Scope. The final characteristic to be examined is the scope of a regime, that is, the number of issues encompassed in it. Two interrelated factors can be adduced to explain regime scope. First, it may be affected by increasing competition. In the case of textile trade, as producers in developed countries face increasing competition across a wide variety of products, they are likely to demand restraints on imports. Given the explanation for why regimes are chosen over bilateral or unilateral restraints, we might expect governments to press for an expansion in the scope of an existing regime as a second-best solution.

Second, the type of meta-regime in existence may affect this choice. If countries agree that trade in cotton textiles should be regulated by bilateral accords, what will happen when problems arise in wool or manmade fiber textile trade? The intellectual coherence of issues is critical in this situation. If the meta-regime is based on a norm of regulation of problems arising in the *textile* issue, then it seems logical to expect that increasing conflict in other fiber-based products will lead to a regime with broader scope. But if countries feel that the meta-regime was intended only for the specific fiber type, there may be resistance to including other fiber-based products—especially if exporters believe that national controls are not likely in these goods. In such a situation, growth in the scope of the regime creates conflict and is not simply a procedural issue.

THE ROLE OF DOMESTIC STRUCTURE AND DECISION MAKERS IN REGIME TRANSFORMATION

International factors provide us with important insight into the process of regime transformation. Still, domestic factors and the characteristics of individuals influence bargaining outcomes. Under what conditions will such factors play a decisive role? If we could easily answer this question, it would be a major step forward in the development of theory on regime change. Unfortunately, this may be an issue that does not lend itself to generalization or prediction. To avoid a random introduction of variables in constructing an explanation of regime change, I suggest some possible conditions below.

Domestic Structure and Regime Change

A number of domestic factors might influence the transformation of regimes. For purposes of economy, I focus only on domestic *structure*—the relationship between state and society in countries and the organization of the state and social groups. I do not examine political parties, economic systems, or other such factors indicating "content." When will domestic structure be most significant in the regime transformation process? Under hegemonic conditions in textile trade, the development of a regime should be more straightforward and shorter in duration. By contrast, the absence of a hegemon should lead to a more protracted struggle among the participants and thus allow domestic structure to make more of an impact on the international negotiations. In a non-hegemonic situation, domestic interests should have more of an opportunity to become involved and to gather domestic support for their position. Having suggested the conditions under which domestic structure should play a key role in international negotiations, I turn now to an analysis of the influence of domestic structure on the development and characteristics of regimes.

From the perspective of protectionist-oriented domestic producers, the ideal form of state intervention in the market would be a unilaterally imposed global quota. Such mechanisms as tariffs are less desirable since they do not fix the absolute quantity of imports; they depend instead on the price competitiveness of exporters. If efforts to secure a global quota are not successful, bilateral accords with all offending countries would be a second-best solution. Essentially, this would be the equivalent of a country by country unilateral quota. Under what conditions would domestic import competing groups desire an international regime? Considering a regime as a multilateral accord that regulates intervention by countries, the desire of these groups for a regime would be inextricably tied to the regime's characteristics. They would welcome a strong protectionist regime or a weak regime that permitted a great deal of protectionist action. The worst of all possible worlds from their perspective would of course be a strong liberal regime.

The ability of the state to resist protectionist pressures (or to protect or liberalize selectively, as it sees fit) depends on the strength or weakness of the state vis-à-vis societal interests.[33] In countries whose political systems contain multiple access points and relatively fragmented state power, domestic groups would be more successful in attaining their objective. The instruments the state possesses to influence societal actors are critical: if the state can work through the banking system, through public firms as market leaders, or directly through subsidies, it will be able to resist domestic pressures and manipulate domestic actors. With respect to domestic groups themselves, the success with which import-competing groups organize into peak associations and ally themselves with other like-minded groups will bolster their economic and political power.[34]

While an analysis of overall structural relationships between state and society is helpful in other contexts, we must pay greater attention to the issue-specific domestic "textile" structure to explain the policy process in textile negotiations. The relationship of textile and apparel groups to the state varies across countries.[35]

The U.S. state, in relative terms, is domestically weak. It possesses few instruments to manipulate sectors and is itself fragmented at the aggregate level (legislative, judicial, and executive branches) and even within its most unified component, the executive branch (multiple departments with different constituencies). By contrast, the textile and apparel industries have developed a strong political organization from the 1950s to the 1980s. Through such peak political organizations as the American Textile Manufacturers Institute (ATMI) and the American Apparel Manufacturers Association, these industries have great political power.

These peak associations are particularly significant. There are many firms in the textile industry and even more in apparel. Given the relative political weakness of firms, the peak associations tend to set policy based on the lowest common denominator. This arrangement encourages broadbased protectionist policies and rules out selective state intervention. Finally, while labor is organized in the textile and apparel industries in various peak organizations, most workers are not members of unions. Management is therefore more likely to set the tone for demands on the state.

We would expect the peak associations in the textile and apparel industries to play an increasingly key role in international negotiations over textile regimes as a result of two developments at the international level: the system in textile trade capabilities evolved from a unipolar to a more bipolar system in the 1970s; and, during the 1960s, these peak associations became more powerful vis-à-vis the state. Taking into consideration domestic factors, the U.S. state appears to have few instruments and is too organizationally fragmented to pursue a coherent policy separate from, or provide coherent resistance to, business (and labor) demands.

Since the early 1970s international policymaking in the European Economic Community has been increasingly delegated to the EEC Commission. Prior to the 1970s, members of the EEC and United Kingdom followed quite diverse policies, in part because of their domestic structures.[36] While the United States may be hampered domestically in determining policy on international textile trade, the Commission is even more constrained. The formal delegation of power to the Commission is misleading, for the Council of Ministers sets policy in textiles (as in other important issues).[37] As a result, policymaking is extremely slow, and key member countries must be satisfied before serious negotiations can proceed. For example, the protectionist turn in the United Kingdom in the

1970s allied it with France and Italy in opposing the more liberal trading position of West Germany.

The Commission has undertaken a number of efforts to manipulate member state textile policies and to promote adjustment in the industry but, given its weak enforcement powers, such efforts have come to nothing. By contrast, the development in the later 1960s of the textile industry's community-wide peak association, Comitextil, has allowed it to exert significant power. Thus we would expect the Commission to favor a regime to bolster its own powers over member states, and not to favor individual accords, which would require much haggling among the Council of Ministers or in Article 113 committee meetings.[38] A regime would give the Commission power to interpret the regime's binding effect on actions.

There is tremendous variation among LDCs in state-society relations. The most active textile and apparel exporters are newly industrializing countries such as South Korea, Taiwan, and Singapore which for the most part possess strong states.[39] Since LDCs also receive much more leeway under the GATT and do not have to offer reciprocity in trade negotiations, these countries can satisfy both import-competing and export-oriented textile and apparel interests. Because of this fact and the obvious weakness of these countries in the international system, we might expect domestic textile and apparel interests to support their governments as they strive to develop a regime that would protect their export-oriented interests.

The characteristics of regimes—their strength, nature, and scope—are intimately intertwined from the perspective of domestic interests. In countries where protectionist interests are powerful, domestic groups would welcome a strong, protectionist, and broad regime that forced the country to impose restrictions on imports. By contrast, if the state was pressing for a liberal regime, such interests would prefer a weak and narrow regime that would allow them to continue pressing for restraints on a case-by-case basis, unhampered by an international accord. But if the state were unable to resist protectionist pressures, it might press for a weak regime that gave it more leeway in bilateral negotiations, rather than allow a strong protectionist regime to develop which forced it to be protectionist.[40]

Individual-Level Factors and Regime Change

Although decision makers are constrained by the international system and domestic structure, certain factors may make it possible for them to have leeway in their bargaining choices. In this respect I examine the role of perception, the impact of learning, and the bargaining skill brought to bear on the international negotiations by decision makers. Before considering these somewhat interrelated factors in detail, some comments on the conditions under which individual-level factors will be particularly salient are warranted. A recent study has examined the conditions under which individual characteristics—specifically, the belief systems of officials—will be decisive. These include highly ambiguous situations, non-routine decisions, unanticipated events, long-range planning, and cases where decisions are made by top-level government officials.[41]

The perception and misperception of "reality" is at the center of decision making. If events are continuously misperceived by decision makers in an unpredictable fashion, any effort to develop international structural (or domestic structure) theories will founder. This study presupposes that, for the most part, decision makers are likely to correctly perceive, and thus respond to, international and domestic constraints. Sometimes, however, officials will not react "rationally" to structural constraints. In such cases, knowledge about their belief systems, which affect the processing of information, is invaluable. In addition, if we determine that because of time pressure or other constraints officials are likely to act on the basis of quite limited information, then we might again expect our international system model to be misleading. However, the analysis of all relevant decision makers' belief systems is neither feasible nor helpful in developing a parsimonious theory of regime change. As long as the international structure model (supplemented by domestic factors when needed) provides an adequate interpretation of regime change, it is not necessary to focus on belief systems and information constraints. But in cases where factors at other levels are not sufficient, characteristics of officials are discussed.

International negotiations will at times be influenced by the growth of knowledge and the growing experience of officials. Haas has argued that as negotiators find it necessary to cooperate with their counterparts in other countries, and as consensual knowledge on a particular issue increases, countries are likely to develop institutional mechanisms (such as regimes) to coordinate their activities.[42] Though he uses this approach to examine regime transformation in general, I would argue that consensual knowledge should be used to predict the development of principles and norms rather than rules or procedures. These principles and norms (or meta-regimes) can be used, in turn, to account for the development of regimes since the nature or scope of regimes is likely to be affected by the existing meta-regime.

Decision-makers engaged in negotiations over regime development will also be affected by changing knowledge: more knowledgeable negotiators may bargain more effectively. Similarly, negotiators with greater experience may also be more successful. The strategy pursued by decision makers, particularly in the type of linkages they employ in bargaining, potentially affects the process of regime transformation. In analyzing the use of linkages, it is useful to distinguish between within-issue linkages and across-issue linkages. Within-issue linkages concern the use of market power—oligopsonistic or oligopolistic—to influence outcomes. This is the classical deviation from the ideal economic world of perfect markets where no individual can influence the price of goods. Across-issue linkages refer to links across two or more issue-areas.

If a country is dissatisfied with the behavior of other actors in an issue-area (A), it might be expected to use its issue-specific capabilities to influence the outcomes in this area. But if its capabilities in this area are not sufficient to achieve the desired outcome, that country might be expected to make across-issue linkages (say, a link to Issue B) where it is more powerful. Such linkages could allow it to achieve its objective since its predominance in that Issue (B) could make up for its lack of issue-specific capabilities. At the same time, this kind of linkage might prove costly. This linkage of Issue B to Issue A may undermine the country's objectives in Issue B. In this case, the country may in fact be constrained from using such linkages, at least overtly. Following this logic one step further, the country may even be hesitant to use its capabilities in Issue A to influence outcomes since its relations with the target country in Issue B are so important that it wishes to make concessions (or is at least unwilling to coerce the target country) in Issue A. Thus it is misleading to assume that the country that is more powerful in a specific issue will necessarily win.

We have examined some of the other factors that might be used to explain the transformation of regimes if the international structural approach proves insufficient. At the national level, we have explored domestic structure—the relationship between state and society in general and, more specifically, their relationship vis-à-vis the textile industry. At the individual level, we considered perception and misperception, learning (from a growth in scientific knowledge), and the role of experience and linkage strategies in bargaining.

THE METHODOLOGY: COMPARATIVE CASE STUDIES AND
PROCESS-TRACING

Evaluating the relative contribution of factors on the international, domestic, and individual levels in explaining the transformation of textile regimes would be a relatively easy task if we had a large number of cases. Following a standard statistical approach, we could hold constant two of the three "levels" and allow the third to vary. The large number of cases would then provide statistical evidence on the differing contribution of the explanatory factors. Unfortunately, this approach is not possible as there are relatively few cases of regime transformation in textiles.

This does not mean, however, that we can only describe what has happened in textile trade in a historical fashion. Two qualitative techniques are helpful in developing and testing theory: structured, focused comparison and process-tracing.[43] These qualitative techniques are interrelated and address different facets of the problem of working with few cases.[44] The method of structured, focused comparison can potentially handle the problem of controlling variables when the analyst must work with only a few cases. It is "focused" in that a historical case must be converted for analytical purposes: certain aspects of the case which are interesting from a theoretical perspective provide the focus. This contrasts with the use of a historical period simply for the purposes of describing as many aspects of the period as possible. Furthermore, the analysis must be "structured"; the analyst should "ask" the same questions of the different cases to provide methodological rigor.

The analysis of case studies in this study follows a similar procedure, but rather than pursuing an inductive analysis and using questions to discover a potential causal pattern, I use the expectations generated from the theoretical ideas discussed earlier to investigate regime transformation. This method provides the first step in utilizing cases systematically.

The problem of how to evaluate the success of the theoretical approach still remains. Even though there may be consistency between our expectations and the outcomes, the correlation found might be spurious. The method of process-tracing can be used to contend with this potential problem. Process-tracing examines the path through which the postulated theoretical model affects decision makers. Information obtained from interviews and other sources is used to examine the role of different factors in explaining the process leading to particular outcomes.[45] If we find decision makers responding in a predictable fashion to international structural factors, then our confidence in the expectations generated by the theoretical models is bolstered. More than simple description, much of the analysis in the case studies that follow is a systematic tracing of the decisions taken by officials in the negotiations leading to regime transformation. This method has a further advantage: it identifies possible anomalies, given the expectations generated by the international structural model. Domestic and individual factors can then be introduced systematically into our explanation to generate a more complete understanding of regime change, and, in so doing, improve our understanding of international collaboration.

PART II
THE CYCLE OF
REGIME TRANSFORMATION

In the night of BRAHMAN, Nature is inert and cannot dance till Shiva wills it: He rises from His rapture, and dancing sends through inert matter pulsing waves of awakening sound, and lo! matter also dances, appearing as a glory round about Him. Dancing, He sustains its manifold phenomena. In the fullness of time, still dancing, He destroys all forms and names by fire and gives new rest. This is poetry, but nonetheless science.

—A. K. Coomaraswamy,
The Dance of Shiva, 1969

3
Nonexistence: The Pre-Regime Period, 1950-1959

The decade of the 1950s started out well for developed country textile producers. In the first few years, developed countries successfully competed in the world market and their industries were in many cases advocates of free trade. By the mid-1950s, however, the first protectionist cries from the domestic industries began to emerge—even though for the most part imports were insignificant and posed little threat. But once governments in the industrial countries succumbed to this protectionist sentiment, they found themselves in the position of the little Dutch boy and the dike: as they plugged holes in the dike, new leaks sprang up; restricting imports from one country merely allowed others to jump into the competition for developed country markets. Both the United States and the United Kingdom proved unwilling to impose a severely restrictive overall quota on imports since this would undermine their global objectives. By the end of the 1950s, it became clear to all that a multilateral solution to the problem of growing controls on imports of textiles was needed.

The development of bilateral accords, while important for understanding the process of regime transformation, is important in its own right as an example of international bargaining. In the mid-1950s the United States successfully persuaded the Japanese to restrain their exports of cotton textiles and clothing. As Hong Kong replaced Japanese in this trade, American textile manufacturers forced the U.S. government to seek restraints from Hong Kong. When these negotiations failed, however, Hong Kong continued to export textiles and clothing to the United States. Although this allowed Hong Kong to enjoy short-term gains, it was later singled out by the United States for restrictive treatment.

The United Kingdom also made use of VERs, managing to have India, Pakistan, and Hong Kong commit themselves to a slower rate of British market penetration. The continental European countries, by contrast, did not bother with bilateral negotiations: they simply slapped import quotas on all offending LDC suppliers. International systemic theory successfully illuminates some of the struggles in these bilateral negotiations. When supplemented by domestic and individual factors, these cases of negotiation vividly demonstrate the political aspects of trade.

THE EARLY PERIOD, 1950-1954

Before World War II, the United States ran a persistent deficit in textile trade. While the war left American and British textile and apparel industries relatively intact, Japan—the leading producer of the 1920s and 1930s—had over three-fourths of its textile capacity destroyed.[1] Therefore it is not surprising that the U.S. and British industries forged ahead and dominated textile trade while the rest of the world sought to rebuild. By 1947 the American textile and apparel industries experienced a trade surplus of unprecedented proportions. As a result of this boom, the American industries (and, to a lesser extent, those in Britain) became overconfident and began to see a surplus as a normal pattern rather than as a clearly abnormal situation resulting from the wartime destruction of other producers. In fact, the textile and apparel manufacturers in the United States were so confident of their position that they willingly participated in the development of the Japanese textile and apparel industries, even organized a technical mission in 1948 to assist Japan's textile industry.[2]

By the early 1950s Japan resumed its preeminent position in textile trade,[3] and American producers began to worry—even though imports were less than 1 percent of American consumption.[4] The ACMI (the peak cotton textile producers association) began to plan the battle against imports. Commenting on a public relations proposal, the chairman of its Foreign Trade Committee reported that

it was but one of the strategic moves planned by the industry in its campaign to combat the deluge of free trade propaganda flooding the country.... In the struggle ahead, the industry [should] be careful to avoid pitfalls and not allow misguided zeal to jeopardize the industry's position.[5]

Textile producers particularly resented the U.S. government's active contributions to the growth and development of foreign textile and apparel industries. As part of its policy of fostering economic growth in the less developed countries for strategic and overall trade reasons, American officials implemented a number of aid schemes.[6] In addition to general aid programs, a ten-member mission sponsored by the U.S. government studied the problems of Japan's textile industry.[7] These programs subsequently were seized upon by protectionist interests in the American textile industry as being the cause of Japan's increased competitiveness. While U.S. aid may have made some contribution to the recovery of Japan's textile industry, it is unlikely that it was the most important factor. Japan's competitiveness resulted from its use of more modern equipment than the United States, and its lower wage scale.

The British textile and apparel industries were less sanguine about their postwar prospects than their American counterparts. They pressured the Japanese to restrict textile exports to the United Kingdom as early as 1950, first at a Tokyo conference and again at a conference in Buxton, England. Ironically, the U.S. industries assisted the Japanese in resisting the United Kingdom's efforts to close off its market to Japan.[8] Continental European governments also felt some pressure from their textile industries to restrict imports. But this was not merely a phenomenon specific to textiles: it was true in a wide range of industries because of their war-weakened position.

For the most part, then, there was not an overwhelming concern with import restraints specific to the textile and apparel industries. Developed country producers faced little competition from LDCs in the late 1940s and early 1950s in textile and apparel trade and therefore had few incentives to work toward securing import restraints. Naturally, all producers wished to restrain imports to protect their market shares; the textile and apparel industries were not unique in this regard.

Experiencing general weakness in their economies, European countries imposed restrictions on much of their trade—but they did so by invoking Article 12 of the GATT which permitted such restraints for balance of payments reasons. As a hegemon, the United States preferred not to intervene in trade because of its overall trade and strategic objectives. With few problems specific to the textile and apparel industries, countries simply took actions under the GATT. As might be anticipated from the structure of the textile system, then, a regime in textile trade was unnecessary.

THE AMERICAN BILATERAL AGREEMENTS, 1955-1959: SUCCESS WITH JAPAN

The year 1955 marked two contradictory movements in trade. On the one hand, it was the year that Japan—with persistent American support—obtained admission to the "trader's club" of GATT.[9] On the other hand, it was the year in which the liberal trade regime of GATT began to fray. In textiles, Japan was subtly pressured into instituting the first post-

World War II textile-specific restriction, euphemistically termed a voluntary export restraint. The United States subsequently demanded further restraint from Japan and them made an unsuccessful attempt to prevent Hong Kong from stepping into Japan's vacated place. International bargaining in this case and the U.K. cases (discussed later) took place on a bilateral basis rather than a multilateral one. International systemic theory supplemented by domestic and individual factors illuminates the bilateral struggles.[10]

THE FIRST RESTRAINT ACTION

In the latter half of 1954, the American textile industry responded to a rapid growth in Japanese textile imports with its first postwar foray into the political arena—it decided to resist passage of a bill, H.R. 1, that would have allowed tariff reductions.[11] Though the industry's first effort failed, it learned to extract concessions from the government by threatening to have its congressional supporters block general tariff reduction bills. In the future this type of leverage would be used with great success by both the textile and apparel industries to obtain restraints on imports.

Undaunted by this first loss, the textile industry vigorously pursued restraints in a number of different arenas. First, it defeated a bill to set up an Organization for Trade Cooperation to administer the GATT—an organization initially sought by the United States as the International Trade Organization. It then asked for restraints under the 1951 Trade Agreements Extension Act "escape clause" provision.[12] Textile producers sought protection at every opportunity, regardless of the strength of their case. For instance, they called for import controls under Section 22 of the Agricultural Act which allowed restraints to be imposed if a domestic price support system was being harmed. They argued that imports of textiles harmed the cotton support system. This effort failed when the acting secretary of agriculture noted that the cotton content of imports was equivalent to less than 1 percent of the American cotton crop.[13]

These actions put pressure on the U.S. government to do something about textile imports and worried the Japanese. They set the stage for the industry's campaign to have a quota imposed directly on Japanese imports due to their "low-wage competition." The outcome was the first VER in the postwar period.

U.S. Policy Choice. Both strategic and overall trade concerns restrained the Americans from taking unilateral actions, and led them to negotiate with the Japanese for voluntary export restraints. The American position in the negotiations with Japan reflects the importance of nesting. From a strategic standpoint, Japan had been increasingly seen as a bulwark against communism by U.S. decision makers, especially after the Korean debacle. Moreover, it had been part of American strategic policy to promote the Kuomintang government on Taiwan as the "true" China. The United States had encouraged Japanese relations with Taiwan, and Japan concluded a bilateral peace treaty with Taiwan in 1952.[14] Knowing that Japan had lost the China market—a key outlet for its pre-World War II exports—the United States feared that Japan might turn back to the mainland if its exports to the United States were restricted.[15] As Frederick Mueller, the under secretary of commerce remarked, "Of course, our foreign policy has taken away their natural market, and that in this particular instance is an overriding [concern]."[16] Such sentiments were echoed by the secretary of state, John Foster Dulles, who also feared that Japan might turn to China.

Legislation to establish import quotas on Japanese textiles would be unfortunate . . . it would serve to restrict trade at a time when the free world must depend for so much of its strength on the expansion of trade and economic viability of countries such as Japan.[17]

In light of talk of Sino-Japanese rapprochement, this was not an idle worry.

The United States was especially concerned with the overall international trading system. It had been making a major effort to enable Japan to become a full member of the GATT.[18] Restricting Japanese exports directly would only serve to substantiate European accusations that Japan was engaging in unfair trading practices. In addition, the GATT directly served to constrain the use of quotas. Although quotas could be imposed under Article 19 of the GATT, it had to be done on a nondiscriminatory ("most-favored-nation") basis. Since the Europeans and all others would be affected by such quotas and the United States would be forced to pay compensation to the affected parties, this path to restrain Japanese exports appeared undesirable. There was also a policy contradiction in the use of unilateral quotas: the United States had been making an effort (which continued for a number of years)[19] to have the Europeans stop the use of the restrictive provisions of the GATT and pursue free trade instead. While serving to restrain American *unilateral* actions, such strategic and overall trade concerns did not rule out "voluntary" action by the Japanese.

Domestic structure also affected the U.S. decision to press for voluntary restraints from the Japanese. The weak U.S. state had given little thought to industrial adjustment and no textile/apparel-specific program had been set up to address their numerous problems—most of them unrelated to imports.[20] Furthermore, industries that were dependent on exports had failed to develop a powerful organization to counter protectionist demands. Faced with strong demands from textile producers, the United States pursued the course that would satisfy these interests and at the same time meet its strategic and overall trading objectives.

Japan's Policy Choice. International systemic considerations at the strategic, overall trade level and the textile-specific level influenced the Japanese policy choice. Japan depended quite heavily on the United States in many ways. At the strategic level, the United States was responsible for defending Japan as its military forces were restricted by its constitution to a very small "Self-Defense" force—hardly a deterrent in an age of nuclear weapons. Moreover, a peace treaty had only recently been signed in San Francisco with a number of countries, under American guidance, and a mutual security pact had been concluded between Japan and the United States, effective April 28, 1952.[21] Another consideration at the strategic level was U.S. interest in Japan as a bulwark against communism. This motivated the United States to attempt to secure GATT benefits for Japan in the face of strong European opposition.

Of more immediate consequence to trade in textile and apparel products, at the overall trade level Japan found itself in a precarious position. Long dependent on raw materials, it needed to rapidly expand its exports to pay its large import bill. General Kojio Sato compared Japan's quest for resources to "the root system of a tree seeking sustenance"; if these outlets were blocked, it would die.[22] The United States served as an important market for Japan. Trade with the United States was more than eight times higher than with any other country and 20 percent of Japan's exports in 1956 was destined for the United States.[23] In light of this dependence, American requests for textile export restraints could not be treated lightly.

The story of Japan's effort to enter the GATT is long and complex.[24] In brief, after an extension of the Reciprocal Trade Agreements Act in 1954 allowing the State Department to conduct tariff negotiations with Japan, intense diplomatic activity took place by both Japan and the United States to secure a place for Japan in the GATT. Finally, in summer 1955, Japan entered the GATT—although with second-class status. Throughout the early 1950s, Great Britain and other countries strongly opposed Japan's admission and threatened to invoke Article XXXV of the GATT, which permitted members to withhold most-favored-nation preferences from new entrants, if Japan was admitted.[25] In April 1955, the United Kingdom, France, and twelve other countries carried out their threat and invoked this article in anticipation of Japan's admission. Japan needed and desired American assistance in having these countries drop their Article XXXV action.

Finally, Japan was also highly dependent on the United States in textile and apparel trade. In 1956, Japan sent over 22 percent of its total textile and apparel exports to the United States. Moreover, textile and apparel products accounted for over 33 percent of Japan's total exports (amounting to $551.6 million) to the United States.[26] Prior to World War II, Japan had surpassed the United Kingdom as the largest exporter of cotton textile products. By 1955, Japan's annual industrial production finally reached prewar levels, but its cotton textile exports still lagged far behind.[27] As Japan continued its efforts to expand its cotton exports, it faced problems in recapturing its old markets in Indonesia, Thailand, Pakistan, and Burma.[28] These countries, experiencing a fall in their foreign exchange earnings, imported fewer Japanese goods. Some countries, such as India and Pakistan, had embarked on their own major domestic development efforts in the textile industry and were mounting their own export drives. The Japanese thus had mixed feelings: while they needed and wished to expand their textile exports to the United States, their high dependence on the American market made them acutely aware of the pitfalls in antagonizing their most important customer.

These structural factors impinged on Japanese perceptions. As early as July 1955 the Japanese ambassador to the United States argued in Japan that "for the sake of maintaining amicable U.S.-Japanese relations the Japanese government ought to take steps to curb the anti-Japanese protectionist movement in America."[29] This led the Japanese Ministry for International Trade and Industry (MITI) to take the first steps toward restraining exports. It conducted negotiations with Japanese industry officials and set up a system to impose restraints on exports, and subsequently developed an American Market Problems Special Committee to study plans for an overall restraint agreement.[30]

One factor at the domestic level may have encouraged Japan to be flexible in negotiations with the United States. As part of a broader industrial policy, Japan had been promoting the synthetic fiber industry and was interested in phasing out its cotton industry. Mike Masaoka, a lobbyist for Japan, argued at U.S. congressional hearings on the problems of the textile industry that U.S. cotton textile producers need not fear Japan for long since MITI was promoting synthetics.[31] In light of this industrial policy, one might argue that Japan was willing to see restraints on its exports. There is little doubt that Japan would have been happier to determine the rate at which its cotton textile industry was phased out, but its plan to encourage synthetic fiber production probably diminished Japanese resistance to restraints and made them more willing to compromise.

International Negotiations and the Outcome. In this instance, the "negotiations" were genuinely short-lived. In fall 1955, Dulles secretly advised the Japanese government that they should "exercise restraint in their exports and not attempt to capture so much of the American market that an American industry will be injured."[32] Soon thereafter, in November 1955, MITI imposed a temporary ban on textile exports.[33] This was followed by an announcement on December 21, 1955 that Japan would unilaterally restrain the export of cotton fabrics, blouses, velveteens, and ginghams.[34] The Japanese were at pains to point out that the agreement was intended to "promote mutually beneficial relations."[35] American producers did not share this view; their appetites whetted, they continued to press for greater concessions. This first Japanese restraint agreement was only the first of many.

The Second Japanese Restraint Agreement

The American textile industry pushed on with its campaign to restrain Japanese exports by advocating a bilateral agreement administered by the United States rather than Japan. Only one week after the Japanese announced the VER, the ACMI petitioned the State Department, arguing quite explicitly that

the American industry declines to accept the suggestion that this danger [Japanese imports] can be removed by imposing upon Japan the sole responsibility of determining and controlling the character and volume of its cotton goods exports to the U.S.[36]

The industry called for U.S. government control of imports. In addition, it advocated a quota based on 150 percent of Japanese exports in 1953 and 1954. As these exports more than doubled during 1955, this figure represented a cutback of more than 25 percent.[37]

From the Japanese perspective, the most damage appears to have resulted from a campaign in the United States at the local level to restrict commerce in Japanese textiles. Various boycotts were instituted (with limited success) and stores in South Carolina began placing signs, in compliance with a newly passed law, declaring that they sold Japanese textiles. This and other laws and actions, such as a debate in the U.S. Congress on instituting quotas, set the stage for Japan's next restraint action.

U.S. Policy Choice. While the international structural constraints remained the same in this case, the U.S. government realized it would have to pursue further restraint actions in light of strong domestic pressure from the industry. Perceiving that a unilateral quota would again be harmful to American strategic and overall trading interests, the United States sought another VER—but this time, with greater government involvement.

Japan's Policy Choice. Increasing domestic protectionist pressure in the United States gravely worried the Japanese. They recognized that their unilateral restraint action of December 1955 had not satisfied American producers. Yet the international structural conditions remained the same as with the first restraint agreement: Japan was still very dependent on the American market. In late January 1956, they sent Takashi Murayama, a high official in the Japanese cotton textile association, to examine the situation in the United States. He reported almost immediately that given Japan's precarious position and the growing domestic pressure in the United States, the Japanese should vary their export items, use American merchandising methods and sales houses, and improve their image through a public relations campaign.[38] The Japanese press also reported fear of possible damage to overall Japanese trading interests. One publication noted that the "Japanese side is anxious to go as far as they can without duly sacrificing the national interest."[39]

Once again, given the circumstances, the Japanese sought to retain as much control as possible over the terms of any restraint agreement in the hope of making the best of a bad situation. Ignoring American demands would have been suicidal. In the international bargaining that followed, American pressure on Japan led to their acceptance of more formal export controls.

International Bargaining. The negotiations this time were much more involved—throughout September the two sides bargained almost daily. Although an American trade publication reported that "government officials . . . stress that the U.S. is *not making any formal request or recommendations to the Japanese and is in no way bargaining or trying to reach an agreement,"* this statement was apparently meant for public consumption.[40] The United States continued its pressure. Finally, on September 27, the Japanese notified the State Department that they would impose restraints on their textile and apparel exports based on the 1955 export level. Moreover, Japan agreed to subdivide their export quota into individual ceilings by categories, reduce exports of the most sensitive products (velveteens and ginghams), and seasonally distribute exports to prevent undue concentration at particular times.[41]

As a bargaining strategy, Japan made a within-issue linkage, tying its export restraint offer explicitly to an expectation that

all feasible actions will be taken by the U.S. Government to solve the problem of discriminatory state textile legislation and to prevent further restrictive action with regard to the importation of Japanese textiles to the United States.[42]

The linkage issue is complex, however. By refusing to challenge state actions during the initial negotiations, the U.S. government had successfully used the anti-Japanese laws as leverage in bargaining with Japan. In this sense, the Japanese did not secure any particular advantage from the United States.

A great deal of bargaining was still to take place on the specifics of the agreement before the formal announcement on January 16, 1957. Japan and the United States disagreed on the exact levels of the former's exports to the United States in 1955: Japan argued for an export ceiling of at least 270 million square yards, the United States for a ceiling of 220 million square yards. Even the amount in specific categories was in dispute. Partly by coincidence and partly by design, a number of U.S. actions put pressure on the Japanese. First, and most directly, the Tariff Commission (a body responsible for evaluating the impact of imports on domestic producers), announced on October 24, 1956 that velveteen producers were being harmed by imports.[43] Since the president could legally override a decision of the Tariff Commission without congressional oversight,[44] President Eisenhower delayed his decision on implementing the commission's recommendation to secure leverage against the Japanese with regard to velveteen imports.[45] The administration increased its leverage further by asking that the commission delay its hearing on a petition brought by the Association of Cotton Textile Manufacturers to restrict ginghams.

The second American action was the decision after a lengthy debate to raise the tariff on wool cloth. After international negotiations on tariffs in 1947, the United States had lowered its tariff on wool cloth to 25 percent. But it reserved the right (known as the Geneva reservation) to temporarily return the tariff to 45 percent if American imports exceeded 5 percent of domestic production at any point in the year.[46] Even though American wool textile producers had been demanding since 1953 that the government raise the tariff on imports of wool cloth, the United States now decided to invoke the Geneva reservation for the first time, effective October 27, 1956. Since Japan wished to increase its wool product exports to the United States this served as an important threat.

Japanese negotiations responded to these American actions by shifting from their rigid position and lowering their demands for a large aggregate limit on exports. The negotiations were successfully concluded on December 22, 1956.[47]

Transactions. The terms of the five-year agreement were made public on January 16, 1957 in a news release by the Departments of State, Commerce, and Agriculture.[48] The final agreement called for an overall export limit of 235 million square yard equivalents (sye) and a division of this quota into five categories of products. Flexibility was limited to 10 percent (i.e., the amount one could transfer between groups if one area was not filled), and sublimits were imposed even within the five broad categories of cotton cloth, made-up goods, woven apparel, knit goods, and miscellaneous textiles.[49]

Soon after the conclusion of the agreement, on January 22, 1957, the president rejected the Tariff Commission suggestion that tariffs be raised on velveteens. This action, along with the gingham manufacturers' withdrawal of their application to the Tariff Commission on January 29, 1957,[50] was welcomed by the Japanese. Although they had been forced to institute export restraints, the flexibility of the agreement had allowed them to preserve some control over their exports.

Still, the Japanese lost their competitive position relative to uncontrolled suppliers—even though Japanese exporters managed to fill most of their quota because of an efficient system of administering the export controls. Table 4 shows the rapid textile export growth of uncontrolled suppliers and the decline of Japan's position. While the value of Japan's overall cotton manufactures dropped from $84 million in 1956 to about $66 million in 1957, the quantity of their cotton fabric exports dropped even more sharply—from 150 million sye in 1955 to only 90 million sye in 1957.[51]

TABLE 4

U.S. IMPORTS OF COTTON MANUFACTURES (IN MILLION DOLLARS)

Countries	1956	1957	1958	1959	1960	1961
Total from all countries	154.3	136.2	150.0	201.3	248.3	203.3
Japan	84.1	65.8	71.7	76.7	74.1	69.4
Hong Kong	0.7	5.8	17.4	45.8	63.6	47.0
Other Asian countries	15.3	13.0	14.3	24.0	34.0	25.0
Egypt	0.4	0.5	0.3	0.3	5.9	1.0
Spain	0.3	0.3	0.4	1.6	7.2	3.2
Portugal	0.0	0.1	0.3	1.0	5.2	2.3

SOURCE: Hunsberger (1964), p. 325.

Restrictions on Japan did not satisfy American producers. As imports from Hong Kong filled the gap, the United States decided to attack this problem with the same approach—another bilateral contracting arrangement. In this case, however, the somewhat different international structural conditions characterizing U.S.-Hong Kong relations—and the domestic political process and individual-level factors in both Hong Kong and the United States—led to a failure in the negotiations for restraints.

THE U.K. AGREEMENT WITH EXPORTING COUNTRIES

The cotton textile industry has been at the forefront of British industrial development. Through astute use of import restrictions and increased mechanization, the United Kingdom managed to capture markets in China and India, as well as throughout much of the rest of the
world, before World War II. But by the 1920s, Japan had become a key
competitor, and by 1933 it surpassed the United Kingdom in cloth
exports.[52] India also became a major producer of cotton textiles in the
1920s and 1930s. Thus the United Kingdom was affected by two key
trends: competition from other exporters and import substitution by former markets. From a position as exporter of half of the world's cotton
textiles in 1913 (and up to 75 percent of world exports in the nineteenth
century),[53] the United Kingdom found itself by the late 1950s in the position of being a net *importer* of cotton textiles.[54] The result was massive
overcapacity in this industry.

World War II had a beneficial, if temporary, effect on the British textile
industry. As one of the few major producers to have survived with its
capacity unscathed, the United Kingdom moved quickly to fill export
orders throughout the world. But this surge, recalling the glorious days
of British supremacy, was short-lived. Japan, India, Hong Kong, and
others entered into the production and export of cotton textiles—leading
to severe contraction in the British textile industry. The overcapacity
problem thus was further aggravated by low-cost imports from a number
of LDCs. In response, the British textile industry pressed for protection
from the government. This industry—which had provided the basis for
the birth and development of the theory and ideology of free trade—now
had become a bastion of neomercantilism.

In the early 1950s, as a first step, the industry asked British African
colonies to restrict imports of cotton textiles. When this effort failed,
British producers pursued restraints on imports into the United Kingdom.[55] Although the British government made an effort to promote
industrial adjustment to reduce surplus capacity in the textile industry, it
did so in the context of the Lancashire Pact—a grouping of bilateral contracts or VERs (concluded in 1959-60) affecting imports from Hong
Kong, India, and Pakistan. Other countries also found themselves faced
with restraints when they tried to enter the U.K. market. The events of
this period increased U.S. desire to develop an international regime in
textile and apparel trade.

U.K. POLICY CHOICE

In 1956 the British government decided on its policy concerning
imports from India, a policy that would also be pursued vis-à-vis Hong

Kong and Pakistan. On July 14, the prime minister made the first public reference to a restraint agreement. At a party rally he explained:

I mentioned this matter to Mr. Nehru when he was here and suggested to him that it would be in the interest of both the United Kingdom and India if there were discussions between the representatives of the textile industries of our two countries. Personally, I should regard such talks as useful, and I think Mr. Nehru shares that view.[56]

What international factors influenced his decision to pursue bilateral discussions instead of unilaterally instituted quotas? Turning first to the overall international system, strategic interests clearly played an important role. Like the United States, the United Kingdom perceived the importance of the struggle with communism (although not to the same extent as the United States, given its position in the international system). In a speech to the cotton industry, the prime minister asserted that

it is a matter of pure self-interest that we should see that developing countries are able to develop on democratic lines—for otherwise they may well be tempted to try the Communist system instead.[57]

In addition, U.K. officials expressed concern that the security of Hong Kong would be endangered by restraints on its exports due to the resulting rise in unemployment.

In this connection, although in large part for economic reasons, the United Kingdom was worried about the British Commonwealth arrangement. The Commonwealth Office, for example, saw the possible introduction of restraints on India and Pakistan as leading to the collapse of the Ottawa Agreement,[58] which gave Commonwealth countries duty-free access to the British market. It feared that violation of the Ottawa Agreement would undermine the whole Commonwealth arrangement since the imposition of quotas would politically antagonize these countries.[59]

Considerations deriving from the overall trading system also affected British calculations. With respect to the distribution of capabilities, the United Kingdom was not concerned solely about the political implications of the potential demise of the Commonwealth system; it was also concerned about its trading arrangements. The Ottawa Agreement provided the United Kingdom with large markets for its goods. Moreover, preferences and traditional ties facilitated the competitiveness of British goods in these markets. The president of the Board of Trade expressed his concern, arguing that imposing restrictions on "imports from India and Pakistan would strike at the root of the Imperial Preference System."[60] A country with limited trade capabilities, the United Kingdom was also worried about possible retaliation against its products. (As is discussed in chap. 5, Singapore did actually retaliate against British restraints on textile products by imposing a temporary embargo on all imports from the United Kingdom.) In addition, the British were making an effort to take Hong Kong's pressure off their market (the United States was trying to do the same with Japan) by encouraging other industrialized countries to accept more imports. A restrictive action against Hong Kong obviously would undermine this objective.

The GATT regime also constrained British actions: Article XIX required the United Kingdom to impose quotas on a most-favored-nation basis. Moreover, since this article called for compensation, this would be a heavy burden. The alternative of a high tariff was out of the question. Unless the tariff was prohibitively high, it would not restrict goods from LDCs since they were selling goods at very low prices.

Finally, at the international level, the distribution of capabilities in textile trade favored the United Kingdom vis-à-vis LDC exporters. Britain was not exporting textiles and apparel to the LDCs in significant quantities. Therefore, retaliation by others in this issue-area was not a major threat. However, the United Kingdom was an important market for a number of LDCs—particularly Commonwealth exporters. A threat to close off its market access would provide important leverage in international bargaining.

Domestic pressures to restrict imports from LDCs increased sharply in the mid-1950s. In the early post-World War II period, the United Kingdom regulated imports from Japan, its major competitor in cotton textiles, under the Anglo-Japanese Sterling Payments Agreement.[61] But as the likelihood of Japan's accession to the GATT increased, cries of unfair competition and the need for protection grew as well.

The United Kingdom led the battle against Japan's accession to the GATT, but it was a losing battle as the United States strongly pressured other developed countries to accept Japan into the organization.[62] Accordingly, the British textile industry was very worried. On July 8, 1954, responding to pressure from various segments of the industry, the Cotton Board (an organization set up by the government to represent cotton textile interests) asked for continued restraints against Japan and for restrictions on the growing exports of textile goods from India.[63] The government, wishing to minimize intervention in industry and constrained by international factors, decided to resist formal import restraints. Responding to domestic pressure, the United Kingdom stated in April 1955 that it would invoke Article XXXV of the GATT, which allowed it to withhold concessions from the Japanese and permitted it to continue restricting Japanese imports under the Anglo-Japanese Sterling Payments Agreement. Furthermore, responding to British government pressure, India reduced its tariff on U.K. textile goods as a concession to exporters. But the United Kingdom refused to formally restrain imports from India.[64]

This liberal policy was soon to change. The parallels between the United States and the United Kingdom with regard to the domestic coalition-building process in the textile and apparel industries are striking. As in the United States, the British textile and apparel industries were not unified initially. But it soon became clear to apparel producers that they had to throw in their lot with those in textiles as imports of apparel more than doubled between 1953 and 1955.[65] Rather than continue individual efforts at the sectional level, textile and apparel groups chose to band together and put their combined weight behind the leadership of the Cotton Board. Furthermore, the industries managed to get the Federation of British Industries (representing producers of goods in all industries) to pass a resolution calling for the Commonwealth countries to restrain exports of certain textile products to the United Kingdom. They also worked through the Labour and Conservative parties to put pressure on the government. In this effort, they secured the support of numerous members of parliament for restrictive measures on imports.

The government itself recognized that although there was not massive unemployment in the Lancashire area, where most textiles were produced, there was a problem with diminishing production and employment in the industry. Moreover, the government was being pressured through multiple channels. With international pressures to pursue an open policy and domestic pressures to impose a quota, the British government decided to follow a compromise path and promote an inter-industry bilateral agreement.[66]

POLICY CHOICES OF INDIA, PAKISTAN, AND HONG KONG

The three Commonwealth members facing British restraints had started to increase their cotton textile exports in the early 1950s.[67] With the European market closed off through various quota restrictions, the United States and the United Kingdom were the only significant open markets. Duty-free access to the British market under the Ottawa Agreement enabled these countries to maintain an edge over countries, such as China and Japan, who were also very interested in the British market. Aware of their privileged position, all three Commonwealth states preferred to maximize their access to the British market by pressing on with their export drive in cotton cloth to secure much-needed foreign exchange for their industrialization policies.

These countries realized, however, that political constraints dictated some restraint on their part. They realized that the Japanese had been restrained through the Anglo-Japanese Sterling Payments Agreement (and that they benefited as a consequence). They also were aware that domestic interests were putting pressure on the British government and that the threatened restraints had been used before. For instance, the United Kingdom had restricted goods from China with import quotas. From the perspective of India, Pakistan, and Hong Kong, then, although some restraint appeared to be necessary, they wished to retain maximum control over restrictive actions. A number of Indian leaders were apparently willing to have some industry-level restrictions on exports of cotton textiles so long as overall textile and apparel exports were not cut back. Hong Kong industrialists (in the absence of government policy on this issue) were also willing to institute restraints—but only on gray cloth and only if other countries were restricted as well. Hong Kong apparently felt that as a colony of the United Kingdom it had somewhat more leverage than India and Pakistan and was much more resistant to restraints.[68] But all these states were wary of unilateral restrictions and realized that they were in a relatively weak position. The alternative to an interindustry agreement was quotas, clearly the worst of two evils.

INTERNATIONAL BARGAINING

The interindustry talks were marked by increasing British government involvement over a period of three years. Shortly after Prime Minister Eden's speech in July 1956 (in which he mentioned that interindustry talks had been brought up with Prime Minister Nehru), talks commenced between British and Indian officials. The British realized that they could not simply restrain Indian exports; growing exports from Hong Kong and Pakistan also had to be addressed. Hong Kong had increased its share of U.K. imports of cotton yarn and woven fabric, in terms of value, from 2 percent in 1953 to 18 percent in 1955 and 30 percent in 1958. In gray cloth, Hong Kong increased its share of U.K. imports, in terms of quantity, from 1 percent in 1953 to 34 percent in 1958.[69] Hong Kong, India, and Pakistan were replacing Japan in the U.K. market because of quota restraints on Japanese imports of these goods. (Japan's share of cotton yarn and woven fabric had dropped from 20 percent of the U.K. market in 1953 to 8 percent in 1958; its share of gray cloth fell from 50 percent in 1953 to 12 percent in 1958.)[70] The president of the Board of Trade therefore made plans to have interindustry talks with Hong Kong as well.

Under the auspices of the British government, Sir Cuthbert Clegg, former chairman of the Cotton Spinners and Manufacturers Association, led the first mission to India and Hong Kong in January 1957.[71] The well-publicized British position that quotas were out of the question did not help its bargaining position. The president of the Board of Trade told the Cotton Board that they "were not authorized to threaten the Indians" and that the British government would not unilaterally impose quotas.[72] Although this was a private admonition, various public discussions in the United Kingdom made it evident to the Indians that the British were reluctant to impose quotas. Hong Kong also perceived this reluctance. A Hong Kong publication reported that "the British Government had thus far repeatedly said that it would be unwise to impose unilaterally any restrictions on imports of Commonwealth cotton goods."[73] As Hong Kong was much more dependent than India on the British market (the latter's exports to the United Kingdom amounted to only 2 percent of production), the ensuing problems were not surprising.

Though Indian officials were willing to restrain their exports if Hong Kong and Pakistan did so,[74] Hong Kong refused. India was warier of damaging relations with the United Kingdom over a relatively minor issue. Hong Kong was more dependent on cotton textile exports to the U.K. market and did not have a government representative to negotiate on its behalf. Hong Kong industrialists bargained for time to boost their exports and stressed that unlike India, Hong Kong "had no large home market and was much more dependent on exports of its manufactures, having lost much of its entrepot trade."[75] As they judged that the British government was unwilling to impose a quota (and as they were very dependent on the U.K. market), Hong Kong producers saw no reason to go along with restraints unless threatened. With the colonial secretary, Alan Lennox-Boyd, providing support in the United Kingdom, Hong Kong was confident that it could avoid restraints for some time to come.

With Clegg's mission having failed to encourage the Hong Kong industrialists to practice self-restraint, the British government decided to increase its pressure. It asked the governor of the colony, Sir Alexander Graham, to confer with the industrialists in an effort to have them restrain their exports. Yet the industrialists continued to resist. In addition to their delaying tactics, the industrialists' fragmentation was no doubt a factor in their resistance: since each industrialist was trying to improve his market share in the United Kingdom, no leader was able to develop an effective restraint system. Ironically, this worked in their favor by creating a delay, during which they built up their exports. With India and Pakistan willing to restrain their exports only if Hong Kong agreed as well, matters were at a standstill.

Pressure from the U.K. industry once again provided the needed impetus to continue the negotiations. Still wary of imposing quotas for

the reasons discussed above, the government made a renewed effort to
have Hong Kong voluntarily restrain its exports. This time, the permanent secretary of the Board of Trade, Sir Frank Lee, was sent to India,
Pakistan, and Hong Kong.[76]

In late 1957, the United Kingdom imposed an import quota on goods
from China which froze imports for 1958 at the 1957 level. The action
against China indirectly increased pressure on Hong Kong by demonstrating the United Kingdom's resolve to control imports. After a series
of negotiations in March 1958 with a committee of Hong Kong industrialists chaired by J. D. Clague, chairman of the Hong Kong General
Chamber of Commerce, Lee warned that "there was a considerable difference between reaching a voluntary agreement and the imposition of
restrictive measures."[77] This "observation" was not lost on Hong Kong.
In light of the seriousness of the United Kingdom's effort and the presence
of a senior member of the government as negotiator, Hong Kong agreed
to have further talks with Cotton Board officials in an effort to reach an
accord. But in agreeing to do so, Hong Kong set a number of its own conditions: it was willing to consider restrictions on gray cloth only; further
quotas in other areas would not be permitted; and the agreement would
be invalid if used as a precedent for other countries. Two linkages were
also important: (1) a restraint action in cotton goods was not to be generalized to other products, and (2) it asked for help in solving its unemployment and refugee problems.[78]

After securing this very tentative commitment from Hong Kong, the
British government proceeded with negotiations on a trilateral basis with
Pakistan and India. These talks took place in early May in London. India
and Pakistan tentatively agreed to specify levels at which they would
restrain their exports if Hong Kong did the same. India and Pakistan
were attempting to use Hong Kong's resistance to improve their own
position. Since their agreement was based on Hong Kong's accepting an
agreement, they could continue to ask for changes until the final signing.
This shifted the pressure onto Hong Kong once again.

A number of actions by the United Kingdom and Hong Kong affected
the negotiating process before the Cotton Board's mission to Hong Kong
in September 1958. The United Kingdom decided to pursue an industrial
adjustment policy in its cotton industry to reduce excess capacity. Prime
Minister Harold Macmillan took the initiative for this action in July 1958
when he contacted a few cotton industry leaders regarding possible
adjustment. This plan was kept closely under wraps, however, since it
was thought that industry would not support such a scheme without
restrictions on imports from Commonwealth countries as a prerequisite.
It was also thought that investment in new plant and equipment might

not take place under such a plan without a guaranteed market for U.K. producers.

Hong Kong's actions were more directly related to the negotiations. Its General Chamber of Commerce pursued various avenues in an effort to improve their negotiating position. Among the most significant were a public relations pamphlet that was circulated among firms exporting to Hong Kong and the fostering of transnational allies in the United Kingdom (the China Association in London, retired Hong businessmen there, and others in favor of free trade).[79]

In late September 1958 the third U.K. mission arrived in Hong Kong, with Cotton Board chairman Clegg, and two other Cotton Board appointees.[80] The Hong Kong negotiating team was once again led by Clague. The bargaining was marked by an interesting strategic move by Hong Kong which paid off only partially. Whereas Hong Kong had tentatively agreed to institute restraints only if India and Pakistan did the same, it now realized that a tentative agreement such as those negotiated by these countries would not satisfy its needs.

Hong Kong negotiators decided to argue that their position was unique (being a colony and without a large home market) and that a different method should be used to calculate the future quota. The United Kingdom wanted to base the quota on the average of exports over the previous three years; Hong Kong argued for a quota based on the preceding six *months*.[81] Moreover, the United Kingdom wanted across-the-board restrictions that would include garments and all made-up goods (in addition to cotton textiles); Hong Kong argued that only gray cloth should be covered in the agreement. The difference in methods of quota estimation was significant. Under the proposed U.K. scheme, Hong Kong would obtain a quota of about 74 million sye. Hong Kong's approach, however, would give it a quota of 120 million sye. The sharp differences in position led to difficult negotiations and an apparent deadlock.

The turning point in the negotiations came on the day of the British mission's planned departure. In a telegram, Macmillan "urged both sides to make further efforts to agree."[82] Hong Kong perceived this as a request to make further concessions. In response to his pressure, they agreed to some concessions, which the British negotiators made a bit easier by tentatively agreeing to somewhat higher quotas. One mission member, Lord Rochdale, returned to England with the news and noted that some progress had been made. Still, details had to be worked out and there was no full agreement on quota levels or coverage of the agreement. The United Kingdom subsequently submitted a new position, which was partially accepted by early November. But Hong Kong resisted reaching a final agreement.

Finally, the United Kingdom resorted to a threat to use its market power in textiles to force an agreement. Macmillan directed the governor of the colony to tell the negotiators that "the British Government would impose unilateral quotas if 'voluntary' limitations were not enforced."[83] His additional threat that quota levels would be lower than those in the tentative agreement was enough to secure restraint from Hong Kong.

THE OUTCOME AND THE EFFECT ON TRANSACTIONS

The terms of the agreement covered most cotton textile articles, but the ceiling was quite high: Hong Kong was allowed to ship 115 million sye of cotton products per year for a period of three years. And though no fixed quota was set on cotton made-up goods and apparel, there was an indirect quota that would be triggered if exports of these products exceeded 46 million sye. In such an event, growth above 46 million sye would be taken away from the cotton fabric quota of 115 million sye. Finally, any amount of the total quota which was left unused could be carried forward to the first half of the following year.

By following a bargaining strategy of delays and arguing for its unique position, Hong Kong managed to secure a much higher quota than India or Pakistan and an agreement that covered fewer products. But this relative success was short-lived: India and Pakistan immediately pressed to have their agreement renegotiated and improved. Through tough bargaining, India and Pakistan managed to delay the negotiations and secure much higher quota levels than they had tentatively accepted earlier. The agreement was concluded in September 1959. India agreed to an overall restraint level of 175 million sye; Pakistan agreed to 38 million sye. These figures were about 20 percent higher than those stipulated in the tentative agreement reached the previous year. With Indian exports running at a yearly rate of only 144 million sye based on the first eight months of 1959, the new agreement was hailed as a great success—even by Indian industrialists.[84]

Hong Kong producers sharply criticized the British delay in securing restraints on Indian and Pakistani exports. They argued that they had agreed to restrain their own exports only if India and Pakistan were restrained immediately. When their government pointed out that this was not true, the producers argued that "when we signed the undertaking we had the knowledge that India and Pakistan would follow."[85] Such protests continued, with appeals of one sort or another being made to the Hong Kong government. Attention soon shifted to the ongoing negotiations with the United States which were beginning to heat up. Hong Kong had hoped that the dislocation they were experiencing (estimated at

30 million sye owing to restrictions from October 1959 to January 1960) would be made up by having "manufacturers... redirect [their] dislocated goods" to the U.S. market.[86] In part their resistance to American pressure for VERs resulted from this effort.

U.S. ATTEMPTS TO RESTRAIN HONG KONG EXPORTS

The increasing success of other countries in penetrating the U.S. market was one major outcome of the restraint on Japan (see table 4). In response, the American industries demanded restraints against the new suppliers. Most important, as Hong Kong was especially interested in the export of apparel, the growth of American imports of these goods encouraged apparel producers to join the cotton textile manufacturers in a powerful protectionist coalition.[87]

U.S. POLICY CHOICE

American textile and apparel producers joined hands to argue for a strict unilateral quota before the Senate's Pastore committee, which was investigating the problems of the textile industry.[88] The committee proved sympathetic; Senator Pastore commented with gusto on Japan's voluntary export restraint of 1957: "I say this. If we are going to have a quota in America, it ought to be an American quota."[89] This statement was not merely a flag-waving effort. American producers were unhappy with the flexibility in the VER negotiated with Japan (allowed by the United States because of strategic and overall trade interests) and hoped to have a quota that would allow for stricter control of imports.

As in the Japanese case, U.S. strategic interests discouraged the imposition of a quota. Though Hong Kong was not seen to be so strategic an area as Japan, it was a showpiece of free enterprise and a magnet for Chinese refugees. In addition, Hong Kong was a listening post for eavesdropping on the mainland. Finally, Hong Kong was a colony of the United Kingdom. It pursued its own foreign economic policy, but Britain acted as its guardian. As one British official put it, "The Foreign Office thinks it is wrong to have Hong Kong discriminated against vis-à-vis LDCs of similar strength."[90] Given the nature of U.S.-U.K. relations, the United States was somewhat wary of imposing quotas on Hong Kong imports.

At the trade system level, U.S. officials recognized other constraints. On May 12, 1958, Secretary of Commerce Sinclair Weeks, who strongly opposed quotas, warned:

Any general resort to quotas on the part of the United States would weaken our current efforts to reduce foreign quantitative restrictions against our own exports. . . . As a large exporter and efficient producer of products wanted by other countries, we have more to gain by avoiding quotas and more to lose by any action on our part which encourages their greater use throughout the world.[91]

Finally, the American textile and apparel market for Hong Kong goods was not as large as in the Japanese case. The United States accounted for less than 12 percent of Hong Kong's total textile and apparel exports in 1958.[92]

The net result of international constraints on the United States was its desire to avoid unilateral quotas. In the words of Henry Kearns, U.S. assistant secretary of commerce for international affairs, assigned to negotiate with Hong Kong, the United States sought a "voluntary export restraint to go both ways at the same time"—that is, it sought to maintain an open trading stance while responding to domestic pressure for restraints.[93] Given the constraints on U.S. policymaking and the reduced leverage over Hong Kong, American decision makers asked Hong Kong to diversify its activities to take pressure off particular categories of textile and apparel products.[94] Even this limited objective proved difficult to achieve.

HONG KONG POLICY CHOICE

Numerous constraints operated on the Hong Kong textile and apparel producers. With the United Kingdom as its guardian, Hong Kong did not feel threatened strategically. At the overall trading level, in 1958 the United States furnished a market for less than 11 percent of Hong Kong's goods (versus over 20 percent for Japan's). This lesser overall trade dependence, combined with the relatively minor importance of the U.S. market for textiles and apparel exports, appears to have given Hong Kong greater confidence in its ability to resist the United States. Hong Kong's heavy *overall* dependence on textiles and apparel (over 40 percent of its exports) gave it added incentive to resist. Industrialists argued that the balance of trade was in the "American favor to the tune of H.K. $113 million";[95] it was their view that the United States had no right to ask for restraints.

Hong Kong saw its actions as being consistent with the changing international division of labor. One editorial commented that some industrial nations, such as West Germany, were more enlightened than others. It referred to a German official's speech, in which he declared, "The newly developing countries should be given a chance to market the products of their new industries abroad." He went on to state, "The highly industrialized countries might even suspend manufactures of simple, basic products and concentrate on more complex equipment which the space age demands."[96] Although quoted approvingly by Hong Kong, this enlightened view was not shared by all countries. The United States was responding to a growth in competition with protectionist moves, which Hong Kong saw as a flaw in the American adjustment strategy, criticizing American and other Western leaders as "reluctant heroes of neoprotectionism."[97]

With respect to trade norms, Hong Kong felt that it had been a fair player. Criticizing the People's Republic of China (PRC) for "failing to stick to the rules of free trade—that you do not sell below cost,"[98] it argued that the PRC was rightly paying the penalty for undercutting other producers and forcing them out of the market. But it saw itself as being wronged. As one editorial noted, "Now the players who have abided by the rules are being disqualified."[99] Playing by the rules was also an issue raised by textile industrialists, who argued that "Hong Kong had suffered a great deal by faithfully observing the trade embargo enforced by the United Nations, and it was a matter of regret that the U.S., a member of that world body should seek to restrict Hong Kong's exports, thereby strangling its development."[100]

Domestic factors and "learning" bolstered Hong Kong's desire to resist American pressure for restraints. Hong Kong's government had not been a very active participant in textile policymaking because of its strong commitment to laissez-faire. In fact, the chief U.S. negotiator with Hong Kong found his task difficult due to the "loose nature of the economy."[101] The British had encountered the same problem with Hong Kong: there was "no body authorized to speak on behalf of the Hong Kong producers...."[102] The key to the negotiations in Hong Kong, then, was various industry organizations representing spinners, weavers, garment manufacturers, and the like. Moreover, other groups were clearly weak compared to the mainstay of Hong Kong's economy—textile and apparel producers. Without a single spokesman and with different groups having different objectives, it was not an easy matter for the United States to exert pressure on Hong Kong.

Hong Kong manufacturers of textiles and apparel products were intent on securing maximum access to the American market. Forced to restrict exports to the United Kingdom, Hong Kong producers increasingly turned to the United States. But there were other reasons that made Hong Kong particularly resistant to restrictions.

Hong Kong producers had learned three things from their negotiations with the United Kingdom. First, they now felt that it was unwise to give in to demands for restraints from importers unless all exporters were being restrained. Hong Kong was unhappy with British efforts to restrain its exports and continuously pointed out that India and Pakistan still had not been restrained by the United Kingdom. As a consequence, they argued that "so long as Hong Kong is the only one with a self-imposed ceiling, it would merely hurt Hong Kong without benefiting Lanca-shire."[103] In fact, Pakistan and India were rapidly building up their exports to the United Kingdom to secure higher quota levels in anticipa-tion of being restrained.

Second, Hong Kong producers learned from negotiations with the United Kingdom that it paid to hold out as long as possible. As one reader of the *Far Eastern Economic Review* (*FEER*) pointed out in a letter concerning negotiations with the United States, "Is it not arguable that Hong Kong should build up her past performance record for all she is worth, banking on at least another nine months or a year of freedom?"[104] In negotiations with the United Kingdom, Hong Kong had stalled for a long time, which allowed its producers to build up their exports to obtain a higher subsequent quota.

Third, Hong Kong producers were afraid of setting a precedent. Dur-ing the British negotiations, other developed countries had responded to the British attempt to secure restraints by seeking their own accords: France had moved to restrict imports of textiles from Hong Kong into its territories in Africa, and West Germany and Switzerland had considered restraints on Hong Kong imports.[105]

These lessons, when applied to the American context, proved to be Hong Kong's undoing. While it had learned to bargain to avoid restraints in the short run and would succeed in using a delaying strategy to avoid U.S. restraints, textile producers failed to learn two important lessons: (1) if they maintained good relations with the United States they could possibly avoid more severe restraints in the future; and (2) efforts to maximize revenue in the short run could prove disastrous to their long-run trading position. While Hong Kong's restraint toward the United Kingdom had diminished its rate of export growth, the VER did provide guaranteed access. Moreover, the access they received was better than that given to a number of other countries. But this lesson escaped many Hong Kong producers and, in the absence of restraints, they subse-quently overextended themselves in the U.S. market.

Three other factors proved to be important in Hong Kong's decision to resist restraints. First, Hong Kong was ideologically committed to free trade—a view that was bolstered by its rapid growth from successfully exporting to world markets. As a result, Hong Kong perceived that the United States would be sympathetic and would see restraints as being "a most undesirable departure from American traditions as presented to the world."[106] "Orderly" marketing would also mean the direct participation of the government in organizing and administering a restraint action—an intervention that would disrupt the laissez-faire emphasis (and the freedom of producers) in the colony.

Second, after Hong Kong producers restrained their exports to the United Kingdom, the British government assured them that it would "oppose vigorously the unilateral imposition of restrictions by other countries on imports of Hong Kong goods."[107] Having complied with its request for restraints, producers expected the United Kingdom to help them out.

Third, textile and apparel interests resented the previous American action to restrain Hong Kong exports by prohibiting imports of goods that might have originated in China.[108] This action, combined with the lack of any aid or much investment from the United States, led to the view that "the Colony owes nothing to the U.S. . . . We have received no official economic assistance—the reverse in fact with the strict conditions of the Foreign Assets Controls ever before us."[109]

In summary, factors at the international, domestic, and individual levels encouraged Hong Kong to resist American efforts to secure restraints on its exports. Of course not all producers in Hong Kong were sanguine about succeeding with the United States. In March 1958, long before the visit of American negotiators, some were concerned that the United States might force restraints on Hong Kong. And instead of the tough stance discussed above, a high official in the key producers' association, the Garment Manufacturers' Union, warned of "excessive concentration on the American market," pointing out that "the United States might restrict imports of many important clothing items in the future."[110] But his was a lone voice in the crowd. The majority view is more aptly summed up in this editorial:

Let us be firm. Entertain any American plaintiffs who may come; show them our industries, our many relief projects. Then send them away with the understanding that we concede none of our trade to any foreign power.[111]

International Bargaining

The negotiations between the United States and Hong Kong were quite prolonged. Discussions of one sort or another continued from the beginning of 1959 to the middle of 1960. But two trips by Kearns to Hong Kong—in February and November 1959—formed the basis for talks. Although a major group of producers in Hong Kong agreed to restraints, in the end U.S. domestic pressure sabotaged the talks.

Kearns first went to Hong Kong on February 13, 1959 for three days, *after* meeting with American producers to ascertain their views on restraints. Approaching Hong Kong in a friendly manner, he argued that they should diversify their exports to the United States to "diminish pressure from industry" to impose quotas on imports from Hong Kong.[112] Furthermore, the United States decided to address only trade in cotton-based exports—even though some officials recognized that synthetics might be a problem in the near future.[113] Summarizing the American position to the press, Kearns argued that "we can buy a lot from Hongkong—with the great purchasing power of the U.S.—but if Hongkong concentrated to a great extent on five items then they would be bound to cause a problem."[114]

Kearns's suggestion to diversify did not have the desired effect. The reception the U.S. proposal received was "almost hostile."[115] All the major representatives of textile and clothing producers for the U.S. market rejected Kearns's overtures. The Hong Kong General Chamber of Commerce was the only group that responded to his seemingly innocuous request. The chairman of that body simply said that "note would be taken of Mr. Kearns' suggestion that Hongkong should diversify its exports to America."[116]

Kearns returned to the United States hoping that something might come of the Chamber of Commerce's willingness to listen to his pleas for diversification. But within a few months Hong Kong sharply increased its market share in a number of clothing categories. For example, in cotton shirts, a major export item, Hong Kong's share in only the first *two* months of 1959 was 50 percent of the American import market—in contrast to their total share of 35 percent for all of 1958.[117] In fact, while Japan's exports of cotton products were stationary, Hong Kong's grew from $5.8 million in 1957 to $17.4 million in 1958 and $45.8 million in 1959.[118] In an effort to relieve growing protectionist pressures in the United States, the Commerce Department argued in April 1959 that Hong Kong was likely to restrict its exports.[119] But with the Pastore committee strongly advocating quotas in its February 1959 report, the domestic industry had no reason to diminish its pressure on the U.S. government—especially in light of the rapid growth in exports from Hong Kong.

Nonetheless, Kearns continued his domestic politicking to contain protectionist demands. At one point he remarked, "You don't kick a good customer in the teeth."[120] Although this reasoning was valid since the United States had an overall trading surplus with Hong Kong, specific sectoral interests were able to exert more political impact than the diffuse exporters benefiting from Hong Kong trade. Having encountered major problems in encouraging Hong Kong to diversify, in May 1954 Kearns turned his efforts toward the United States. He met with numerous major importers and retailers in the United States in an effort to have *them* diversify their purchases from Hong Kong. But while Kearns optimistically noted that he was "confident that they will review their buying practices and revise them where indicated to help prevent a worsening of the problem,"[121] this was not to be the case. With heavy competition among retail outlets in the United States, any diversification move would have impaired their relative market position. This effort, then, also came to nothing.

Attempting to influence both the importers and exporters, Kearns's aides mentioned that "mandatory controls would become necessary if the steep rise in imports from Hong Kong was not checked by early December."[122] The U.S. cotton producers association (the National Cotton Council) decision to ask the Department of Agriculture to investigate the extent to which harm was being done to the cotton price support program from cotton *textile* imports put further pressure on Hong Kong. These two actions greatly concerned Hong Kong. In an editorial, the influential *FEER* shifted its position from one originally advocating free trade and a desire to send the Americans "packing" to a call for the Hong Kong government to monitor a system of restraints.

If the small manufacturers will not agree to temper their ambition of joining the bandwagon of the currently expanding American market, and if the pursuance of those ambitions will jeopardize Hongkong's retention of that part of the market it has already gained, *then an element of force must be introduced by government.*[123]

The press was not the only element having second thoughts. Leaders of the Hong Kong garment manufacturing industry asked the government whether a voluntary ceiling on exports was advisable. Concerned about U.S. pressure, they saw a quota as the alternative to VERs—an action they perceived as much worse. They were aware that, according to U.S. (and GATT) law, quotas would be imposed on a nondiscriminatory basis and would be based on performance for the last seven years. Aside from the inherent inflexibility of a quota, then, Hong Kong would lose out to Japan since the latter had been exporting larger quantities of textiles for a much longer time.[124] The Hong Kong government's attitude was not very helpful: it merely offered to "administer any agreement made unanimously among the manufacturers."[125]

A lack of consensus in the ranks of manufacturers was at the root of Hong Kong's problems. Small firms were succeeding in their efforts to increase their share of Hong Kong's trade with the United States. Large firms were willing to have restraints since they would freeze existing market shares, guaranteeing them a market, and avoid what they felt was excessive competition among firms which was cutting into profit margins as labor and materials become scarcer.[126] This struggle eventually led to a split in the Hong Kong producers' position.

Discussions among the members of the Garment Manufacturers' Union led Kearns to see some prospects for restraints. At the end of August he announced that he "expected voluntary quotas by the end of October and would talk figures on his next visit to the Colony."[127] To enhance Kearns's bargaining power, President Eisenhower asked the Tariff Commission to investigate the effect of VERs on the U.S. cotton subsidy program under Section 22 of the Agricultural Act.[128] If problems were found by the Tariff Commission, the president could ask for a penalty fee on imports to compensate for the fact that these countries were obtaining American cotton at a price subsidized by the American government—a price unavailable to American textile producers.[129]

The United States took a second action to encourage cooperation from Hong Kong. This request, made by the president, was in the form of a carrot rather than a stick. Eisenhower instructed Kearns to investigate the future prospects for investment in Hong Kong. Hong Kong officials perceived the link to export restraints. As one observer in Hong Kong put it, "There is some speculation in the Colony that this might be a *quid pro quo* for Hongkong's cooperation in beginning serious negotiations on a quota."[130] Meanwhile, Hong Kong countered with its own strategy. The Hong Kong General Chamber of Commerce asked a major law firm in Washington, Covington and Burling, in which Dean Acheson was a partner, to investigate the likelihood of American import restraints.[131] The stage was now set for Kearns's second visit.

A major rift among Hong Kong producers developed during Kearns's second visit to Hong Kong from November 18 to 23. Shortly before his arrival, small and large manufacturers were sharply divided on restraining exports. Since producers were still debating what Hong Kong's position would be, they could not agree on who would represent Hong Kong in the negotiations. They finally compromised and a special subcommittee was instructed to hear the proposals; it would not, however, be allowed to make a decision on restraints.[132] Within three days after Kearns's arrival, the split became institutionalized. Eighteen large producers broke away from the Garment Manufacturers' Union after it voted to reject a voluntary export restraint. These producers represented over 80 percent of Hong Kong's garment exports to the United States and approximately 32 percent of total garment production in the colony.[133] Immediately after the split the new organization's chairman stated: "We agree to the restriction of Hongkong's garment exports to the U.S. because we don't want to lose this market."[134]

The small manufacturers sharply criticized the restraint proposed by the group of larger firms. They had been told by Covington and Burling that unilateral restrictions were unlikely. Moreover, the "stick" (the investigation of the cotton subsidy program) failed to have its desired effect: as one producer noted, the restraint action was foolish because "a penalty fee was likely to be imposed on cotton textile imports."[135] Thus the American action did not give Kearns the intended leverage.

The newly formed rebel association, the Hong-kong Garment Manufacturers' (for the U.S.A. Association), gained a number of other members soon after the split. But the conflict between large and small manufacturers continued. In attempting to pressure the government, a producer involved with the older association argued that

the few dissident garment makers might send 80% of total garment exports to the U.S. But nearly 1,000 garment manufacturers with no less than 100,000 people in their employment could not submit to a few people's whims at the risk of losing their rice bowls.[136]

THE OUTCOME AND TRANSACTIONS

As the battle heated up between the two associations, the Colonial government warned the garment manufacturers that the United States was likely to impose quota restraints in the absence of a VER on their part. It had therefore decided to pursue the initiative taken by the new association. In a letter to the U.S. Consul General in late December 1959, the terms of the proposed agreement were spelled out. Only five garment types were to be restrained for a period of three years. The agreement specified high growth (10 percent to 15 percent) and "carry forward" (the future use of unused quotas) in all categories.[137] In submitting this accord, the Hong Kong government stated that it endorsed this action because the new association represented the greatest share of exports to the United States.

Although Hong Kong hoped that this "generous offer" would be accepted in the "spirit of international understandings and cooperation in which it is offered,"[138] the American textile and apparel industries were not feeling very generous. Both the ACMI and the Southern Garment Association immediately opposed the proposed action.

Meanwhile, in Hong Kong, the older Garment Manufacturers' Union continued to oppose the restraint plan. The chairman of the Chinese Manufacturers' Association, a broadly based trade group, argued: "Since this very minor group embraces some factories with either American or

Japanese capital, many of which are factories newly established, therefore such a group cannot be considered qualified to come to any agreement limiting the exports of the garment industry."[139] The result of this internal bickering and U.S. rejection of the proposed agreement was the collapse of the negotiations. Although the American producers suggested a counterproposal, it was far beyond what Hong Kong was willing to accept—especially in light of the ongoing struggle between various associations. By the end of February 1960 the talks had broken down completely.

U.S. failure to secure restraints from Hong Kong can be attributed to the complexities of domestic politics (in Hong Kong and the United States) and the weaker international leverage that the United States had vis-à-vis Hong Kong as compared to Japan. We have already seen that Hong Kong was less dependent on the United States than Japan. Moreover, with Hong Kong a colony of the United Kingdom, and with mixed American objectives, it was difficult for the United States to make it clear that "the alternative to a VER was worse."[140] In addition, the American threat to impose a penalty fee on cotton imports backfired since it appeared that such a fee would be imposed regardless of what Hong Kong did. Many Hong Kong producers therefore took the short-term view that as "Hong Kong cotton goods will become less competitive in foreign markets generally [due to a rise in the price of raw cotton and wages] it is therefore folly voluntarily to limit exports to their most important market."[141]

Hong Kong failed to benefit from an absence of American restraints. As shortages of labor and raw materials increased, contracts as initially negotiated with American buyers could not be fulfilled, resulting in a large number of cancellations (worth over $14 million by March 1960).[142] These problems were aggravated by the efforts of a number of producers to build up "performance" records in anticipation of U.S. quotas, which were to be based on such past performance. Without quality control, Hong Kong experienced major problems and their exports fell sharply. Surplus capacity, resulting from the entry into the market of numerous producers who tried to fulfill the frenzied buying by American importers fearing quotas, led to price-cutting and disruption of the market as a whole. In 1961, garment exports fell by 33 percent and overall cotton manufactured exports dropped over 25 percent.[143]

Ironically, then, by "winning" in the negotiations, Hong Kong lost potential benefits from trade—in part because of the *anticipation* of quotas on its exports. Bhagwati and Srinivasan[144] have argued that countries are harmed as a result of uncertainty created by potential VERs and quota restraints since it leads them into the production of alternative products instead of fully utilizing their potential in a particular area. The overproduction of textiles in anticipation of quotas proved to be just as harmful.

When the Short-Term Arrangement went into effect, Hong Kong suffered because of its previous and continued recalcitrance. In February 1962 the United States asked Hong Kong to restrain exports of eight categories of cotton products. While Hong Kong initially acceded to American wishes for restraint, it resumed its exports under strong domestic pressure from its producers. In early March, the United States embargoed Hong Kong cotton product exports. After arduous bargaining, thirty categories of cotton textiles were subjected to a ceiling by the United States.[145] In the intermediate term, then, Hong Kong lost out. In later bargaining, however, Hong Kong was more forthcoming, and subsequently took advantage of the flexibility provided for in the Long-Term Arrangement.

THE EUROPEAN ARRANGEMENTS

The European countries had been imposing restraints on the imports of developing countries through a number of different mechanisms. At least until 1958 they did so in a rather straightforward manner, facilitated by Article XII of the GATT which allowed restraints on imports due to balance-of-payment difficulties. Many of the industrialized countries in Europe simply imposed quotas on textile and apparel imports under this provision. In 1958, however, with the return of convertibility, a number of European countries instituted various quotas in violation of the GATT as well as the restrictive arrangement among cotton textile producers which was known as the Noordwijk Agreement.[146]

The cotton trade associations of Germany, Austria, Belgium, the Netherlands, Italy, France, Switzerland, and Norway concluded the Noordwijk Agreement on May 9, 1958. This agreement—monitored and enforced by the governments of these countries—forbade the reexport to participating countries of gray cloth admitted temporarily on a duty-free basis into other countries for finishing. By following such a strategy, these associations tried to ensure that existing quotas would not be undermined through this practice.

Through this agreement countries improved the position of their domestic producers of gray cloth at the expense of some finishers and the Asians. In fact, the agreement specifically called for restraints on Japan, China, India, Pakistan, and Hong Kong. These countries complained bitterly since under the STA and LTA such restraint agreements were supposed to be eliminated. The agreement persisted, however, and was only discarded when the EC countries phased in their Common External Tariff, which eliminated incentives for this kind of accord.

Various European countries also invoked Article XXV of the GATT against Japan. This allowed countries to withhold GATT preferences from Japan until they had obtained some kind of voluntary restraint on exports of goods that were most politically sensitive.

Finally, a number of European countries used illegal restraint measures and administrative mechanisms to protect their industries. Through various systems of licensing and quotas, the Scandinavian countries restricted imports from Taiwan, Korea, Colombia, Turkey, and others.[147] Countries such as Germany, France, Italy, and other members of the EEC had restrictions of one sort or another on cotton textile imports from India, Pakistan, Taiwan, the U.A.R., South Korea, and other developing countries. The United States, as we shall see, was interested in having the EEC (and other developed countries) eventually eliminate these illegal restraints and open up their markets.

SUMMARY

For the most part, the importance of the international system factors discussed in chapter 2 is borne out by the process-tracing analysis here. During the first period considered—1950 to 1954—we found an absence of textile-specific restrictions. The lack of competition from the LDCs serves to explain this absence. American textile industrialists seemed quite willing, in fact, to help the Japanese develop their industry. Also, the Europeans appeared unconcerned with the textile industry per se; their problems stemmed more from their overall weakened economic situation. In response, as expected, they pursued restraints under the GATT rules that allowed the use of restraints for balance-of-payment reasons. Only in the United Kingdom was there a major push (specific to the area of textiles) for restraints. But, although the industries preferred quotas, the government resisted their pressure because of its perceived overall interests in promoting free trade.

From 1955 to 1959, changing international conditions would lead us to expect that bilateral agreements would be concluded as countries faced growing competition from new suppliers to their markets. It was a cheaper method of imposing restraints (the organizational cost argument) and did not violate the international agreement regulating the imposition of overall trade controls—the GATT. U.S. actions did lead to bilateral accords with Japan: the first was a more genuinely voluntary restraint action by the Japanese (in 1955); the second was one that Japan was more overtly pressured into (in 1957).

The process-tracing analysis of the decision making demonstrated that the United States was very concerned with and constrained by both overall trade and strategic issues. Key American officials deflected calls for unilaterally imposed quotas against Japan by repeatedly emphasizing other American interests. Japan perceived its relatively weak position at all levels and was quite willing to give up its desire for an open American market in exchange for at least some control over the terms and flexibility of the textile restraint action.

When the first action proved unsuccessful, the U.S. government, under heavy pressure from its industry, again sought an agreement that would control to some extent the influx of imports without overtly violating the GATT. This action—marked by various kinds of pressure by the United States—resulted in another bilateral accord, but one requiring more government involvement. Once again, the kinds of international systemic level factors that I argued would be important played a key role in decision makers' calculations. The United States did not make overt linkages to the overall trading and strategic levels: the threat to cut off Japan's access to the U.S. textile market was sufficient since Japan readily perceived its high degree of dependence in this and other issue areas.

The next effort undertaken by the United States was also expected given the international factors we have examined. As other entrants came into the market the U.S. government sought to restrain Hong Kong. But the result was unexpected: Hong Kong refused to restrain exports to the United States. How can this be explained? In addition to the somewhat weaker leverage the United States had from a structural standpoint, we saw that three factors on the domestic and individual levels came into play. First, the complexities of domestic politics both in the United States and in Hong Kong proved to be important. Second, in many ways, including the failure of American decision makers to lobby effectively at home, the United States did not bargain well. Third, Hong Kong's previous experience and greater sophistication in negotiating proved to be crucial elements in American failure to secure restraints from Hong Kong.

In the case of the U.S.-Hong Kong negotiations, then, international structural factors were not sufficient to explain the outcome. Although the asymmetry in capabilities in the U.S.-Hong Kong case were not as great as in the U.S.-Japan case, we should still have seen the development of a bilateral agreement. Given the American attempt and the near success of this effort, international conditions clearly "favored" the development of a bilateral agreement.

The United States was not the only country which concluded bilateral arrangements. As we have seen, the United Kingdom developed bilateral accords with Hong Kong, India, and Pakistan. Once again, international factors were important in constraining the behavior of British and LDC decision makers. The United Kingdom did not wish to impose a quota, and the LDCs were willing to go along with some kind of restrictive agreement in view of the likely alternative. One important point should be mentioned. Although there was variation in the negotiating strategies of LDCs and, in the short term, greater success for Hong Kong than India or Pakistan in securing large quotas, this difference did not last long. The latter two countries not only benefited, after some delay, from higher quotas but also had unrestricted market access for a longer time than did Hong Kong.

The cases examined here lend support to the role of the international system level elements discussed in the previous chapter, but they also indicate the need to consider factors on the domestic and individual levels. The EEC also developed an agreement to restrain LDC imports. However, these countries subsequently turned to illegal restraints in addition to their bilateral agreements. These illegal restraints did not remain undisturbed for long: they were seen by the United States as undermining the GATT and soon became the subject of the first regime in textile and apparel trade—the STA.

4
Creation: The Short-Term and Long-Term Arrangements, 1960-1962

Considering the changes that took place in textile trade in the late 1950s, and the international factors discussed in chapter 2, we might anticipate that the United States would seek to develop an international regime. New entrants competing with the domestic textile industry would encourage the Americans to seek protection. Bilateral agreements proved to be a costly and ineffective way of regulating imports—when Japan was restricted, Hong Kong filled the gap. Moreover, the conclusion of such agreements or unilateral restraints would undermine the principle of multilateralism of the GATT meta-regime and conflict with American strategic and overall trading objectives. A regime in textiles would allow the hegemon (the United States) to regulate the behavior of LDCs and possibly take pressure off its market by forcing European countries to accept more imports.

With regard to the characteristics of the regime, as the preeminent power in textile trade the United States could force other countries to go along with a strong regime. With regard to the degree of restrictiveness of the regime (nature), there are two opposing factors. On the one hand, the hegemon would be able to impose a very restrictive regime that would satisfy its domestic producers. On the other hand, a multilateral arrangement would then fail to satisfy the goal of controlling the behavior of other importing countries—that is, to force them to pursue more liberal policies to take pressure off the hegemon's market. A regime of moderate openness could satisfy these competing demands. Finally, since the "problem" was limited to cotton-based products, one might expect the regime to be similarly limited in scope.

The first step toward a regime in textile trade was actually taken by the Eisenhower administration in 1959. At that time, the United States asked GATT members to work toward developing a system for coping with low-cost imports. The United States was apparently motivated by a

desire to assuage European fears of giving Japan further market access
under the GATT, since the Dillon Round was just getting under way. On
November 20, 1959, GATT participants agreed on a procedure to deal
with market disruption. The document setting forth the procedure noted
that "useful experience would be gained by taking up a specific case of
market disruption in the near future."[1] The first case was not long in
coming; the United States decided to base the STA on this concept.

POLICY CHOICES

The United States

International factors (discussed in Part I) account for American efforts
to develop the STA and LTA. Nesting considerations proved especially
important. While U.S. textile interests pressed for increasing protection,
American policymakers clearly perceived the constraints imposed by the
bipolar struggle with the Soviet Union. In congressional hearings on the
problems of the textile industry in 1958 (just prior to the development of
the STA), the deputy assistant secretary of state for economic affairs,
Wilson Beale, noted that

since the Soviet bloc started on its economic offensive in 1954, as of the middle of
1958, it has offered 17 textile plants to 8 different countries and additional textile
machinery to 4 countries.[2]

Commenting on government procurement from Japanese textile manufacturers, Leonard Saccio, deputy director of the International Cooperation Administration (ICA), argued that this "aid" had "helped Japan
ward off economic penetration from Red China. . . ."[3]

The best evidence of the paramount importance of the bipolar struggle
in the formulation of foreign economic policy, and specifically with
regard to the textile industry, is indicated by the frustration Senator Pastore (a strong protectionist) expressed in the hearings bearing his name.

The minute you take these [restrictive measures on imports] you get these protes-
tations from Japan or you get them from Italy, you get them from France, you get
them from England—that unless you do thus and so we are going to be overrun
by communism. That becomes a big problem in the State Department. I can
imagine what happens at your meetings the minute you begin to feel one little
measure is going to accelerate the possibility of communistic infiltration. Then it
becomes a big political question.[4]

The bipolar distribution of capabilities impinged on the perceptions of
decision-makers in the formulation of policy. Simply forcing Japanese
and Europeans to accept American demands would not suffice.

A second key factor in the U.S. decision to pursue a multilateral arrangement was the importance of the international trading system—most notably, the preservation of GATT. In a White House report issued in September 1961, President Kennedy noted that the "refusal of many countries to undertake full GATT obligations towards Japan continues to be of serious concern to the United States and other countries."[5] As the *Daily News Record (DNR)* put it, "The cotton textile pact is to be cited as an ideal example of how the U.S. can liberalize its trade policies while still protecting specialized industries from market disruption."[6]

The American negotiating team at the STA talks also remarked on the proliferation of restrictions undermining the GATT. The proposal presented by the United States argued that "attempts of countries to deal unilaterally with such disruptive imports tend to take the form of restrictive measures, including quantitative limitations, that invite retaliation and impede the expansion of international trade."[7] Some of the quantitative restrictions being used by the Europeans were expressly forbidden by the GATT regime. As countries imposed various controls, American decision makers felt that it was necessary to take action to forestall this growing protectionism. Douglas Dillon, under secretary of state under Eisenhower, warned that "orderly expansion of international trade could be endangered by import restrictions imposed by countries seeking to protect themselves from a sudden influx of low-cost goods."[8] The U.S. delegation's proposal at the STA talks emphasized control of other countries' policies, and, in particular, opening up European markets: "Such a mechanism should permit the distribution of cotton textile trade over a large number of importing countries."[9] Thus, the nested nature of textile trade within the overall and international trading system and a desire to control other countries' behavior provided the U.S. with considerable incentive to press for some kind of arrangement to regulate the imposition of trade controls while at the same time responding to domestic industry pressure to restrict the growth of imports.

With regard to the regime's characteristics, American decision makers perceived that with a regime they could force open European markets and at the same time satisfy domestic producers. Beale had remarked that the proposed agreement provides "an opportunity for the importing countries to share equitably the increase in imports among themselves so as to ensure that the impact on any one market becomes much less."[10] Speaking directly to the strength and nature of the STA, the *DNR* surmised that American motivation in seeking a multilateral arrangement was a hope that the agreement's "objectives will definitely commit European nations to a more liberal import policy, while pledging Asian exporting countries to a policy of restraint."[11]

On the domestic front, the position of the textile and apparel industries was very clear by 1961 (immediately prior to the STA negotiations). They demanded a "total product by product worldwide quota based upon the imports during some pre-1957 period."[12] As we saw in chapter 3, the United States had sought initially to restrict the exports of only the "offending" parties, Japan (successfully) and then Hong Kong (unsuccessfully). When demands by the industries to institute quotas increased in intensity, however, U.S. decision makers realized that more needed to be done about imports. Bilateral arrangements were rejected by the textile and apparel industries. In the absence of international structural constraints, the simplest solution would appear to have been a highly restrictive unilateral quota on the import of textile and apparel products as desired by industry interests.

The United Kingdom

The United Kingdom disagreed with the American proposal on the STA. The British representative expressed a clear preference for a bilateral arrangement:

There should be no attempt to elaborate a generalized plan . . . maximum effort should be made to liberalize trade in accordance with GATT obligations . . . should problems arise, these should be dealt with through bilateral negotiations.[13]

The British reiterated this view throughout the negotiations for the STA and the LTA. After the STA was signed and preparations were being made to develop a longer agreement, the *DNR* reported that "the British view [is] that more can be achieved through quiet, bilateral arrangements than by any grandiose international agreement."[14] Maintaining this position in the discussion about the proposed Long-Term Arrangement, the British delegation argued that "the details for restraint should continue to be a matter for bilateral negotiation within the broad framework of the arrangements."[15]

The United Kingdom found itself in the position of a middle-level power at the strategic, overall economic, and textile levels: it did not have the incentives of a hegemon to ensure world "order," nor did it fear that it was too weak vis-à-vis LDCs to be able to restrain their trade effectively without a regime. In such a situation, simply concluding bilateral arrangements with Commonwealth suppliers—with which it was having success—and unilaterally restraining imports from other countries appeared to be the preferred policy. With Hong Kong a part of the British delegation, but with increasing pressure from its textile industry, the United Kingdom's representative had to steer a careful path between protectionism and liberalism. Furthermore, the government was pursuing a domestic intervention scheme, known as the 1959 Act, to cut excess capacity in the textile and apparel industries. As part of this scheme, the government had promised to control imports from major exporters to increase the industries' confidence and encourage investment in more modern capacity while phasing out obsolete equipment.

With respect to the United Kingdom's views on the characteristics of the international cotton regime, I have already noted that it wished to pursue independent policies—unconstrained by a regime. But recognizing that the United States was interested in some kind of international arrangement, the United Kingdom needed to respond to the American initiative. In its proposal regarding the LTA, it argued that

the United Kingdom policy had long been to afford an open market to the trade of less-developed countries, with particular reference to cotton textiles where we had reached the point that 40 per cent of the British market is met from imports, the bulk of which come from less-developed countries... we should not be asked to accept any new commitment in the GATT to do more, at least until others had made a comparable contribution.[16]

And in this context, the United Kingdom advocated a "growth formula which varies according to the proportion of imports to domestic consumption."[17]

The effect of international factors on the British position versus the preferences of domestic groups is reflected in the original attempts of the Cotton Board. It had argued that "the LTA should require all industrialized countries to take no less than 10% and no more than 20% of their domestic consumption of cotton goods from low cost countries."[18] As a large importer, the United Kingdom would readily benefit from this scheme. Yet this proposal was rejected by the British delegation. Cognizant of American power and objectives, it felt that the United States (and other countries) would not accept such a proposal and therefore did not even advance this idea at the talks.

The EEC Countries

For the most part, the member countries of the EEC were pursuing independent policies. During the international negotiations, however, they were represented by a single spokesman. In the initial stages of the negotiations the EEC sought to stem discussion on liberalization of imports. As the EEC representative noted, "The emphasis in fact should more properly be on diversification of production and harmonization of economic activity rather than on access to textile markets."[19] Moreover, with the success the EEC countries were having in using the GATT regime to restrict the influx of textile and apparel products into their countries, they argued that "whatever arrangements were made should be adaptable to the normal machinery and procedures available within GATT."[20] In the actual discussions on the LTA, each major participant submitted an alternative proposal for the agreement. The EEC's view on the choice of a bilateral versus a multilateral agreement was quite different from that of the United States. The EEC noted that "no provision of the agreement should preclude the negotiation of mutually acceptable bilateral agreements containing other stipulations."[21]

With a fragile unity in the EEC, the common denominator appeared to be a drive to maintain the independence of member states—both because of their international positions and their internal political situations. From the standpoint of their positions in the international economic system, the EEC countries did not fear that GATT was being undermined. At least in their view (with four out of six countries invoking Article XXXV against Japan), things were satisfactory as they stood. Of their 1960 textile imports, only 9 percent were from the LDCs and Japan, in contrast to the corresponding figures of 34 percent and 26 percent for the United States.[22] Yet it is clear that the EEC countries would not have come to the international negotiations except for their fear that further expansion of international trade would be undermined (particularly with respect to a further opening of the American market). The EEC member states had been under great pressure from their domestic industries to keep imports of low-priced textile goods out of their respective countries. With this pressure, the EEC did not wish to have a regime that might force them to open up their markets. If a regime were to be created, however, it should remain weak to preserve the freedom of EEC member states to invoke restrictions at will.

The international structure prevented the EEC states from completely ignoring American requests.[23] They argued that the LDCs needed to diversify and that, in any case, any arrangements that needed to be made "should be adaptable to the normal machinery and procedures available within GATT."[24] Of course, this was not a tenable position. More realistically, the EEC sought in the LTA to weaken the proposed arrangement by eliminating any language that would commit them to restrict LDC exports in a manner that did not suit them.

THE LDCs AND JAPAN

In many ways, the LDCs and Japan had mixed feelings about the whole STA/LTA program. They feared (and, in retrospect, with good reason) that the United States and the Europeans might simply turn the agreements into a global quota system, thereby diminishing their market access even further. They were willing to have a regime, but wished to see a strong, liberal one that would serve to increase their export potential. For example, Japan noted that although "the bilateral approach was very important, it was difficult to find solutions without there being something on a multilateral basis."[25]

India continued to insist that "it was essential that no agreement reached during the meeting should be able to supercede the principles of GATT."[26] Although India was being harmed by the voluntary export restraints it had with the United Kingdom and by unilateral restrictions employed by the EEC, as a large country with an important international role it apparently felt that it had sufficient political clout to conclude bilateral agreements without having a multilateral program. Hong Kong, by contrast, preferred a multilateral agreement. As its delegate put it,

there were some disadvantages in multilateral arrangements alone, while the same was true of a bilateral system which was completely unregulated. Hong Kong, therefore, would support an arrangement where bilateral agreements could be entered into under some general framework of principles conforming as closely as possible to the principles of GATT.[27]

THE NEGOTIATIONS

INTERNATIONAL BARGAINING

The United States was successful in its drive to set up an international regime in textile and apparel trade to control the behavior of other countries. As we shall see below, although the United States was forced to compromise on some specifics of the agreements, for the most part the characteristics of the STA and the LTA were in accord with American policy choices.

At the GATT textiles committee meeting in 1961, the Americans, led by Under Secretary of State George Ball, argued for a multilateral arrangement in textile and apparel trade.[28] Specifically, the United States felt that the "participants have a common responsibility to take comparative and constructive action to facilitate the expansion of world trade."[29] Part II of the U.S. proposal, the "Guiding Principles," specified the measures and conditions under which participating countries would be allowed to intervene in the market. In the ensuing debate, the Americans reiterated that "the most promising approach would appear to be the bilateral approach within a multilateral framework."[30] The STA was only intended as a one-year stopgap to permit the development of a formal regime. In its proposal for a longer-term arrangement, the United States argued:

Such a mechanism, too, should be a substitute for unilateral restrictions on cotton textile imports in various markets with a view to bringing about a situation in which international trade in cotton textiles will take place on the freest basis possible, but within the framework of a multilateral arrangement which avoids disruption.[31]

As with the STA, the emphasis was on controlling the behavior of other countries and ending unilateral measures.

With respect to the strength and nature of the regime, the United States proposal asserted that importing countries should have "a schedule for annual minimum relaxation of quantitative restrictions [which] would be drawn up at the time the arrangement is negotiated."[32] American emphasis on international regulation of national action is indicated by Provision II-3 in its proposal: "Countries not presently maintaining quantitative restrictions would agree not to impose them during the arrangement, except as authorized by GATT or by the arrangement itself."[33]

Finally, in contrast to the proposal put forth by the EEC (which called for bilateral negotiations to increase quota shares but without international supervision of negotiations), the United States proposed that access to the markets of importing countries should be expanded by a specified percentage over existing quota restrictions.[34] The United States repeatedly took the EEC to task for not accepting sufficient quantities of LDC exports of cotton textiles. In one statement, it proposed:

Participating countries which presently impose quantitative restrictions on imports of cotton textiles shall significantly increase access to their markets by the progressive relaxation of such restrictions to an agreed level within an agreed period of time.[35]

Furthermore, the United States took the position that restrictions not contemplated by the STA or the GATT would also be forbidden. Other provisions in the U.S. proposal called for an international textile committee whose only real task would be to monitor the agreement; it would not have any enforcement powers.

With regard to the future LTA, the U.S. proposal called for "provisions making it possible for participating countries to share fairly in expanding market opportunities resulting from the *growth* of cotton textile consumption."[36] Measures preventing nonparticipants from benefiting from restraints by the signatories and measures preventing participants from cheating on the agreement were also included. As in the STA, there were rules specifying the conditions under which signatories of the

LTA could invoke restrictions on textile and apparel imports in cases of domestic market disruption. Furthermore, if countries chose to restrict imports, they were required to allow a minimum growth rate of at least 6 percent in the quotas they imposed. Finally, the proposal bound importing states to a schedule mandating a relaxation of import controls.[37]

Both the STA and LTA regimes proposed by the United States addressed only cotton textile and apparel products. Although American producers wanted to include wool products in the agreement, the United States resisted this potential expansion in scope.

During the discussions leading to the development of the STA, Ball made it clear that the United States would not allow states to stay aloof from the proposed arrangement: "It will be necessary to take some action against those who refuse to participate in the forthcoming international textile trade talks."[38] And indicating that the United States would use its market in textiles as leverage, he stated that "there is no reason why countries which refuse to cooperate in the world textile marketing program should benefit by their refusal and have unlimited access to the U.S. market while cooperating nations hold down."[39] Further, in the debate on the STA, the Americans threatened to close off their market:

There were strong domestic political pressures urging the U.S. Government to take unilateral action and establish import quotas. As action of this type would be contrary to the generally liberal trade policies of the U.S. in recent years, this government has advanced its proposals for a multilaterally acceptable solution.[40]

As anticipated, then, the United States was willing to employ its hegemonic market access resources in the textile and apparel issue to induce others to join the STA.

The United States also used its market power to influence the negotiations leading to the LTA. Whether by direct intent or not, President Kennedy's request in November 1961 that the Tariff Commission determine if an "equalization fee" was in order to compensate for the higher price of U.S. cotton certainly did not please the Japanese.[41] After the LTA was signed, the administration encouraged other states to join the agreement by announcing that it was ready to embargo imports from nonsignatories as soon as it received necessary authority from the legislature.[42]

Finally, in two other instances, the Americans used their textile market power to induce compliance. For the LDCs, American attempts to open up the European market through the promotion of a regime served as an inducement to join the regime. The Europeans, however, perceived American threats to close off its market as a "stick" since LDC exports would then be diverted to Europe. The *DNR*, in commenting on the difficulty the United States was encountering with other countries, noted that "Americans are presumably faced with the problem of selling Western European nations the idea of absorbing whatever imports the United States is cutting down from Asian countries."[43] Japan, for example, saw the possibility of entering the European market as a real inducement. In the negotiations on the STA, the *DNR* reported that

Japanese delegates have privately assured U.S. representatives that they will accept the document. Japan certainly does not want to be excluded from any possible opening up of markets by EEC nations.[44]

To increase its leverage, the United States also manipulated linkages to the international trading system. While his statement was probably intended for internal consumption, Senator Edmund Muskie's observation that the administration faced "real difficulty" on renewal of the Trade Agreements Act unless it could work out a "realistic solution to the problem of textile imports" was not lost on officials of other countries.[45] The U.S. market was of key importance to the Europeans; while they would have preferred to be allowed to continue to discriminate against the United States (in implicit violation of the GATT), they recognized that undermining GATT would in the end be more harmful to them (as nations more dependent on trade) than to the United States. This concern was best illustrated in the negotiation of the LTA.

European countries are sympathetic to the overall trade aims of the American Administration and would like to give the President as much help as possible in the great debate that will take place in the Congress. Otherwise, observers here frankly say that it would be impossible to conclude an agreement at this time.[46]

W. Willard Wirtz, the American under secretary of labor, emphasized the link to overall trade, arguing that "the conclusion of a successful agreement in textiles was an integral part of the development of the international trading program."[47] In ongoing discussions following the conclusion of the STA, Wirtz was even more direct:

It was precisely those individuals who came to Geneva in July to negotiate a world textile agreement . . . who returned to Washington to work with the President on the world trade program. Had there been no agreement, there might not have been such a program.[48]

This type of linkage was not necessarily directed only to the multilateral/bilateral aspect of the arrangement, but to its strength and nature as well. Unlike Tinbergen's dictum that the number of policy instruments should be equal to the number of policy objectives, political linkages do not suffer from the same constraint. A big stick can be used to beat people on a variety of subissues.

The linkages to the international trading system became very clear. As the *DNR* noted during one particularly difficult struggle: "The biggest plus factor going for the American program is the realization by the negotiating nations that this textile agreement is desperately needed by the US Administration in its fight to push freer trade policies through Congress."[49] In linking textiles to overall trade, Wirtz identified three areas of American displeasure with respect to regime characteristics: (1) the number of categories that would be included (which would facilitate or impede determinations of market disruption); (2) a "suitable" base year; and (3) the EEC itself. With regard to the latter point, he noted: "If we are to succeed in our present endeavor, every effort must be made to increase these quantities."[50]

Shortly thereafter, the EEC increased its prospective import quota, Japan went along with the U.S. market disruption formula, and the United States gave up on its proposal for a growth rate of imports tied to the domestic growth rate and for using 1960 as a base year. While the outcome was not as favorable to the United States as might be expected (given its preponderant capabilities in the international system), it should be recognized that it was constrained by the GATT regime and its own strategic interests. The EEC countries were always more than willing to indicate to the United States that they were following legal policies under Article XXXV of the GATT. Since Japan was the major exporter of textile products, this use of Article XXXV was a major bargaining point for the Europeans.

With respect to an international monitoring body, Hong Kong proposed an impartial body that would pass judgment on whether market disruption is taking place rather than leaving it to individual importing countries. The U.S. delegate, in classic understatement, "expressed doubts" as to whether it would be practical to include such a clause in the long-term arrangement. Needless to say, this proposal was not incorporated in the LTA.

THE OUTCOME

The Short-Term Arrangement largely resembled the original U.S. proposal. Though modified to some extent by pressure from the LDCs, for the most part other countries decided to focus their attention on the LTA. Since the STA was only proposed for a one-year period, this was a reasonable strategy for relatively weak countries.

The final LTA text also followed the U.S. proposal closely. Turning first to the meta-regime (principles and norms) of the STA/LTA, we find the underlying principle to be a belief in liberalism, *modified* to take into account the problems and costs of adjustment. Recognizing that excessively rapid change may be detrimental to the industries in importing countries, the participants resolved to control rates of growth of imports into developed countries. Of course in arguing that this is the principle behind the textile regimes, I am not asserting that either the industries in developed countries or the LDCs fully subscribe to these goals; they may (and generally do) see these regimes as the next best thing to unilateral import restraints. Consistent with my arguments on nesting, most government officials saw this kind of collaborative arrangement as being consistent with the GATT but still meeting their objectives for pursuing organized trade.

With respect to its norms, the STA/LTA agreement drew on the GATT arrangement but called for certain modifications. In a recent paper, Finlayson and Zacher[51] summarize the norms of the GATT. They identify five substantive norms—nondiscrimination, liberalization, reciprocity, development, and safeguards—and argue that there are two procedural norms—multilateralism and the major supplier concept—in negotiations. Consistent with my nesting notion,[52] some of the norms of the GATT are found in the textile regime, while others have been modified in various ways.

Those norms found in the textile regime are development, safeguards, and multilateralism. The development norm was incorporated in the STA preamble, which stated that collaborative action in this area was being taken with a "view to the development of world trade and that such action [cooperation] should be designed to facilitate economic expansion and in particular to promote the development of the less developed countries by providing increased access for their exports of manufactured products."[53]

The safeguard norm was the key to the STA/LTA. It provided for an elaborate scheme regulating the imposition of safeguards and attempted to specify quite carefully (although not easily defined in practice) the conditions under which countries could institute unilateral and bilateral restraints. It modified the concept of safeguards embodied in Article XIX of the GATT, which allows restraints but only if they are instituted on a most-favored-nation basis.

The third norm maintained more or less intact was multilateralism. Pointing to the proliferation of restrictions that were undermining the GATT, the LTA called for multilateralism in dealing with the problems arising from low-cost imports. Article 1 of the LTA stated that the participants "are of the opinion that it may be desirable to apply, during the next few years, special practical measures of *international co-operation* which will assist in any adjustment that may be required."⁵⁴

Two GATT norms were clearly modified in the LTA: nondiscrimination and liberalization. In the GATT, nondiscrimination has been a key norm (until recently), and almost any restrictive measure instituted or removed was to be on a most-favored-nation basis. The LTA regime moved away from this norm, and allowed restraints to be imposed against imports from the offending country only. This, in fact, was one of the motivations in developing the STA regime since Article XIX of the GATT was seen to create many problems and forced countries to pay compensation. As we saw in chapter 3, countries therefore used illegal unilateral restraints or bilateral accords—measures the United States saw as undermining the GATT. Yet, while the nondiscrimination norm was modified in the textile regime, important elements were still preserved: Article 2 of the LTA stated that "the participating countries concerned shall administer their remaining restrictions on imports of cotton textiles from participating countries in an equitable manner."⁵⁵ By laying down specific rules and procedures to be followed when restraints are imposed, the agreement also tried to ensure that there would be nondiscrimination in its use—even though this use may single out offending countries. In addition, Article 6 stated that nonparticipants in the LTA should not be given more favorable treatment than participating countries who face restraints. As we shall see, this clause encouraged a growth in membership in the LTA since it guaranteed the most favored treatment possible for the class of "restrained" countries.

The liberalization norm also found its way into the LTA in modified form. The preamble and Article 2 called on countries to expand their markets for cotton textiles.⁵⁶ Of course there was a delicate balance between liberalization and safeguards. This balance was more difficult to maintain than the one in GATT since the LTA makes it relatively easy to impose restraints—albeit restraints regulated by multilateral agreement. And while the *minimum* rate of growth for restrained imports was 5 percent in the LTA, in practice this was generally the maximum. Reciprocity and the major supplier rule were not incorporated in the LTA.

With respect to the LTA's rules and procedures, the EEC countries committed themselves to increasing their level of imports by specific percentages, and the United States managed to have the following phrase incorporated in the LTA: "It would be desirable that each annual increase should correspond as closely as possible to one fifth of the overall increase."⁵⁷ But the United States gave up its demand for keying the growth rate of imports to the increase in the domestic growth rate of the importing country's market. As to the question of the strength of the agreement and the conclusion of bilateral arrangements, the United States went along with the notion of "mutually acceptable bilateral arrangements" but obtained the phrase, "not inconsistent with the basic objectives of this agreement."[58] This gave the United States freedom of action but still bound the EEC countries to accept more imports. Finally, the absence of an international monitoring body was a noticeable omission: only the importing country would be allowed to determine whether imports were causing "market disruption." This, again, preserved American freedom of action.

BEHAVIOR OF COUNTRIES AND TRANSACTIONS

Much has been written about the effect of the STA and LTA on international trade.[59] In general, the debate has been between those who see free trade as the alternative to these regimes and those who see uncontrolled national actions leading to greater protectionism as the alternative. In my opinion, the latter view is more realistic given the political pressure for unilateral measures in developed countries. As Bardan notes in summarizing the effect of the LTA,

"if the LTA has not operated according to the highest canons of liberalism, it has at least served to curtail protectionism, and has helped to make the world cotton textile trade much less restricted than it otherwise would have been."[60]

While this statement cannot be tested, the experience in industries such as steel, autos, and television, where regimes have not come into being, demonstrates that unilateral and bilateral controls are very common responses to protectionist pressures. The earlier textile regimes (until 1977) appear to be a force for liberalism.

BEHAVIOR OF COUNTRIES

Let us first consider some of the control actions taken by countries under the STA and LTA.[61] Some thirty countries participated in the LTA during the period from 1962 to 1965, with a trade coverage amounting to three-fourths of world trade in cotton textiles.[62] The industrialized countries can be divided for convenience into four groups: the United States, the EEC, the United Kingdom, and others (including the Scandinavian countries, Canada, Austria, Australia, and Switzerland). With the exception of the bilateral agreement (discussed in chap. 3) with Japan, the United States had no restrictions on its imports at the inception of the agreement. In the first year of the agreement the United States invoked

Article 3 (calling for unilateral restraints in the event of market disruption) against eighteen countries. Using these unilateral actions as leverage, it subsequently converted them to bilateral agreements under Article 4. By 1964 the United States concluded eighteen bilaterals that were of longer duration than the Article 3 restraints (which had to be renewed every year), and was left with only five unilateral restraints. The bilaterals were preferred by the United States and the developing countries because they minimized the time and effort the United States had to devote to this area and they gave the LDCs greater flexibility and longer-range security than unilateral actions.

The EEC member countries were pursuing independent policies at the time of the LTA negotiations and continued to do so under the first LTA. While the Benelux countries and Italy removed their restraints completely in the first year of the LTA, France and Germany maintained theirs. Germany liberalized a number of categories of goods, however, and allowed the mandated growth in restricted categories. As for the use of other provisions of the LTA, Germany invoked Article 3 to restrain a few categories of goods from Hong Kong. France, by contrast, was quite stingy with its liberalization: it liberalized only a very few items and its total imports (discussed below) were very small. Moreover, France continued to use various impediments of an administrative nature to keep imports out of its market.

The United Kingdom had negotiated agreements (the Lancashire Pact) with India, Pakistan, and Hong Kong prior to the development of the LTA. These arrangements continued under the LTA, and the United Kingdom also moved to conclude a number of bilateral accords with new suppliers such as Israel, Taiwan, and Spain. Yet these accords did not satisfy its domestic producers, and responding to their demands, the United Kingdom violated the LTA in 1966 with a global quota.

Finally, among other industrialized states, the Scandinavian countries had a variety of restrictions in place at the LTA's inception. Norway, Denmark, and Finland had a few restraints and also had a licensing arrangement to monitor imports. Sweden had restraints on Japanese textile imports. Subsequently, under the LTA, these countries followed the liberalization mandated in the agreement and, in some cases, relaxed the categories under restraint. The LTA was also used by Norway in a restrictive manner: it concluded a bilateral arrangement with Hong Kong during the first year of the arrangement for a period of five years. Canada followed policies somewhat similar to the United States: it was an open market before the LTA, but, as imports grew, imposed numerous unilateral restraints. It did not, however, convert these to bilateral accords. Australia dropped all restraints on its market and did not impose any restraints of a quantitative nature on imports (it did, however, have high tariffs). Finally, Austria liberalized its quotas that were in effect in accord with the provisions of the LTA, but did not drop any quotas completely or impose any new ones.

Countries followed very different policies upon entry into force of the LTA—policies based on their market position, domestic structure, and politics. On the whole, however, the regime served to open up the market in countries having severe restraints, and helped to regulate the imposition of new restraints. The result, as I indicate below, was a more even sharing of imports among countries.

TRANSACTIONS

Since many factors other than restraints affect the flow of trade in textiles and apparel, it is difficult to attribute changes in transactions directly and solely to the regime and national controls discussed above. Imports as a whole from all countries into the developed countries (the latter being known as Group I in the agreement) rose from $134.7 million in 1961 to $184.6 million in 1965. During this period, the Group II (LDCs party to the agreement) share of this trade increased from 21 percent to 24 percent. Japan's share fell from 12 percent to 11 percent, and that of nonparticipating countries inched up from 12 percent to 13 percent.[63] Imports from LDCs grew at a rate of 12 percent per annum, in contrast to the overall growth rate of 8 percent for all countries. Table 5 illustrates the growth rates of different groupings of countries. The major growth took place in cotton clothing—the new focus of LDCs. Thus, for example, while Group II exports in textiles to Group I increased by 8 percent, clothing exports grew by 17 percent. Since clothing was more labor intensive and had higher value added, this was a natural shift.

Among the LDCs, Hong Kong proved to be the most successful exporter. By contrast, India, Pakistan, and the U.A.R. often lost market shares in various developed countries. The poorer competitive ability of these latter countries is illustrated by their performance in markets without any restraints whatsoever. In these cases, Hong Kong captured a larger share of the market. In the United States, however, Hong Kong initially lost ground to others because of its intransigence, which resulted in severe quota restrictions by the United States. It eventually made up for this with its superior competitive position.

Variations in the amount of imports among Group I countries were also quite evident. In terms of value, the United States took $126.4 million from the Group II countries in 1963 and another $89.5 million from Japan. Germany took $36.2 million from Group II in 1962 and another

TABLE 5

AVERAGE ANNUAL GROWTH RATES OF COTTON TEXTILE IMPORTS OF
GROUP I COUNTRIES FROM THE WORLD, GROUP I COUNTRIES,
AND GROUP II COUNTRIES, 1961-1965 (PERCENT)

| *Group I countries* | *World* | Cotton Textile Imports From | |
		Group I countries	*Group II countries*
Australia	1	-5	9
Austria	10	12	4
Canada	-2	-11	20
Denmark	2	-3	21
EEC	19	22	39
Belgium	17	15	42
France	31	28	42
Germany	25	23	35
Italy	20	19	65
Netherlands	19	18	61
Finland	1	-2	40
Norway	-5	-8	5
Sweden	7	3	1
United Kingdom	1	-7	5
United States	11	10	9
Group I	8.2	6.3	12.0

SOURCE: UNCTAD, TD/20/Supp. 3, 12 October 1967.

NOTE: Data for the EEC countries are 1962-1965 annual averages; data for the United States are 1963-1965 annual averages.

$11.5 million from Japan. By contrast, France, with a relatively large market, took only $1.6 million worth of imports from Group II and only $0.3 million from Japan. Even the Netherlands took $4.7 million from the LDCs and another $4.9 million from Japan. The growth figures that were subsequently allowed by various countries as part of the liberalization move[64] must be understood in light of the base levels. The United Kingdom, for example, which had no growth provisions for its import restraints, had a base level of $114.3 million from Group II countries, and another $10.4 million from Japan. The rapid growth of imports from Group II to $194.4 million in 1964 explains some of the drive behind the United Kingdom's desire to have global quotas.[65]

One last point on transactions relating to the utilization of quotas allocated by the developed countries: they vary in relation to the developed country in question, the developing country exporters, and market conditions. From the standpoint of developed countries, the highest fill rates took place in the United Kingdom, the United States, and, to a much lesser extent, West Germany.[66] LDCs encountered the most problems in filling their quotas in France, Austria, and Norway. The other cases fell somewhere in between. The reason for the problems could often be attributed to administrative measures such as the licensing procedures (often delayed) and the issuance of licenses to so many importers that it made trade uneconomical. The most important shift, however, was the growth in man-made fiber (MMF) and wool-based exports from the LDCs and Japan (discussed in chap. 5).

CONCLUSION

We have seen the development of the first regime in textile and apparel trade. Because of a number of structural factors, and for reasons of cost and efficiency, the United States pressed for an international agreement. As is apparent in the statements of decision-makers and in the interview data, various theoretical reasons for instituting a regime (costs, nesting, and control of other countries) were at one point or another seen to be significant. Concerning the characteristics of the regime (strength, nature, scope), the United States was able to secure the kind of agreement it desired: the final agreement was strong enough to force the Europeans to open up their market while allowing the United States to take pressure off its own. In this case, the strength and nature of the regime were intimately connected. Moreover, since the United States was trying to minimize intervention in markets, it saw no need to have any restraints or regulation of restrictions in areas other than cotton-based products.

In the bargaining process, the United States made it clear that it was the most powerful and was determined to have its own way. It successfully engaged in within-issue and across-issue linkages and obtained the desired agreement. Strategic considerations, however, probably constrained the United States as it did not want to undermine its overall objectives vis-à-vis the Soviet Union. Textile power was used effectively against the LDCs to get them to join the regime: not only were they fearful of losing the American market but they also saw an opportunity to go along with the United States to secure market access to other industrialized countries. And in dealing with the EEC, the United States made numerous linkages to the overall trading system and made it clear that it would close off its market (and potentially create a diversion and put even more pressure on the Europeans than they were already experiencing from the LDCs) if the Europeans would not accede to its demands.

5

Maintenance: The Renewal of the LTA and the Development of the MFA, 1963-1974

In the mid-1960s, the effects of the LTA readily became evident: the LDCs made an effort to circumvent the restrictions under the LTA by shifting their exports to man-made fiber and wool-based products. After initial American efforts to conclude an agreement with the Japanese on wool-based products failed, the domestic industry pressured the U.S. government to restrict imports of wool and MMF goods when the LTA came up for renewal in 1966. But American officials resisted this effort, in part because they wished to ensure that the ongoing GATT negotiations, the Kennedy Round, would not be disrupted. By 1969 increasing industry pressure through the Congress and European unilateral and bilateral actions made it imperative for American decision makers to take some action. When their first effort to develop a regime encompassing all fibers met with failure—resulting in large part from poor U.S. bargaining and European resistance—the United States concluded its own bilateral accords with Far Eastern suppliers.

After a long struggle (from 1969 to 1971), the United States successfully concluded accords with Japan and other key suppliers. In response, these countries diverted their exports to the European market, and European governments came under increasing pressure from their own industries to raise import barriers. By 1973 the United States managed to develop a multi-fiber accord. The analysis in this chapter supports the key role of international factors by demonstrating that while such factors may initially be misperceived and lead to unexpected results, in the medium run these international systemic factors act as a powerful constraint. At the same time, the analysis clarifies the role of domestic and individual level factors in regime transformation.

THE UNITED STATES TRIES TO SECURE AN
INTERNATIONAL WOOL AGREEMENT

Although the initial Long-Term Arrangement had largely satisfied cotton textile and apparel producers, it failed to blunt the demands of other sectors of the industry. Both the wool and MMF based industries wished to have restrictions imposed on the imports of products from the LDCs and from certain developed countries such as the United Kingdom, Italy, and Japan.[1] In this instance, however, the Kennedy administration successfully resisted pressure from the industry. The Europeans, meanwhile, had made arrangements to restrict some wool-based products considered to be particularly sensitive. Internationally, then, the United States received little encouragement for any potential "multi-fiber" arrangement. Yet, under the Johnson administration, the industry managed to convince U.S. decision makers to try to secure restraints on exports of wool fibers. This struggle to broaden the LTA (and, at the time, some efforts to restrain MMF products) became one of the key issues in the early bargaining for the renewal of the LTA.

The United States made various efforts to stimulate interest in an international arrangement for wool textiles in the 1960s. As noted earlier, Kennedy's plan to have wool included in the LTA met with resistance from some developed countries, such as the United Kingdom and Italy, who feared that the controls would be used against them.[2] In December 1963, the United States made further efforts to develop some sort of a multilateral accord in wool products. But this effort failed to generate much interest. Wool industry groups from various countries called for an intergovernmental meeting of countries involved with world trade. At the subsequent Paris meeting in May 1964, they agreed that "each industry would be free to advise its own Government in the way it would like this problem resolved."[3] This weak agreement indicates some of the problems involved in this issue-area—each country had very different objectives in wool trade. Continuing its efforts to develop some kind of arrangement, the Johnson administration then called for an autumn conference of exporters and importers of wool products. Yet this effort did not make much headway: the key supplier countries declined to attend the meeting.[4] In contrast to the pressures they could bring to bear on the LDCs, the Americans had quite limited leverage on the developed counries. This failure of American decision makers to understand the limitations of their power led to major problems in the negotiations for restraints of other fibers.

Although the U.S. overture to develop some kind of a regime in the area of wool textiles and apparel was rebuffed, its efforts continued. This time the United States chose to deal directly with the country it perceived to be most amenable to restraining exports—Japan. Yet, unlike the cotton situation, Japan was not so willing to restrain its exports—a fact that would subsequently become the basis for a major crisis in Japanese-American relations from 1969 to 1971.

Negotiations with the Japanese commenced with a summit meeting between Prime Minister Sato and President Johnson in Washington in early 1965.[5] Johnson asked Sato whether he would be willing to receive an industry-government mission to discuss the wool issue; when Sato agreed "in principle" to negotiations, the stage was set. Although industry leaders were pleased at this opportunity, the U.S. government's position had not been fully resolved. There was still debate on the feasibility of an international agreement on wool products; while some thought it impossible, others felt that approaching Japan first might lead to a successful agreement.

The U.S. mission was led by Warren Christopher in his capacity as special representative of the secretary of state, and included five other government representatives and ten observers from the American industry.[6] This rather unusual procedure of having industry representatives at an official intergovernmental negotiation (the idea of interindustry talks having been scrapped because of antitrust regulations) led to a vitriolic meeting on June 7-8, 1965. In the talks with the Japanese, one American official from the National Association of Wool Manufacturers pointedly stated, "If we fail here to develop a solution with your cooperation, a solution will be developed without it." He then went on to threaten, "Should we be forced to go home and report failure of this mission, the consequences would be tragic."[7] The Japanese resisted American initiatives, arguing that the LTA did not allow extension to other fields. They also made it quite clear that they were unwilling to impose any restraints on their wool product exports in light of their unpleasant experiences under the LTA (they had lost part of their market share to other unrestrained suppliers).

On the second day of the meeting a crisis (that finally led to the breakdown in talks) developed. Christopher bolstered the statement made by the wool association official by threatening that "if relief from disruptive imports is not forthcoming, Congress may well take matters into its own hands."[8] This type of threat to use market power was not at all unusual: the United States had applied such pressure successfully in the negotiations leading to the bilateral accords in the 1950s and in the negotiations of the LTA itself. The unusual part was the presence of Japanese and American industrialists, which only served to raise the temperature of the meeting. The response from a Japanese textile spokesman made the

American industry's statements look polite by comparison. After expressing shock at the American presentation, he said:

We too have means for our protection including trade in textiles. Therefore to avoid an ugly showdown, you should check the real facts and change your position. We are not easily frightened and our relationship will suffer. We do not like political threats. We are not North Vietnam. We hope you will make distinctions between your friends and your enemies.[9]

The reference to Vietnam was poorly received and the meeting adjourned abruptly, in spite of an apology from an MITI official. The result was added fuel in the bitter struggle to obtain restraints on wool-based products in the United States. While the Japanese temporarily avoided any restraints on these products, when domestic pressure finally led to negotiations with Japan in the late 1960s the discussions were very unpleasant, and led to severe weakening in close U.S.-Japan relations.

THE RENEWAL OF THE LTA

International factors critically affected the outcome of negotiations to renew the LTA. Specifically, the fact that the textile system was nested within the overall trading system was to be decisive. This affected the American preference for a regime as well as its use of linkages in the negotiations. In addition, the participants' recognition of American hegemonic capabilities in textile trade helped lead to a renewed LTA in accord with American wishes. The actual conduct of the negotiations illustrates that American officials correctly perceived what they could do with U.S. textile power. The rapid conclusion of the negotiations after the United States broke a deadlock in the negotiations by concluding bilateral accords demonstrates the successful use of this power.

POLICY CHOICES

The United States. The American policy choice reflected an awareness of the structure of the international system. U.S. decision makers argued for renewal of the LTA with two key changes in the regime: first, they were willing to provide more liberalization in the bilateral agreements; and second, they agreed to more liberal access to their market through a reduction in tariffs—a linkage to the Kennedy Round originally suggested by Eric Wyndham-White, director general of the GATT and chairman of the Cotton Textiles Committee. The quid pro quo in this deal would be an agreement by the LDCs and DCs to accept a renewed LTA without changes in the strength, nature, or scope of the formal rules and procedures of the arrangement.

A number of international factors led to the American decision to maintain the LTA regime. From an organizational cost standpoint, the United States had successfully concluded a number of bilateral accords with LDCs and had regulated imports at relatively low cost as the LTA had facilitated negotiations. More important, the LTA had encouraged the EEC countries to open up their markets to LDC exports while at the same time permitting the United States to restrain rapid import growth. Thus the LTA had met the American goal of controlling the behavior of other countries through a system of rules.

From a domestic perspective, the LTA had been effective in minimizing pressure from industry groups. For example, even fervent protectionists such as the American Textile Manufacturers Institute, though expressing dissatisfaction with the LTA, grudgingly noted that "it was the only restraint that they have."[10] This view was widespread; one newspaper reported, "In general, U.S. textile men, flushed with prosperity, have been satisfied with the results of the LTA."[11]

Finally, American decision makers were able to capitalize on their previous experience with textile negotiations. They recognized that increasing competition from LDCs would be likely to create a problem. Already pressed to do something about restraining imports of wool and MMF products, they anticipated that there would soon be a need for some kind of broader arrangement. As one source commented on the U.S. view, American decision makers felt that it would be worth it to agree to LDC demands to liberalize the LTA in exchange for its renewal since the cotton accord provides a

precedent for dealing with the problems of rising imports of man-made fiber textile products and the critical wool textile import problem. If an international solution of these problems, as against a United States legislative or unilateral solution, is to continue to be sought an existing LTA may be an indispensable requisite.[12]

With respect to the regime characteristics, the United States wished to maintain the formal rules and procedures without changes. They sought to secure LDC support for renewal by promising liberalization in the renewed LTA's implementation. The nested position of textile trade within the strategic and overall trading system proved important in this context. At the strategic level, the Americans had an incentive to be lenient toward the LDCs. The USSR had been a key supporter of a United Nations conference on trade in their quest to secure increasing influence with the LDCs. The West's response—to form the United Nations Conference on Trade and Development (UNCTAD)—was a reluctant concession in this direction.[13] As a *New York Times* (*NYT*) article on the LDCs' disillusionment with the ongoing GATT Kennedy Round talks commented:

In terms of overall world trade it would have been easy to ignore them. But in practical political terms none of the rich nations has wanted to risk being charged with failing to heed the demands of the poor. From the very outset of the Kennedy Round talks, the U.S. has insisted that the realistic expectations of the developing countries should be met.[14]

U.S. interest in a successful conclusion to the overall trade negotiations of the Kennedy Round also led the Americans to consider tariff cuts and increased quotas for the LDCs. The Kennedy Round talks, initiated in 1962, were reaching a climax, and intensive discussions began in September 1966. The final rounds of bargaining had been slated for early 1967—the same time that the U.S. Trade Expansion Act allowing American negotiators to bargain for tariff concessions would expire. The United States had been making an all-out effort to conclude the negotiations with obtaining tariff reductions on a variety of products and wished to ensure that all countries would improve access to their markets.

With the LTA discussions taking place at the same time, decision makers needed to resolve numerous problems. For example, a high U.S. official discussing prospects for an expanded LTA stated that wool and manmade fibers would not be included in the agreement.[15] The *DNR* then observed that "the official, who had just returned from Geneva, was much too concerned with serious Kennedy Round problems to concern himself with other avenues of relief."[16] This illustrates the tension surrounding the Kennedy Round negotiations at this time and the participants' perceptions that the success of the whole venture was still up in the air. As one administration official remarked, there was only a "60-40 chance of the talks succeeding—and that figure sometimes seems more like a 40-60 chance, at other times impossible." When asked by the *DNR* what would happen if the talks were not accelerated or if the administration was not able to easily secure further negotiating authority, he replied, "I think we've had it."[17]

The magnitude of American concern over the successful conclusion of the Kennedy Round derived in part from structural changes in the international trading system. The United States still held a competitive edge in international trade in a wide variety of politically important industries and remained interested in preserving open markets. But in contrast to the late 1940s, the United States was no longer a hegemon in the overall trading system. The Common Market countries, represented by the commission, negotiated in the Kennedy Round for the first time as a unified actor (although with major problems among themselves). In addition, the EEC provided a large potential market for American goods. Therefore, the United States could not simply assert its will in overall trade: it needed to coordinate its policies with the EEC. Finally, the United States wished to appear as a friend of the LDCs so that they would maintain a positive attitude toward American business (vis-à-vis the EEC). Thus, in the negotiations, each major importing area wished to make the other appear to be the intransigent party to curry favor with the LDCs. Minor concessions to secure LDC support for the LTA and to maintain momentum in the Kennedy Round were a small price for the United States to pay from an *overall* trading perspective.

Last, with respect to international influences on regime characteristics, the United States continued to be a hegemon in textile trade—with almost two-thirds of imports from LDCs into the combined markets of the United States and EEC countries.[18] This asymmetry allowed the United States to maintain an international regime in this area.

Domestically, the wool sector pressed the U.S. government to impose restraints on the import of wool goods—both directly and through the Congress. While the government had tried to satisfy wool interests by restraining Japan and developing an international arrangement of some sort in this area, after these efforts failed it did not feel compelled to respond to wool-based producers by developing an all-fiber regime. The wool sector was weak domestically, and producers of MMF products exerted only minor pressure on the government, while cotton interests privately expressed satisfaction with the operation of the LTA.

The EEC. EEC countries on the whole felt satisfied with the LTA. While the regime had forced them to open up their markets, this "burden" had not been excessive. By going along with the LTA, the EEC countries mollified American demands, while still retaining a good deal of control over market access. The textile and apparel industries in most European countries did not suffer from excessive import competition and, as a result, offered only weak calls for protection. But while member states agreed on the benefits of renewing the LTA, they still failed to fully coordinate their policies—as in the Kennedy Round negotiations. Instead, the European states were still trying to decide whether to negotiate with the LDCs separately or en bloc.

With respect to regime characteristics, the EEC member states realized that they had to improve LDC access to their markets. The United States was seeking tariff reductions of 50 percent in all categories in the Kennedy Round and wanted the EEC to liberalize its access to the LDCs in textiles to take the strain off the American market. Furthermore, the United States had agreed to be more liberal in implementing the LTA. This placed added pressure on EEC member states since the LDCs could point to this concession to argue that the Europeans were being inflexible.

Dissension among EEC member states also made it difficult for the commission to take a firm position in the negotiations. The French led the protectionists, while the Germans pursued a liberal line with their willingness to accept more imports. The Germans were particularly concerned with the success of the Kennedy Round as export promotion was one of their major objectives.

While the EEC countries recognized they would have to be more liberal if they wished to secure a renewed LTA, they preferred to move in this direction by granting tariff reductions rather than by giving LDCs more liberal quota access. The advantage of such a policy was quite clear: since LDCs were highly competitive on a price basis, lower tariffs would not really allow them much greater access to the EEC's market. As we shall see, however, the EEC was forced to change this position and agree to greater market access for LDCs.

The United Kingdom. The United Kingdom actively supported a strong and highly liberal LTA. The Wilson government wished to take pressure off the U.K. market since high import penetration had led to complaints from industrial groups. Under the first LTA, the United Kingdom had failed to regulate imports. In the early 1960s, many new suppliers began exporting to the United Kingdom. Although under the LTA the British did not have to allow increased market shares for the LDCs they restrained, they were still overwhelmed by new entrants. Under the LTA, the United Kingdom had to wait sixty days before they were allowed to use a unilateral quota to clamp down on imports. Complaints by domestic producers led the United Kingdom to institute a global quota in 1965. In December of that year, the United Kingdom went to the GATT textiles committee to seek approval from other countries for this action. LDCs strenuously objected to the U.K. scheme and, in response, the United Kingdom made some modifications and concessions on a bilateral basis to garner support for its plan. Moreover, the United Kingdom promised to help the LDCs secure a more liberal LTA in the forthcoming negotiations.[19] Since the United Kingdom had essentially exempted itself from the LTA, any changes that forced other developed countries to take a large share of imports would be to its advantage.

The LDCs and Japan. The LDCs and Japan were aware of the international structural constraints on their bargaining. They realized that the LTA was to their advantage since more restrictive unilateral restraints would be the most likely alternative. Of course this did not discourage them from making sharp demands in the bargaining, but these were tactical moves. Recognizing that completely free trade was out of the question, the LDCs pressed for increased access through bilateral agreements and a clearer definition of "market injury" to prevent DCs from arbitrarily restricting imports.

In many cases, however, LDCs had sharply different interests. Countries such as Japan, Hong Kong, and South Korea were interested in open competition since they were the most competitive exporters. By contrast, some LDCs such as Pakistan, India, and especially the Latin American countries were succeeding in their export drive in a number of categories *only* because of the restraints on other supplying countries who were very competitive. Thus, while liberalization of the regime was in the interest of most countries (or better, liberalization in specific categories), most wished to secure improved bilaterals for themselves and themselves alone. This sometimes led to splits among LDCs, on which the developed countries would be able to capitalize.

The LDCs and Japan thus sought an improved regime to meet their interests. The *DNR* stated that "Japan reportedly would support renewal, but wants more flexibility in categorization practices and an improved position in controlled expansion of markets."[20] India (along with Pakistan), while opposing the extension of the LTA in its public bargaining position, appeared to recognize that this was not a credible position and hoped to secure better access through bilateral bargaining. The *DNR* noted that if India was "pressed [it] would probably adopt the Japanese position—which is that the disruption clause should be modified to give better access to industrialized country markets."[21]

A number of other LDCs also had a vested interest in the renewal of the LTA. For example, even a highly competitive state such as Hong Kong, while a preeminent exporter in man-made fiber-based products, was losing some of its comparative advantage in the production of traditional cotton-based goods. As one source commented, "Hong Kong, a notoriously cheap producer, has on occasion protested pricing practices of new entry nations in the cotton textile export field who produce more cheaply than Hong Kong."[22] As long as Hong Kong maintained a large quota for itself, it would stand to profit from guaranteed market access— if its exporters continued to supply products at lower prices than the domestic producers in importing countries. This was not a particularly difficult task given the comparatively high wages in the developed world. On the whole, LDCs and Japan sought to secure favorable bilateral agreements and would accept a renewed LTA on that condition.

International Bargaining over the LTA's Renewal

The GATT Secretariat was heavily involved in the 1967 LTA renewal. In addition to publishing a major study on the functioning of the LTA and the state of the cotton textile industry in the world, the director general of GATT, Eric Wyndham White, suggested a plan to tie the Kennedy Round to the renewal of the LTA. Developed countries would reduce their tariffs to the greatest possible extent and would administer the LTA in a more liberal manner (essentially, through improved bilaterals) in exchange for continuing the LTA in its present form.[23] This idea, disseminated in private memorandums to the parties to the LTA in August 1965, set the agenda for the ensuing negotiations: the basic conflict revolved around (1) how much liberalization there would actually be in the administration of the LTA and to what extent this would be formalized in the regime rules; (2) how large the tariff reductions were to be; and most important, (3) whether the importing countries should make concessions before or after the exporters accepted a renewed LTA.

As the key power in the negotiations, the American strategy was crucial. The United States took the lead in the negotiations and attempted to secure a rapid conclusion to the talks. It proposed a five-year extension of the LTA and asked that the LDCs commit themselves to a renewed LTA *prior* to U.S. tariff cuts and increased liberalization. This linkage (at least from a temporal standpoint) did not prove to be entirely successful: India, Pakistan, and other LDCs resisted this notion of agreeing to a renewed regime before other aspects of the package were negotiated, modified, or discontinued.[24]

The Pakistani delegate to the Cotton Textiles Committee avowed that his government would not sign the renewal in the vague hope that access for its cotton textiles would be enlarged through reduction of tariffs and a "more liberal administration" of the agreement.[25] Similarly, the Indian delegate stressed his unhappiness with the LTA, agreeing wholeheartedly with the Pakistani's comments. Moreover, he argued that the procedure for establishing market disruption (which allowed countries to restrain imports) was arbitrary and unfair. He went on to suggest a scheme whereby such disruption would be defined in a more objective manner and procedures to determine disruption would be laid down.

The Americans immediately responded by rejecting these suggestions that the United States should specify in advance what changes they would make. Any changes in strength, nature, or scope were to be made in the bilateral implementation—*not* on an agreed multilateral basis. As the American delegate bluntly put it, "The U.S. had no reason to believe that the countries now participating in the Arrangement could find a better basis for mutual agreement than the terms of the Arrangement as it now stood."[26]

Further discussion in the textiles committee meeting indicated the differences among the various LDCs. South Korea, a new entrant into the field of cotton textiles (soon to become one of the most competitive countries in the textiles field as a whole), strongly promoted its particular interests at the expense of other exporters. While criticizing the importing countries for maintaining a low level of imports from developing countries, the Korean delegate also pointed out that his country, "as a newcomer to the international market had probably been subjected to more severe restrictions than other exporting countries."[27] But most important—and serving as an entree for the importing countries to split the LDC coalition—he argued: "Unused quotas granted to some exporting countries should be made available to other countries which could easily fill them."[28] In summing up the discussion of the December 1965 meeting, Wyndham-White observed that although countries appeared to agree with his suggestions, many did not accept the American position that renewal should precede concessions.[29]

Following the "breakdown of multilateral sector talks" in December,[30] the United States set out to negotiate bilateral agreements with key exporting countries. The American strategy was to preserve the regime by using its large market to lure LDCs into bilateral accords. Japan was the first country which agreed to conclude a bilateral agreement with the United States. In exchange for an American promise of increased liberalization, Japan expressed support for the LTA's renewal. In late January 1966, one source commenting on the successful negotiations between the United States and Japan stated, "with Japan committed, there is an implied warning to other countries that a bandwagon would be in the making, and that those exporters which are slow in clambering on board may lose out."[31] The American offers of more liberal bilaterals also put pressure on the EEC to cooperate with them. The Europeans did not want to antagonize the LDCs any more than necessary. As the key power in textile trade, the United States successfully secured such "bandwagoning."[32]

Along with inducements came threats. In a talk to ATMI, the U.S. secretary of commerce, John T. Connor, suggested that if the LTA was not extended or if successful bilaterals were not concluded, then legislation allowing *unilateral* action should be pushed. He virtually asked them to lobby Congress, advising them that "your industry, in particular, will have a heavy responsibility in this respect."[33] In commenting on the secretary's advice, the *DNR* noted:

There appears to be little doubt that the pressure will mount from the industry for legislation and that more pressure will be placed on foreign governments to soften their negative attitudes.[34]

While Connor's efforts may be seen as reflecting bureaucratic infighting over the U.S. policy stance, it undoubtedly affected the views of LDCs and their willingness to make concessions: a unilateral system of restraints was the action they feared most.

As the proposed September 1966 meeting of the GATT Cotton Textiles Committee drew near, the United States busily continued to conclude bilateral agreements with key supplying countries in the hope of securing a quick renewal of the LTA. The American bilateral arrangement with Hong Kong, for example, was "viewed in some quarters as a shrewd move to forestall changes in the LTA."[35] Shortly before the September meeting the United States softened its bargaining position. Whereas the United States had previously hinted that a man-made fibers arrangement might be sought in addition to the LTA, the Americans now made it clear they only desired an extension of the LTA, and would worry about the man-made fiber and wool trade at a later date.[36]

At the September meeting of the Textiles Committee, the LDCs still resisted American calls for a renewed LTA, arguing that the importing countries should spell out what measures they would take to liberalize access to their markets. But while the United States had managed to line up a number of LDCs on its side through bilateral bargaining to support a renewed arrangement, the EEC's failure to agree on a unified policy stance undermined American strategy. The LDCs blamed the EEC for the delay and stated that they would not agree to renewal unless they made a firm offer.[37] This placed the United States in a very awkward position since it could hardly criticize the LDCs in light of the EEC's failure to make an offer. The negotiations were once again delayed, leading Wyndham-White to admit that his concept of a package deal was falling through and forcing him to adjourn the meeting once again until bilateral talks had been conducted.[38] This delay, caused by the EEC, forced the United States to continue juggling the various parties to prevent any modification in the arrangement. Since the United States was very concerned with Kennedy Round talks, this delay proved to be a major thorn in the American side.

The EEC continued to encounter problems in concluding bilateral agreements with exporting countries, an issue that became a matter of concern at the November meeting of the Textiles Committee. The EEC spokesman himself admitted that member states were having the "problem of formulating a common commercial policy"—a problem illustrating their weakness in the negotiations.[39] Since the EEC negotiated jointly on tariffs but separately on the LTA, it was difficult for them to use their full economic muscle. As the *DNR* reported, the "EEC hopes to improve their own fighting position by thrashing out a common policy within their joint Council of Ministers in Brussels."[40]

The United States continued to express its displeasure with the delays and increased its pressure on the EEC and the LDCs to reach an agreement. It argued that tariff negotiations—of clear concern to the EEC—would be delayed unless a quick renewal was agreed to. Moreover, it increased its pressure on the LDCs by warning them that the liberalization that the United States had agreed to bilaterally with the exporting countries would not go into effect until the agreement on the LTA was signed.

In early March 1967, the EEC was able to arrive at a joint position. It offered to cut tariffs by 50 percent, but promised little increased quota access. The LDCs, however, continued to press for greater market access. At the EEC Council of Ministers meeting on March 6, Germany led the battle to make concessions on the LTA and GATT negotiations. As a major exporter, it wished to increase its market access to LDCs and DCs and pressed for greater concessions from the other EEC member states.[41] German pressure on its partners led to a compromise more favorable to the LDCs: larger quotas but a 20 percent tariff cut instead of the original 50 percent offer. Quotas would increase by 35 percent in overall terms over and above the 1967 level.

Armed with Council of Ministers' authorization to make new concessions, the council representatives set out to bargain with the less developed countries and Japan.[42]

Even with the EEC's new mandate, the talks broke down once again. Both India and Japan now claimed they might call for a complete reexamination of the LTA and might block a quick renewal of the LTA as desired by the United States. Thus, both these countries were holding up renewal of the regime to bargain for concessions in the bilateral talks. Although the LDCs needed the regime, they played a game of brinkmanship, hoping that the EEC and the United States wanted the LTA more than they did. The United States pressed the LDCs and the EEC to bargain more vigorously, warning that liberalized market access that had been promised to LDCs would be delayed and that the Kennedy Round negotiations were in jeopardy.[43]

The meetings resumed after a forty-eight hour break on March 22. In response to the EEC's statement that much of the bilateral negotiating had been concluded, the chairman of the committee suggested the members make a decision in principle to extend the LTA. Once again, the issue of timing arose, with the Americans holding to the position that LTA renewal was a precondition for liberalization, and the LDCs wanting to know what liberalization they were entitled to before signing an agreement. The meeting concluded with a note by the chairman that he would have a draft protocol prepared. This set the stage for the conflict over the wording of the protocol—a conflict that would demonstrate American power.

THE AGREEMENT

In the period between the basic agreement to go ahead with the protocol and the April meeting, American negotiators reported back to Congress. Although a number of congressmen had been supporting the industries' demands for a longer and more protectionist regime, many of them were relieved to learn that an agreement had been reached at all. Some had feared that the negotiators would "give away" even more, resulting in greater industry pressure on them. As the *DNR* commented, "A three year extension conceivably might have been more than they really expected."[44]

The April meeting began with various importing countries reporting the growth figures they would accept over the next three-year period. A struggle then developed over whether or not the protocol would refer to the decision to further liberalize the implementation of the LTA (although any liberalization would be agreed to bilaterally). The Americans feared that any mention of such liberalization in the agreement might lead to tremendous pressures from congressional supporters of the industry.

Commenting on the chairman's earlier statement that some multilateral recognition be given to the bilaterally agreed to intentions of the importing countries, the Indian delegate argued that there was a need for the "protocol . . . [to] reflect the liberalized principles which the bilaterals were supposed to have brought in to operation and secure multilateral recognition of these intentions."[45] The American delegate immediately opposed the Indian demand, arguing that liberalization had been agreed to on a bilateral basis. The United Kingdom supported the American delegate. As a country pursuing an increasingly restrictionist policy, it did not wish to be called upon to abide by any provisions calling for more liberalization, although it had feebly offered to help the LDCs in their bilateral negotiations with the other importing countries. As the EEC was starting from a very closed stance and had already made its firm offer of import growth, a statement calling for greater liberalization in implementation did not greatly concern them.

The bickering continued, with the United States, Canada, and the United Kingdom on one side, and the Indians on the other side. Other countries remained on the sidelines. The American delegate again expressed his concern about the delay that this might cause in the Kennedy Round, a delay India encouraged since it was still in the midst of conducting bilateral negotiations with a number of countries. Furthermore, India wished to find out exactly what kind of liberalization would take place in the Kennedy Round tariff negotiations. The United States now shifted its attack to make it appear that India was harming the interests of other

LDCs by forcing delay of its promised liberalization measures. The U.S. government

> regretted that the measures of liberalization promised to the exporting countries, as distinct from those which were granted to them in the course of the discussion had not been in effect since the September meeting; the United States had been prepared to put these in practice had a decision at that time been reached to extend the Arrangement.[46]

The United States, then, was holding out these concessions as incentives for the LDCs to agree to a quick renewal.

While strong resistance from the LDCs and the indecisiveness on the part of the EEC frustrated American efforts to secure a rapid decision on renewal, the United States did prevent any changes in the LTA. Moreover, the United States avoided making tariff cuts until after it had secured renewal of the LTA.

In the subsequent tariff negotiations on textiles, American tariff cuts averaged 14 percent on a trade-weighted basis. Although cotton textile duties were cut by 21 percent, wool textiles duties were only cut by 2 percent. This tiny cut in wool tariffs was the result of massive pressure for some kind of restraint in the wool sector by domestic producers. In man-made fiber products, the United States cut duties on apparel by only 6 percent, fabrics by 18 percent, and yarn by 37 percent—the cuts following the stages of processing, with lower cuts corresponding to the higher value added products. The European Common Market also reduced its tariffs on cotton textiles to the same degree, with cuts averaging 20 percent.[47] The key concession by the EEC—as I discussed above—was a decision to enlarge quota access to its market. But the EEC also made a key reservation that was to be used in the future: they linked their tariff reductions to a renewal of the LTA in three years.[48] Soon thereafter, the United States also linked its tariff reductions to the LTA's renewal.

Although technically liberalized, then, the LTA was seen by both major importing areas as a method of facilitating import restraints— restraints that would otherwise be costly to negotiate individually. And although the LDCs continued to protest the LTA, the alternatives were bleak. The story, however, would soon shift from cotton textiles and apparel to the area where LDCs were now becoming highly competitive in response to restraints in cotton textiles—the MMF area.

Behavior of Countries and Transactions

Behavior. As we have seen, the United States and EEC concluded numerous bilateral agreements in cotton textile products during the LTA talks. The United States continued to negotiate additional bilateral agreements with exporters; by 1970 it had 27 bilateral agreements and had undertaken 8 unilateral restraint actions.[49] The EEC, meanwhile, followed a policy of replacing its unilateral restraints with bilateral agreements—a process initiated in the final stages of the LTA talks. For example, it finalized previously negotiated tentative agreements with India and Pakistan in 1968 and concluded a bilateral agreement with Japan in 1969. The United Kingdom continued to pursue its illegal global quota scheme. Moreover, prior to the introduction of this scheme, it had imposed a temporary surcharge on textile imports. These measures effectively reduced the growth of LDC imports into the U.K. market.

Other countries, particularly the Scandinavian states, instituted various new restraints on cotton textile goods. In a few cases, however, they pursued some liberalization.[50] Denmark imposed a quota on imports from South Korea in 1968 but discontinued its restraints on imports from Colombia in 1969. Its preexisting quota on Japanese goods was not renewed. Sweden concluded a bilateral accord with Hong Kong, effective June 1, 1968. In 1969, Australia moved to restrain imports from Hong Kong; Austria replaced its unilateral restraints on numerous LDCs with bilateral accords; and Canada continued to restrict imports from a growing number of LDCs.

The most disturbing development from the LDCs' perspective, however, was the trend toward restraint on products of MMF and wool—goods that Japan and the LDCs were just beginning to export successfully. Among the EEC countries, restraints on man-made fiber and wool-based products had only been imposed on the Eastern bloc countries;[51] in the late 1960s, EEC states began to restrict garments of man-made fibers imported from Japan. As these restraints were not comprehensive in nature (and thus not very restrictive), when the United States responded to domestic pressure from its man-made fiber and wool manufacturers by concluding bilateral agreements with Far Eastern suppliers in 1971, LDCs diverted a large portion of their exports to the EEC's market. While the United Kingdom had instituted a global quota on cotton products, it did not have a similar scheme for MMF and wool-based products. It did, however, restrain goods from the Eastern bloc countries and, starting in 1970, negotiated a voluntary export restraint accord with Japan on a variety of man-made fiber products. The LDCs were not affected by these actions.

Finally, the Scandinavians had a variety of restraints. For example, Sweden, a traditionally open market, extended its cotton bilateral agreements with Hong Kong in 1968 to encompass products of other fibers. In 1970, Norway followed Sweden and asked Hong Kong to restrain products of other fibers. Denmark imposed a variety of quotas on MMF products against the LDCs in addition to its various controls with Eastern bloc countries which were imposed in 1972. Throughout the 1960s, Canada had been regulating Japanese imports of MMF products. Such restraints were subsequently extended to South Korea in 1967, Hong Kong and Poland in 1968, and India, Rumania, Trinidad and Tobago, Malaysia, and Taiwan in 1970-71.

The rapid shift in LDC exports from cotton to MMF and wool-based products led the developed countries to these new textile import controls. This shift was partially encouraged by the LTA itself. As the LTA defined "cotton" products as goods having 50 percent or more cotton content, the textile exporters' logical strategy was to have products of 49 percent cotton content to avoid trade barriers.

Transactions. While there are some discrepancies in the data, on the whole the LDCs and Japan (Group II countries) appear to have continued their relative penetration of the industrialized (Group I) countries' markets in cotton products. One source states that the relative share of Group II countries had risen from 21 percent in 1961 to 28 percent in 1970.[52] Further data from the GATT also bears out this relative increase. Comparing two different years, 1962 and 1968, Group II countries increased their share of the Group I market from 26 percent to 30.5 percent.[53] Japan, in contrast, lost some of its share of cotton product exports in Group I. Their exports experienced a decline from 12 percent to 9 percent during the nine-year period from 1961 to 1970. For textiles as a whole, however, this is somewhat misleading: MMF products were the key to Japan's and the LDCs' textile exports.

The real growth in textiles and apparel trade took place in the area of MMF and, to a much lesser extent, wool-based products. Considering MMF imports into the United States, for example, imports increased from 328,430 sye in 1964 to 2,750,820 sye in 1970 (and to 4,319,520 sye in 1971).[54] Of this total, the developing countries increased their exports of these goods to the United States from 31,216 sye in 1964 to 777,114 sye in 1970. Meanwhile, Hong Kong and Japan increased their share from 174,699 to 962,059 sye. This phenomenon, repeated in markets throughout the industrialized world, illustrates the magnitude of the import "flood" leading to protectionist measures. In wool-based goods, imports of developing countries and Hong Kong and Japan into the United States increased from 59,182 sye to 98,463 sye. But in the case of wool, there was a great deal of fluctuation, and in fact U.S. wool-based imports overall were lower in 1971 than in 1963.

Imports of MMF-based goods into the EEC increased rapidly from a value of $1,421.7 million to $2,794.1 million from 1967 to 1970. Yet developing countries did not make the same inroads as they did into the U.S. market. Their share only increased from $68.4 million to $212.8 million. Japan rapidly gained an increased market share, with its exports growing from $28.2 million to $51.9 million from 1967 to 1969.

The United Kingdom experienced a sharp rise in imports of MMF goods from the LDCs, with imports rising from $57 million to $88 million between 1967 and 1969. Among some of the other countries, penetration into the Canadian market was significant: imports overall rose from $158.6 million to $247.8 million in the two years from 1967 to 1969, with LDC exports rising from $21.5 million to $50.2 million during this period. Japan also increased its share in the Canadian market from $26.5 million to $42.2 million. These were some of the market factors (resulting from a combination of technological change and restraints on cotton goods) leading to the U.S. attempt to negotiate bilateral arrangements in man-made fiber and wool goods.

SUMMARY

The first renewal of the Long-Term Arrangement on Cotton Textiles in 1967 illustrates the use of American power to maintain the textile regime. The United States felt constrained in textile talks by its interests in overall trade and the Kennedy Round talks and, as a result, the LDCs obtained some (temporary) liberalization in quotas and tariff reductions in exchange for renewal of the LTA without formal changes. But, in the end, the United States derailed LDC efforts (especially India's) to make changes in the text. It even refused to promise to reduce its tariffs by specified amounts until the LTA had been renewed. Therefore, although constrained by the overall trading system and some strategic considerations, its textile power allowed the United States to prevail.

EXPANSION OF THE LTA, THE FIRST EFFORT: 1969-1971

With cotton products restrained under the LTA, the LDCs began to export wool- and MMF-based products in ever-increasing quantities. While U.S. imports of cotton textiles and apparel held steady during the late 1960s, those of wool- and MMF-based products surged dramatically (see table 6). In 1968 the volume of wool- and MMF-based imports first exceeded those of cotton, and by 1970 they were double that of the regulated fiber.

As a number of other exporting countries entered into the production of MMF products, we would expect costs of concluding bilaterals and information about market conditions to grow rapidly. We would also

TABLE 6

U.S. IMPORTS OF TEXTILES AND APPAREL (MILLION SYE)

	Total Imports			
	Textiles		Apparel	
Year	Cotton	MMF and wool	Cotton	MMF and wool
1967	1485	1101	475	402
1968	1648	1663	515	638
1969	1652	1974	525	996
1970	1536	2928	478	1216
1971	1611	4340	498	1600
1972	1853	4582	545	1682
1973	1592	3531	449	1641
1974	1463	2948	449	1489
	Rates of Growth (percent)			
	Textiles		Apparel	
Year	Cotton	MMF and wool	Cotton	MMF and wool
1967-8	11.0	51.0	8.4	58.7
1968-9	0.2	18.0	1.9	56.1
1969-0	−7.1	48.3	−8.9	22.1
1970-1	4.8	48.2	4.2	31.6
1971-2	11.5	5.7	9.4	5.1
1972-3	−14.1	−23.0	−17.6	−2.4
1973-4	−8.2	−16.5	0	−9.3

SOURCE: OTEX/TAD Department of Commerce Document, January 1978. Percentages computed by author.

expect the hegemonic state in overall trade, the United States (see table 2), to be wary of undermining GATT through unilateral or unregulated bilateral actions. Once again, a dose of liberal protectionism through an "organized" deviation excising the textile/apparel issue-area from manufacturing trade in general would be a useful method of preserving the stability of the overall trade regime.

As the United States was still the hegemon in textile trade (see table 3) it might be expected to "supply" the regime and use both carrot and stick to secure the cooperation of other states in developing a new arrangement. Exporters could be better controlled with a regime and the importers (such as the EEC) could be forced through regulation to take a "fair" share of imports. Both actions would take pressure off the American market while meeting the American goal of preserving a semblance of liberal trade.

What characteristics of a new arrangement should we expect? As far as the strength of the regime is concerned, American hegemonic capabilities in textiles should allow for the development of a strong regime. With respect to nature, we might expect a moderately protectionist regime, as the United States wished to protect its market. Still, the regime had to be liberal enough to force open EEC and other importers' markets. Finally, as discussed above, we would anticipate the new regime to be of wider scope to handle trade in wool- and MMF-based products.

POLICY CHOICES

The U.S. On entering office, President Nixon decided to seek an expansion of the LTA and to develop a regime covering all fibers. Cognizant of the problems of the 1950s—when numerous LDCs entered the American market after the United States restrained Japanese exports—the United States in this case decided to bypass the bilateral "stage" and seek a wider accord. The Americans did not want their market to become a "dumping ground" for LDC exports barred from European markets, nor did they wish to bow to domestic pressure for legislated import quotas. Instead, the U.S. government sought a multilateral accord that would allow it to regulate imports while constraining the EEC's use of import controls.[55]

Complicating these efforts, however, was the U.S. attempt not only to have an agreement including the Europeans but to make them an *object* of American controls.[56] As we will see, this proved to be a major miscalculation of American power and aggravated the Europeans.

The American policy choice was influenced by a number of factors. Turning first to the overall international system, a number of changes led to a situation that can be characterized as "loose bipolarity." President Nixon sought a lessening of tensions with the Soviet Union through linkages of trade with better political relations. Détente, as the process came to be known, had two important implications: it weakened U.S. leverage over the Europeans by making its role as Europe's guardian against the Soviet Union less important; and it diminished the American fear of seeing the Europeans or Japanese swallowed up by the Communist menace. As a result, the United States more frequently came to see the Europeans and the Japanese as competitors. As Nixon commented in 1971: "When we think in economic terms and economic potentialities there are five great power centers in the world today; both Western Europe and Japan are potent competitors of the United States."[57] This changing strategic situation explains in part why subsequent American efforts to affect

European and Japanese behavior were marked by greater conflict than before.

American capabilities in the overall trading system had declined somewhat after 1960. Growing competition from other countries increased the industries' desires for some form of protection. Still, President Nixon, with his internationalist perspective, sought new legislation to eliminate a number of trade barriers. In 1969 he attempted to obtain congressional authority to allow American participation in new trade negotiations. Fear of undermining the trading system also extended to some members of Congress. For example, a key representative, Wilbur Mills, chairman of the House Ways and Means Committee, argued in a speech to the National Cotton Council that "it appears difficult if not impossible to work out an import quota for one industry, and prevent its extension to other industries."[58] The administration, for tactical purposes, still sought to link success in the textile negotiations to trade liberalization.

Finally, with respect to textile trade, the United States continued to be a hegemon. To what extent did this influence American views? The arrogance of American negotiators (particularly Maurice Stans) was directly related to the knowledge that the United States could unilaterally impose restrictions on the import of textile and apparel products if they did not obtain a satisfactory "voluntary" arrangement. As Stans noted in a speech to the ATMI, in the absence of a voluntary arrangement, "You can count on us to proceed at once with action in the textile import problem."[59] The implications of this statement were clearly recognized by one U.K. observer, the *Financial Times*, which noted: "It looks as if the Administration will press hard for VERs with the threat of quotas or some other form of protective legislation hovering in the background."[60] The United States was aware that American restraints would have important implications for other importing countries. One journal, commenting on American discussions with Japan, reported:

U.S. officials are confident that once an agreement is reached with Japan, other countries will follow suit in order to avoid a deluge of Japanese textiles on their home market.[61]

On the domestic front, when American textile and apparel producers failed to secure an expansion of the LTA to encompass products of other fibers during the 1966-67 discussions, they made unilateral restraints their first priority. ATMI and other textile and apparel organizations managed to extract pledges from *all* the 1968 presidential candidates to restrain imports of MMF- and wool-based products. Candidate Richard Nixon promised to promptly take the step necessary to extend the concept of international trade agreements to all other textile articles involving wool, man-made fibers and blends.[62]

In line with its long-term objectives, ATMI sought to have an arrangement keying the growth rate of imports to the actual growth of domestic consumption in the United States. Moreover, it wished to control the exports of the European countries, and therefore, wanted a broadly based agreement. Few domestic industries fought against the ATMI requests. In addition, government decision makers had failed to develop a coherent domestic industrial policy. Ironically, the only real constraints on the demands of the ATMI were the international constraints influencing U.S. government decision makers.

At the individual level, the Nixon administration's decision to handle negotiations on textiles at a high level possibly contributed to some of the ensuing problems. The aggressive posture taken by Commerce Secretary Maurice Stans toward the Europeans resulted in a strong negative reaction to American proposals. If talks in this area would have been conducted at a lower level in the bureaucracy, some of the idiosyncrasies in the negotiating process might have been avoided.

The EEC. The EEC countries resisted American efforts to develop a multilateral accord covering all fibers. Remarking on the EEC's position, the *Financial Times* stated:

The U.S. has for some time been attempting to get the Europeans to agree to voluntary restrictions of their textile exports to the U.S. But the EEC commission has made it clear that these would not only be bad precedent, but also completely unworkable.[63]

The EEC states had successfully controlled the influx of imports in a number of wool- and MMF-based products through unilateral and bilateral measures. Therefore, they were primarily interested in gaining further access to the lucrative American market for their exporters. Moreover, on an overall basis, the EEC states experienced an export surplus in both wool and MMF products.[64] Once again, with views similar to those in the 1961 STA talks, the EEC member states wished to preserve their freedom to institute controls without being constrained by a regime. Their changing overall international and trade positions fostered these choices.

The EEC feared Soviet military might less as talk of détente grew, and as a result, was not as willing to bow to American demands for an international accord in return for security considerations—especially an agreement that might restrain their own exports. With respect to trading capabilities, the EEC had become increasingly unified after the Kennedy Round negotiations and it follows a trading power to reckon with.

Within the EEC, variations among member states also affected the EEC's attitude toward the American proposal to expand the LTA. German industrialists were not particularly upset by the influx of low-priced imports, since their government had concluded bilateral agreements in the most "sensitive" categories of textile and apparel products. Moreover, apparel producers emphasized the development of outward processing.[65] However, French producers continuously pressured the government to use a variety of restrictive mechanisms to stop low-priced imports. The Italians were doing extremely well not only in the textile and apparel export business but also in a host of other products,[66] and feared that their overall export push might be nipped in the bud by American protectionist actions.[67] As a result, the Italians were more willing than other Europeans to listen to Stans's pleas for some kind of multilateral arrangement, lest the Americans respond with trade barriers.

As a result, when the United States attempted to institute a multifiber arrangement and indicated that European countries might also be subject to import controls under the arrangement, the EEC naturally resisted. Most EEC countries were quite happy with the status quo; any new agreement would probably work against them. In the negotiations, however, the United States employed its textile capabilities to alter European incentives toward the development of a multifiber agreement.

The United Kingdom. The United Kingdom had independent arrangements in international textile and apparel trade and sought to replace its quota system with a broadly based tariff system. As a medium-size power in the international system, the United Kingdom wished to retain maximum independence of action to follow its own policies and avoid an international accord. At the same time, the British were clearly aware of their rather weak position—both in textile trade and at the overall trade level. For example, U.K. officials recognized that "unilateral action by the U.S. could indirectly affect Britain through the switching of imports to the U.K. market."[68] The significance of American policy for U.K. actions was duly noted by the *Financial Times*:

For what the U.S. manages to achieve in international agreements controlling trade in low-cost textiles will bear heavily on the U.K. Government's decisions regarding future tariff and/or quota restrictions.[69]

On the domestic front, a report by the Textile Council published in May 1969 advocated the abolition of the existing British quota system and its replacement by a uniform tariff to be applied to all cloth regardless of origin.[70] After some discussion within the government, it was decided that this program would take effect at the beginning of January 1972. Yet due to last minute pressure from the domestic textile and apparel industries in Britain, the government did not remove the quota system and put both types of restrictive measures into effect in 1972. The relative success of U.K. exporters in exporting wool products to the American market also influenced British policy. Industrialists in the United Kingdom feared, as did the Europeans, that any multifiber-type agreement would be used to restrict these exports to the United States.

Thus, the United States recognized that it could create problems for the Europeans by closing off its market; and the Europeans and the United Kingdom realized that this action could create a diversion to their markets. In addition, the Europeans and the British were also aware of the interrelationship of textile policy and the overall trading system and their vulnerability in this regard. But in the negotiations with the Europeans, the U.S. attempt to use its capabilities failed, as its initial push to control European exports frightened them off. In this case, it appears the Europeans felt that their loss of exports would more than outweigh the problems incurred by diversion. Yet the American policy of negotiating bilaterals did in fact lead to a diversion of textile and apparel products from the Far East to Europe. This put pressure on European textile and apparel producers who in turn pounced on their respective governments to speed up the formation of the Multi-Fiber Arrangement.

International Bargaining

Stans took it upon himself to implement Nixon's pledge to develop a multilateral arrangement covering man-made fiber and wool products. His first effort, a trip to Europe in April 1969, failed in its objective. He subsequently ran into trouble on a similar trip to Japan. The United States managed to secure bilateral agreements with Far East supplying countries only after two years of strenuous efforts and direct threats.[71]

Round 1: Stans Goes to Europe. Stans's trip to Europe in April 1969 was not met with an enthusiastic response. He initially sought to get the Europeans to voluntarily control their exports to the United States and to cooperate in developing a multilateral agreement for MMF and wool products under the auspices of GATT. When these efforts were rebuffed, Stans called for a preliminary conference on these products. When this proposal also was denounced, he left without any commitment whatsoever.

Stans referred to American textile power and links to overall trade in an effort to get the Europeans to go along with restraints. In a speech to the ATMI he said, "in the absence of such an agreement [voluntary solution on textiles] you can count on us to proceed at once with action on the textile import problem."[72] As the *Financial Times* commented, it "looks as if the Administration will press hard for VERs with the threat of quotas or some other form of protective legislation hovering in the background."[73] More directly, Stans told the Europeans that "while President Nixon was very much against such things as quotas, and did not want to get involved in a round of retaliating restrictions, he could only translate this into policy if other countries cooperated."[74]

Stans did not hesitate to link American action on reducing trade barriers and the development of a new negotiating round to a satisfactory solution of the textile issue. He repeatedly emphasized that the United States desired to have freer world trade, but at the same time he made it quite clear that "American initiatives would depend on cooperation from Europe,"[75] and warned a group of Italian businessmen and government officials that voluntary restraints were a precondition to further trade liberalization.[76] The British also took note of this link, with the *Financial Times* reporting:

The internal political pressure to do something about textile imports is however recognized in London. A protectionist concession might smooth the way for other proposals fulfilling what President Nixon has described as his 'open market' policy for foreign trade.[77]

In textiles specifically, the British recognized the problems that American restrictions might create. A *Financial Times* editorial argued that curbs on imports in the United States would not only lead to retaliation against U.S. exports (presumably by European states who had the capability to effectively retaliate against the United States) but "would also probably lead to a considerable switching of shipment to other markets, including our own."[78] The British (and other Europeans) opposed restraints. The *Financial Times* reported: "Although specific proposals had yet to be framed, Mr. Stans was given to understand that Britain would oppose any suggestion that the present GATT LTA on cotton textiles be extended to include man-made fiber and woolen products."[79]

With the Europeans opposing VERs on exports of textile and apparel products of man-made and wool fibers, Stans abandoned his approach and called for a GATT conference on these products.[80] In an attempt to lure the Europeans to the conference table, Stans argued: "Imports from Britain and other European countries were not a problem . . . although there were one or two exceptions on individual items."[81] This maneuver backfired, however, as the "one or two exceptions" clause proved to be enough of an irritant to put the Europeans on their guard. The British noted that "if the source of Stans's problem was the Far East, then he needed to go there to work out the means of solving it."[82] The Germans responded by arguing that the proposed international conference was an "act of improper solidarization against developing countries."[83] Stans was forced to acknowledge that the "Europeans were not especially enthusiastic about the American proposal for a textile agreement."[84]

In light of the threats the United States was willing to use with their textile and trade power, why did Stans fail to gain European acceptance of restrictions or a conference? The basic answer appears to lie in the asymmetry of motivation. Instead of simply sharing American interests in controlling imports, the Europeans were also major suppliers of the American market. They were therefore reluctant to have any type of international agreement that might potentially threaten their market position. By the time Stans backtracked on restricting European exports, it was too late to convince the Europeans they would be spared. But, while American decision makers could not convince Europeans to go along with their wishes by simply alluding to their textile power linkages to the international trading and security system, they could employ their power to alter European incentives. This could be done, in Stans's view, by first concluding bilateral agreements with Far East suppliers; the resulting diversion of goods to European markets would then encourage them to agree to a multilateral accord.[85]

Round 2: On to Japan. The American effort to secure voluntary restraint of man-made fiber and wool products from Japan and Far East suppliers lasted for two years. The resulting crisis adversely affected Japanese-American relations over an issue with few strategic implications. Although Japan's primary motivation in resisting American demands stemmed from its international structural position, domestic political factors also played a key role in delaying the development of a bilateral arrangement.[86] In the end, the United States had to make the overt threat of restricting Japanese trade and a strategic linkage to the return of Okinawa before the Japanese relented and agreed to restrain their exports.

Having failed to secure European cooperation in setting up a multilateral system of controls in textile and apparel trade, Stans flew to Tokyo on May 10, 1969 to discuss restraint agreements with the Japanese. The Japanese were not any more cooperative than the Europeans as their government officials were under strong pressure from their own industry. This industry was one of the most dynamic sectors in Japan at this time,[87] and was on the "verge of take-off."[88] The situation was further aggravated by U.S. demands for a *comprehensive* agreement on textiles and apparel rather than selective restrictions. Stans returned to the United States without the desired concessions from Japan.

Two international shifts explain the problems the United States encountered in trying to restrain the Japanese. First, international systemic pressures for the United States to help Japan and to preserve an open trading system had declined. Aware of this, the U.S. industries could hardly expect the government to procure a "worse" deal than it had obtained in the 1950s and as a result was adamant about securing a protectionist accord. Second, Japan, as a full-fledged member of GATT, was less open to persuasion on strategic grounds and did not need the United States as its benefactor in opening up markets.

After Stans's first mission failed, talks moved to the highest level. In November 1969, Premier Sato met with President Nixon and secretly agreed to secure Japanese restraints on textile exports in exchange for the United States return of Okinawa and waiver of any claims to use nuclear facilities on the island. But Sato failed to deliver on this agreement as promised and the American industries demanded that the U.S. government increase its pressure on the Japanese. To counter the efforts of domestic textile and apparel interests (who threatened to demand a legislative solution to restrain Japanese imports), Donald Kendall, of the Emergency Committee for American Trade, developed a compromise plan for a negotiated bilateral solution. Although this plan called for temporary restraints of all Japanese textile and apparel exports at 1969 levels, it contained a provision stating that restrictions would only be continued on items which the Tariff Commission had determined to be seriously injured by imports. ATMI and ten other textile and apparel organizations rejected the Kendall plan on March 30, 1970, since they had not had a satisfactory experience with the Tariff Commission on injury findings. Since this plan had failed to gain widespread acceptance in Japan as well, it was doomed.

The textile and apparel industries in the United States were not particularly distressed by the failure to secure a bilateral understanding with the Japanese. In fact, on March 19, 1970, they had called for an end to negotiations with Japan. Their efforts had already shifted toward a legislative solution involving stringent unilateral quotas; Congress had proved a more responsive channel of access. To increase pressure on Congress, the Amalgamated Clothing Workers Union demonstrated against imports from "low-wage" countries by staging a work stoppage. Mills was finally led to introduce a bill, H.R. 16920 (also known as the Mills Bill), to restrict textile, apparel, and footwear imports through the use of quotas. Under the terms of this bill, textile and apparel imports for 1970 would have been limited to the 1967-68 average; growth in the quota would be keyed to changes in consumption in the U.S. domestic market.

The previous alliance of fiber, textile, and apparel manufactures and labor grew even larger as the footwear industry joined the protectionist ranks to lobby for the Mills Bill. However, the textile/apparel coalition was frustrated in its efforts to keep this bill from becoming a "Christmas tree" with multiple amendments to impose quotas on other products—a bill Nixon would surely veto. The original bill was amended to include a provision that automatically conferred quotas on industries that the Tariff Commission determined were being "injured." In addition, the injury determination procedure was specified in terms of the import/consumption ratio without regard to other factors. The bill also permitted quotas to be imposed without great difficulty. In an ironic twist, the textile/apparel alliance joined *anti-quota* forces in an attempt to make the bill "liberal" enough to pass Congress and avoid a presidential veto.

In the meantime, negotiations continued in a fruitless stop-and-go fashion with the Japanese. On November 19, 1970, the House of Representatives passed the Mills trade bill. The textile and apparel alliance saw this as being one step closer to their long sought goal of quotas by country and categories and keyed to the domestic growth rate. As far as they were concerned, there was nothing to be gained from negotiations with the Japanese. The Senate Finance Committee began consideration of the bill and removed the provision to invoke quotas for other products while retaining those for textile, apparel, and footwear. The optimistic outlook for passage of the Mills Bill put pressure on the Japanese government to come to an agreement.

The negotiations between Presidential Assistant Peter Flanigan and Ambassador Nobukhio Ushiba were finally nearing a successful conclusion in December 1970. With only relatively minor differences remaining in the U.S. and Japanese positions, Flanigan initiated discussions with industry leaders at the White House. In a major show of power they rejected the proposed American/Japanese accord. With a strong possibility that the Mills Bill would pass, a moderate position was unnecessary. Their stand led to the collapse of the bilateral talks. Yet, at the same time, the bill was encountering trouble in the Senate, and failed to come to a vote as a result of delaying tactics pursued by a number of senators.

In early 1971, Mills decided to pursue an agreement with the Japanese on his own initiative. He hoped that a unilateral arrangement by the Japanese to restrict their imports might prove satisfactory to the textile and apparel industries. Although the Japanese decided to pursue such a unilateral restriction, political rivalry between Nixon and Mills and the industries' dissatisfaction with the Japanese initiative, led to Nixon's rejection of the unilateral restraint.[89]

Worried that the negotiations would drag on through the election, Nixon escalated the pressure on the Japanese. In a rapid series of events that eventually led to an agreement with the Japanese, Nixon imposed a 10 percent across-the-board import surcharge (on August 15, 1971), and threatened to invoke the "Trading with the Enemy Act" to unilaterally restrain imports of textiles and apparel (on September 21, 1971).[90] With a new U.S. ambassador (David Kennedy) to conduct "negotiations," an agreement with the Japanese was finally concluded on October 15, 1971 (the day the "Trading with the Enemy Act" provision was to take effect).

The agreement was comprehensive in nature, setting group and category ceilings on products as well. The Japanese were able to secure relatively high base levels for growth rates, which were set at 5 percent. In contrast to the five-year accords negotiated with South Korea, Taiwan, and Hong Kong at about the same time,[91] the Japanese accord provided for controls for only three years. The agreement was greeted with great enthusiasm by U.S. textile producers, but apparel interests were dismayed. The latter were particularly unhappy with the high base periods used. The *Daily News Record* noted that apparel interests had not followed the negotiations as closely as the textile industry even though they were more vulnerable to foreign competition and tended to favor stricter agreements.[92]

THE SECOND EFFORT: THE DEVELOPMENT OF THE MFA, 1973

American use of textile power to close off its market to Far East suppliers began to have the desired effect. Growth rates in U.S. textile and apparel imports dropped precipitously in 1972.[93] Goods were diverted from the American market to those in Europe, thus altering European incentives to negotiate an expanded agreement.

Within days after the signing of the bilateral agreements with Far East textile and apparel suppliers, the U.S. industries began their own push for a multilateral agreement in man-made and wool textiles and apparel. These producers, aware of the diversion of goods to Europe caused by the new American controls, happily observed that "such a broad pact might now be welcomed by the Europeans."[94] This was not idle speculation. Responding to the Americans' negotiation of bilaterals with Far East countries, British mill owners warned that "the industry [in the U.K.] could collapse if low priced textile imports weren't strenuously controlled."[95]

In June 1972, following discussion in the GATT Council, a GATT Working Party began a study of the problems associated with world trade in man-made fiber, wool, and cotton textile and apparel products.[96] This group issued a comprehensive report in December 1972. In April 1973, the Council instructed the Working Party to seek possible alternative multilateral solutions to the problems in international textile trade. Their subsequent report set the stage for the negotiations to develop the MFA.

POLICY CHOICES

The United States. The Americans pushed strongly for a multilateral arrangement covering controls in all fibers. As before, the United States was reluctant to impose unilateral controls for fear of undermining the GATT regime; the best option, then, was to get the Europeans to accept their share of the import "burden." One high-level American negotiator, expressing concern for the nested position of textiles within the overall trading system, argued that in the absence of a multilateral multifiber agreement, "unilateral quotas would be the result" and the textile issue would then "flop over into everything else."[97]

The first American attempt to control European exports turned out to be a major error in judgment. Yet by 1973, the Europeans were inundated with diverted goods as a result of the American bilaterals. While the member states of the EEC were quite able to control imports on an individual basis, there was no unified EEC policy. With free circulation within the EEC as allowed by the Treaty of Rome, import barriers could be avoided; imports could enter the community through the country with the lowest barriers and then be reexported to more protected markets. Thus, only the EEC Commission could implement an effective restraint program. The Americans, realizing this, were quite certain that the Europeans would have to agree to multilateral action.[98] As one trade journal noted in April 1973 (before the negotiations in Geneva got under way), "As regards the Geneva talks, the U.S. is confident that some kind of multi-fiber extension of the LTA will be negotiated."[99]

American decision makers recognized the advantages of having a formal regime to control the behavior of other countries. Even though they had succeeded in controlling imports from the most important suppliers (i.e., the Far Eastern countries), they felt that such bilateral controls would not suffice in insulating the American market. As one negotiator pointed out, "We needed the MFA to ensure that nobody else would move in [to replace the Far Eastern suppliers]."[100]

In this case domestic pressures reinforced the American predilection for an international regime. The ATMI concurred with the administration's view, declaring that the Board reaffirms its position that only a multilateral, multifiber arrangement under the GATT and patterned along the existing LTA can fairly and effectively deal with problems arising from international textile trade.[101]

Of course, the ATMI saw a multifiber agreement as a device to facilitate protection. As a vice president of ATMI argued:

[We] hope that the idea will be abandoned once and for all that developed countries would dismantle their textile industries and turn textiles over to less developed parts of the world.[102]

With regard to regime characteristics, the Americans wanted to soften the LDCs' demands for a surveillance body to oversee the negotiation of bilateral accords and imposition of unilateral controls. *Textile Asia* claimed that "the Americans will have nothing to do with international supervision."[103] This may have simply been a bargaining tactic; in the actual American proposal, provision for a surveillance body was explicitly made—although in watered-down form.[104]

A second issue relating to the strength of the agreement concerned the criteria to be used for determining market disruption. The GATT proposal, in summarizing the views of the Working Party, contained a long list of possible factors that had to be present before importing countries could claim market disruption. The U.S. proposal suggested a much weaker version that would constrain its actions much less.

With respect to the nature of the agreement to be negotiated, the American negotiators were being asked by the domestic industry to restrict the growth of imports into the American market to a maximum of 5 percent a year. Here, the importance of international factors emerges clearly. As one key negotiator in the MFA put it, the United States was "trying to be fair" in the negotiations to protect its overall international trading system interests and to try to keep from forcing the LDCs into the Soviet camp. Thus the United States gave LDCs flexible agreements in the 1960s containing higher swing and carry-over provisions in the bilateral agreements to make up for low growth rates.[105]

As American textile groups tended to focus primarily on the growth figures in their demands, the negotiators were given some leeway. As a high State Department official commented, his department would try to temper the protectionist impulses of the representatives of other agencies because State, aware of the multiple interests the United States had with these countries, did not want to jeopardize this relationship for a few yards of cloth.[106]

Finally, with respect to the scope of the regime, the U.S. government resisted European efforts to include other fibers besides cotton, wool, and man-made fiber goods (flax- and ramie-based products) since these were the only products affecting U.S. producers.

The EEC. Shifting textile trade as a result of American bilaterals had two important consequences. First, Europeans worried about increasing American protection leading to a diversion of goods to their markets. According to *Textile Asia*:

> The Europeans in general recognize that the U.S. is determined on another heavy dose of protectionism in its own textile market, and therefore fear that the chief exporting countries may divert their main effort to the EEC market as Hong Kong and Japan have already done to some extent, and indeed in other products such as electronics.[107]

A key American negotiator in the MFA also noted that the "EEC perceived the American bilaterals as leading to diversion. The Macao and Singapore bilaterals [concluded in late 1972 and early 1973] were seen as one more nail in the diversion coffin."[108] This was not an unfounded fear: according to Comitextil, imports to the Common Market rose approximately 52 percent during 1972 as a consequence of the American bilaterals. While the exact figure may be questioned,[109] there *was* a marked growth of imports into the EEC market.

A second important effect of the change in textile trade would only make itself felt in the 1977 MFA renewal. At that time, the preponderant textile capabilities and internal unity of the EEC allowed it to develop an MFA to fit its own needs—in spite of protests by the United States.

In the 1973 development of the MFA, the EEC lacked a unified stance throughout the negotiations. As late as December, shortly before the MFA was signed, *Textile Asia* reported that even as important elements in the draft of the MFA were being hotly debated, "The EEC once more had to explain that its Council of Ministers, preoccupied with the Middle East war, oil problems and internal disharmony, had not yet been able to work out a mandate from the nine governments."[110]

The EEC states, and especially the Commission, were beginning to see the writing on the wall: they would have to agree to a regime. In September 1972, the Commission sent a memorandum to member states pressing them to develop a uniform policy. It argued that

> external developments, and notably the restraining agreements imposed by the U.S. obliged the member states to adopt a common policy, especially as the talks at the multilateral level would probably be long and it would be some time before an international agreement came into force.[111]

Although the EEC could technically pursue restrictionist policies unilaterally, thereby neutralizing any diversion from Far Eastern countries to their markets, "the EEC states wished to avoid criticism from the LDCs," as one negotiator remarked.[112] Of course, as is quite evident, criticism by itself has little efficacy in international politics. More important, the EEC was concerned about diversion in other products besides textiles (e.g., electronics), and recognized that their overall trading interest would be impaired by unilateral restrictionist measures. The EEC was a big exporter of a variety of products to the LDCs. *Textile Asia* reported that part of the difficulty the EEC was experiencing in developing a unified position

seems to stem from the fact that the European Commission, while ready to go part of the way with the industry, especially as regards the Far Eastern exporting countries, feels the need to make concessions to the developing exporter countries.[113]

Internally, EEC states encountered major problems in developing a unified policy. From the Commission's standpoint, the optimal policy consisted of a liberal overall policy with controls negotiated on a bilateral basis and provisions for the surveillance of sensitive categories of imports from the LDCs.[114] By and large, it wished to treat matters on a piecemeal basis since this would allow the EEC countries the maximum flexibility. As *Textile Asia* noted, the

EEC is not in such a hurry to seek a multilateral, multifiber pact. In wool its interests are in keeping the American market open, and on man-made fibers it has as yet no restrictive agreements with any of its suppliers, though some of its individual members, notably Britain and France, have partial "voluntary" restraint agreements with Hong Kong, Japan, South Korea and other exporters.[115]

In the period leading up to the negotiations, EEC member states were pressed by their domestic industries to protect them from exports originally destined for the United States. The United States was thus successful in altering EEC incentives to set up a multilateral agreement (or at a minimum, participating in a conference with the United States and the LDC exporters of textile and apparel products).

The United Kingdom had recently become a member of the EEC. It was most concerned with ensuring that there be equitable sharing of imports within the EEC. The British position had also been influenced by the shift in exports from Far Eastern countries. The British Textile Confederation (the peak textile organization in the United Kingdom)

drew attention to the disruption and demoralization caused by the swelling flood of imports from low cost Far East countries. This was largely the result of diversion of their exports from the U.S. to Europe, and particularly to the "soft" U.K. market.[116]

In spite of these domestic pressures, the net effect of the international structure and the changes that were taking place appears to have been to push the EEC to grudgingly acquiesce to American efforts for a multilateral arrangement.

The lack of consensus among member states affected the EEC's views on the strength of the regime as well. Some EEC countries supported the American calls for "equitable burden sharing" among importers, but for reasons very different from those envisioned by the Americans: these EEC states saw it as a means of ensuring a more equitable distribution of textile imports within the EEC itself.[117]

On the issue of the Textiles Surveillance Body, the EEC went along with American demands to weaken its powers. This is consistent with their desires to maintain as much leeway as possible in the imposition of trade controls. International constraints did not readily alter this policy preference.

With respect to the nature of the regime, when it became obvious that a multilateral arrangement was likely to be negotiated, the EEC—led by France—sought to have a "recession clause" inserted in the agreement. Such a clause would have allowed countries to restrict the growth of imports to a lower level than the proposed 6 percent in case of a recession. At the same time, however, the EEC states were unwilling to accept a higher growth rate when the market was expanding rapidly. As I discuss below, this issue was at the forefront of an important battle between the United States and the EEC; the United States feared that the recession clause would lead to a diversion of goods to the American market.[118]

Japan. Shortly after the conclusion of its 1971 bilateral agreement with the United States, Japan realized that although it had managed to secure a quota of over one billion sye of textiles and clothing, it was no longer as competitive as it had been in the late 1960s. U.S. imports of Japanese textiles and apparel had dropped from 1.282 billion sye in 1971 to only 650 million sye in 1973.[119] This shift appears to have been due to a loss of Japanese comparative advantage relative to the LDCs and the currency realignments in 1971. The result of this change—combined with an increase of Japanese imports from other countries—was to make Japan more amenable to some kind of multilateral agreement.

Although Japan argued for a number of changes in the proposed MFA and repeatedly complained about the restrictions it faced, it recognized that a multilateral accord was in its interest. In spite of its effort to pose as a staunch opponent of a multilateral accord, much of the evidence indicates that its true desires lay elsewhere. In talks with Japanese textile and apparel producers, the Japanese ambassador to Geneva noted that they should accept the fact that an international agreement was going to be negotiated in one form or another.[120] As negotiations with the Japanese on an extension of the bilateral agreement were taking place, the *DNR* reported that the "Japanese are more concerned with getting specific quota liberalization than blocking a pact *per se.*"[121] Furthermore, Japan participated in discussions on the problems of trade in man-made and wool-based goods at the same time that it claimed not to favor a multifiber agreement. In practice, this was not a credible distinction. Thus, one observer commented:

This has led some of the smaller Third World countries represented in the Working Group to suspect that the Japanese may have struck a secret deal with Washington, to go along on textiles in return for a helping hand in the MTN [Multilateral Trade Negotiations]. The Japanese deny this, as they must. Only time will tell.[122]

More evidence of Japanese duplicity comes from a high-level American negotiator, who noted that although the Japanese "never came out front with public support (of the MFA), in their own way, they became quite helpful."[123] The most convincing evidence that the Japanese were quite willing to go along with the MFA and that they were simply bargaining for tactical purposes is the decrease in their exports to the United States and their own growth in imports. As a country that was already restrained, it had little to lose from a rule system that would provide some regulation of bilateral and unilateral controls.

The LDCs. While a number of LDCs professed unity in their view toward the proposed MFA, they actively engaged in behind-the-scenes back-stabbing. This is not unexpected. The interests of southern states were not uniform. On the surface, all wanted greater access to developed country markets and a minimization of disruptive mechanisms impeding trade. This was a frequently espoused position. In summarizing the LDC position, the Spanish delegate claimed that all wanted to "avoid discrimination, have multilateral surveillance of market disruption, and better access to markets (among other points)."[124] But the breakdown of unity begins where the rhetoric ends. This lack of unity minimized the role of the LDCs in the international negotiations and made the U.S.-EEC struggle critical.

Why should LDCs have divergent interests? Simply put, these exporters differed in their competitive position in textile trade. In an uncontrolled market a few of the most competitive suppliers (primarily the Far Eastern countries) would drive everyone else out of the market. Therefore, control of these countries by developed states allowed ordinarily noncompetitive suppliers to enter the market. The difference between established suppliers and the new entrants to the market also led to dissension. Established suppliers had obtained large quotas since quotas were based on "past performance" in exporting; in the face of the importers' resistance to radically increased market access, the only way for new entrants to increase their small quotas would be to "steal" shares from the established exporters.

A large, established exporter like Hong Kong—which had already been controlled in 1971 by the United States—pushed for an early multifiber agreement since it recognized its "political inevitability" and noted that "U.S. might is right."[125] As one Hong Kong official put it, "The trade must go on, that's for sure."[126] However, new entrants into the market wished to delay the MFA pact since "the later the multifibre pact, the more past performance in MMF exports they can notch up and the bigger quotas they can claim."[127]

INTERNATIONAL NEGOTIATIONS AND THE MFA

The EEC had made known its desire for bilateral accords and unilateral controls as opposed to a regime. Therefore, to get maximum mileage out of going along with the U.S. attempt to institute a multilateral arrangement, the EEC pursued a strategy hinted at by one source:

The Eurocrats in Brussels see little reason therefore to help the Americans out of a difficulty of their own making—unless, perhaps, they are assured of some *quid pro quo* in the GATT, on the general MTN [Multilateral Trade Negotiations] for instance.[128]

The EEC did in fact propose such a quid pro quo to the American delegation: it asked the United States to reduce tariffs on textile and apparel products to "compensate" for its acquiescence to a multilateral agreement.[129]

It should now be evident that this was not a totally credible linkage. The EEC did not want to antagonize the LDCs and thus was reluctant to use unilateral measures to control its market. Recognizing this, Anthony Jurich, the chief American textile negotiator, explicitly rejected this tariff linkage to the MFA. At the same time he pointed out that unless an MFA was concluded, there was no chance whatsoever of a reduction in U.S. tariffs. On a more positive note (from the EEC perspective), Jurich indicated that such a tariff reduction would probably happen.[130]

American tactics reinforced its preponderant position. The United States had concluded two bilaterals—one with Macao and another with Singapore in addition to its original accords in 1971 with other Far Eastern exporters. The EEC felt increasingly pressured by the ensuing diversion of LDC exports to its market. Concurrent American efforts to renegotiate its agreements with the Far Eastern suppliers restricted in 1971 increased the pressure on the EEC. Washington worked quickly to strengthen its position and sent representatives to Hong Kong, Taiwan, Japan, and Korea to negotiate a one-year extension of its bilateral cotton textile agreements.[131] While these agreements were primarily directed to bolstering the American position vis-à-vis other developing countries (to convince them to go along with the proposed MFA), the agreements undoubtedly helped to pressure the EEC as well.

The major struggle took place over the proposed regime's characteristics—in particular, development of the TSB, market disruption criteria, and import growth rates. With regard to the first issue—the TSB—there was a split between importers and exporters. To some extent, the United States had an interest in a reasonably strong TSB—although one that would be sufficiently weak to allow it enough leeway to conclude restrictive agreements. Once again, as in the LTA negotiations, the American objective was to allow itself enough leverage to take such actions, while at the same time forcing the Europeans to accept more imports. As *Textile Asia* pointed out:

It was the prime purpose of the MFA [the Multi-fiber Arrangement] that some of the well protected countries in Europe should take a greater share of these exports from developing countries, and the burden thus be more easily distributed.[132]

The EEC does not appear to have been a very active participant in the negotiations over the TSB. The real bargaining appears to have taken place between the United States and Japan (with the LDCs adding their voices as well with somewhat unrealistic demands). Although Jurich argued in the initial stages that the proposed surveillance body came "too close to tampering with nations' economic sovereignty,"[133] in the subsequent negotiations the United States softened its position. In fact, the *DNR* stated that it would appear that the TSB and market disruption were being exchanged for a multifiber, multilateral agreement—a trade that was two bones for exporters and one bone for importers. While Jurich subsequently denied an explicit exchange, he said "that may be the practical effect."[134] For the most part, the concessions would appear to be a result of pressure from Japan, which was willing to go along with an MFA (1) if a TSB-type body was set up; and (2) if safeguards were used only when this body found injury. While the United States went along with the TSB issue, it opposed the market disruption criteria and vehemently opposed the TSB having sole responsibility for determining market disruption.

The United States and the EEC differed sharply on the issue of market disruption, at least overtly. The EEC took a more liberal stance on the issue of criteria for market disruption, possibly in the hope of appearing to be favorable to LDC demands. Since member states could be harsher than the United States in implementing the agreement, because of a difference in the domestic procedure for imposing restrictions,[135] the market disruption criteria did not worry them.

The United States responded by linking a quick conclusion of the MFA to the GATT trade negotiations. This undoubtedly helped to bolster the American position—especially since the EEC had a strong interest in other American markets. In one speech, officials in the U.S. administration argued that

textiles is a specially sensitive issue, best got out of the way quickly so that Congress does not have to deal with it as part of the overall trade package the next GATT round will presumably produce. If the LTA extension is not agreed to by the time the general GATT round gets going in earnest, then the U.S. textile lobby will make things difficult for the GATT round.[136]

While this was not specifically addressed to the EEC or even to the issue of market disruption, such statements obviously softened up the EEC a bit. Sometimes, of course, such subtle indications did not suffice. One such incident came up in the discussion of import growth rates—an issue over which the EEC and United States battled fiercely.

The United States decided to go for broke against the Commission on the issue of a recession clause in the agreement, fearing a diversion of goods to its market if this clause was incorporated. In a speech to the other delegates, Jurich warned that "if the EEC should persist [with a call for a recession clause], the U.S. would be prepared to support an alliance of LDCs."[137] While the EEC members were quite taken aback by this speech (and the LDC delegates applauded after a moment of hesitation), it served its purpose and the recession clause discussion was left to another time.[138]

The arguments over the nature of the regime bear out the fact that LDC opposition was not always of great significance. As noted earlier, while there was a great deal of surface unity, the LDCs bickered among themselves when it came to specifics. One important divisive issue was the entry of new suppliers into the markets of the developed countries. *Textile Asia* noticed this development and reported on an American attempt to have small suppliers obtain the unused quotas of established suppliers:

The Indians, who fall into the latter category [larger suppliers], were provoked by this suggestion into a clash with Sri Lanka and other envious would-be suppliers.[139]

The UNCTAD—as in other trade negotiations—provided a counter to the GATT. As a forum to aggregate LDC interests, it proved to be relatively successful given the inauspicious circumstances. Thus, while on many issues LDCs were sharply divided, the Group of 77 (a caucus group of LDCs) actually united to issue a resolution "demand[ing] abolition of all tariffs and quotas on textile imports from developing countries by a fixed target date."[140] Furthermore, it argued that textiles should be included in the General System of Preferences and that noncotton fiber-based textile and apparel products should be excluded from quota controls.[141] But the LDCs went a little too far in insinuating that Japan was the key exporter creating market disruption. The resolution adopted by the Group of 77 was unanimously rejected by the Americans, Europeans, *and* Japanese.

Finally, with respect to the nature of the regime, the LDCs managed to get some of their objectives accomplished—although as a result of broader American interests. In the negotiations on the minimum quota growth rate that would be allowed, the LDCs demanded 10 percent per year. The American industries had been pushing for a very low growth rate and were reluctant to see even a growth rate of 5 percent. Since the mid-1950s they had consistently wished to see the quota growth rate pegged to consumption in the American domestic market. After complicated negotiations, the United States managed to satisfy the LDCs and to some extent the American industries. As was the case in the 1960s with the American bilaterals, Jurich gave the LDCs greater swing and flexibility in the agreement to compensate for a 6 percent growth rate. The American industries grudgingly accepted this when Jurich explained that the LDCs were pushing strongly for 10 percent.

The Agreement

The text of the MFA incorporated these negotiated provisions in a number of articles, drawn in part from the old LTA. At the meta-regime level, the underlying principle of the regime continued to be an agreement on the need for organized trade. Article 1 of the agreement stated:

The basic objectives shall be to achieve the expansion of trade, the reduction of barriers to such trade and the progressive liberalization of world trade in textile products, while at the same time ensuring the orderly and equitable development of this trade and avoidance of disruptive effects in individual markets and on individual lines of production in both importing and exporting countries.[142]

The regime norms went beyond the LTA in calling on the developed countries to pursue industrial adjustment measures to improve LDC access to their markets. Article 1, paragraph 4, called for the "pursuit of appropriate economic and social policies . . . which . . . would encourage businesses which are less competitive internationally to move progressively into more viable lines of production or into other sectors of the economy."[143] Yet no provision was made for any monitoring of these adjustment policies or penalties for failure to pursue them. Realistically, at best this provision can be seen merely as a recommendation.

The norms contained in the LTA continued in the MFA, although with somewhat different language. For example, as part of the development norm, the preamble addressed the issue of "new entrants"—that is, countries which were just entering the international market in textiles—and noted the importance of giving them favorable treatment. More explicitly, Article 6 of the text asked that special attention be given to the needs of new entrants, and specifically stated:

it shall be considered appropriate and consistent with equity obligations for those importing countries which apply restrictions under this Arrangement affecting the trade of developing countries to provide more favourable terms with regard to such restrictions, including elements such as base level and growth rates, than for other countries.[144]

With respect to the safeguard norm, the MFA went into much greater detail than the LTA on what type of agreements would be permitted between importers and exporters and addressed issues such as swing and flexibility with precise numbers. The multilateralism norm was particularly emphasized in the MFA, the preamble of the accord calling on participants to "take cooperative and constructive action, within a multilateral framework."[145] This was not merely rhetoric: the United States and a number of other countries wished to avoid uncontrolled unilateral or bilateral action and this emphasis on multilateralism was emphasized throughout the text of the MFA. Moreover, this notion was embodied in the Textiles Surveillance Body (discussed in detail below)—an organization whose mandate, though still a matter of much debate, emphasized the conciliation of disputes through a multilateral mechanism.

With respect to the nondiscrimination norm in the MFA, Article 3 asked that "participating countries . . . take into account imports from all countries and . . . seek to preserve a proper measure of equity." It continued in this vein, noting: "They shall seek to avoid discriminatory measures where marked disruption is caused by imports from more than one participating country."[146] On liberalization, the MFA called for "the reduction of trade barriers and the liberalization of world trade in these products."[147] As we shall see below, this norm was operationalized through various rules and procedures in the text of the accord.

One point with respect to the meta-regime worth noting is the potential conflict among various MFA norms. An example of this is Article 6 of the MFA (discussed above), which called for special attention to the needs of new entrants—the embodiment of the development norm. This potentially conflicted with the nondiscrimination norm since "favorable treatment" for some LDCs could be used against LDCs with established market positions. Though Article 6, paragraph 1, warned that "it shall be borne in mind that there should be no prejudice to the interests of established suppliers or serious distortions in existing patterns of trade," in practice the DCs tried to take the quota share of large suppliers and give it away to the new entrants—rather than actually increasing the total quota levels for imports. In summary, just as in the GATT, conflict in norms can be exploited to serve the ends of different countries.

A number of provisions addressed the strength of the regime. There were two major changes and a number of minor provisions addressing this dimension of the arrangement. The major changes—the development of a surveillance body and stricter rules on the procedures to be followed in determining market disruption—were incorporated in Article 11 and Annex A, respectively. The Textiles Surveillance Body was to review all actions taken under the provisions of the arrangement and make "recommendations to the participating countries . . . to facilitate implementation."[148] Another important provision of Article 11 called for rotation of the membership of the TSB. Since the article also calls for "balance" (and in light of political realities), the United States and the EEC have always been members of the TSB.

The Annex addressed the criteria that had to be considered before countries could claim market disruption. These criteria were more stringent than the corresponding provisions of the LTA and included a provision to consider the interests of the exporting countries (in terms of the importance of textiles to its economy, trade balance, overall balance, and so on).[149]

Other provisions of the MFA called for a one-year limit on Article 3 actions (allowing countries to restrict imports when they could demonstrate market disruption), and also noted that Article 4 agreements (bilateral accords rather than unilateral actions) were to be more liberal in their provisions than Article 3 actions. Article 2 called for the elimination of all unilateral and bilateral agreements not in conformity with the newly signed agreement. These articles set out a strict procedure to be followed by countries wishing to restrict imports and referred to Annex B, which described the minimum provisions on growth, swing, and flexibility which had to be included in any agreement.

Turning to the nature of the arrangement, the most important concession to LDCs was provision for mandatory swing and flexibility provisions in Annex B. Thus, although the maximum growth that importing countries were forced to give exporting countries was only 6 percent per annum, the swing and flexibility provisions of the agreement allowed exporting countries a great deal of leeway to ensure that they could maintain their exports to the level of the quota restrictions. Without such provisions, changes in the market could easily lead to a situation where countries would not be able to fulfill their allowable total of aggregate exports. One provision of considerable importance to the Scandinavian countries was the second paragraph of Article 1. This paragraph noted:

In the case of those countries having small markets, an exceptionally high level of imports and a correspondingly low level of domestic production, account should be taken of the avoidance of damage to those countries' minimum viable production of textiles.[150]

This provision came to be known as the Nordic clause among the cognoscenti, and was used by these countries to sharply curtail imports.

Finally, with respect to the scope of the agreement, the primary objective of the whole exercise had been to impose some kind of regulation on trade in man-made fiber and wool-based textile and apparel products. Hand loom fabrics and products of cottage industries were to be excluded from the agreement. This became a significant issue in the subsequent implementation of the agreement, since it is not always possible to clearly distinguish if a product was made without machinery, and opened up the possibility of cheating on the agreement.

BEHAVIOR OF COUNTRIES AND TRANSACTIONS

Changes in imports resulting from American bilaterals with Far Eastern suppliers had an important effect on EEC incentives to go along with the MFA. Similarly, the actions taken by countries under the first MFA had a significant effect on future regime bargaining. The marked difference in the time it took for the United States to conclude bilateral accords versus the time it took the EEC became a major issue. The EEC's sluggishness in negotiating bilaterals led to a rapid rise in imports into its market. Ironically, this gave the EEC much more leverage in the 1977 negotiations since they had become the largest importer by this time.

Behavior of Countries. The United States quickly renegotiated a number of its cotton bilateral agreements to include other fibers and renegotiated its multifiber bilaterals previously concluded with Japan, Hong Kong, Taiwan, South Korea, and Malaysia. By making concessions of one sort or another to these countries, the United States managed by

1975 to control access to its market. Including cotton textile restraints and agreements with state-trading countries, the U.S. had concluded eighteen bilateral accords by October 1, 1977. It supplemented these accords through the use of "consultation" agreements with ten countries; these provided for discussions if imports grew too rapidly.

The liberal but broad agreements concluded by the United States led the Textiles Surveillance Body to report in late November 1976: "On the whole, it appears that access to the market of the United States had increased substantially."[151] While this may be an accurate statement, it provides an interesting contrast to the TSB's report on the EEC's actions. While the EEC was found to be violating the MFA by not eliminating its old restraints quickly enough, overall imports into its market rose much more rapidly than imports into the United States.[152] The reason was attributable of course to the EEC dragging its heels in concluding its bilaterals.

The EEC had myriad restrictions on imports of man-made fiber and wool-based products at the time the MFA came into effect, but their effectiveness was limited by the rules allowing free circulation among member countries of the EEC. While France had quotas on imports of various sorts from at least eleven countries, Italy only restrained goods of man-made fiber and wool from Japan. The Benelux countries similarly restrained Japan, while Germany had restraints of one kind or another with a number of different countries. Therefore resourceful LDCs could simply ship to the uncontrolled country and then arrange to have goods redirected to those having restraints.

These variations in controls led to struggles among the EEC members over how to bring restraints into conformity with the MFA. First, they had to decide whether agreements would be selective or comprehensive—that is, whether to control only those products that were being imported in large enough quantities to cause market disruption, or all categories of goods.[153] After some debate—with Germany pressing for liberalism, and dissension fermenting within the commission over what items to include if there was to be wider coverage—the commission, on behalf of the member states, decided to pursue selective restraints.

A second problem was that of "burden sharing," that is, the mode in which countries would share imports coming into the EEC. After heated discussions, a formula to allocate market shares was decided upon on October 15, 1974.[154] The scheme is depicted in table 7.

The Commission also devised a complex formula that would take into account variable import growth rates in an effort to ensure that over time countries would be taking their "fair share" of imports (which would be based on such factors as past imports, gross national product, and popu-

TABLE 7

KEY TO ALLOCATION OF IMPORTS OF TEXTILE
PRODUCTS AMONG MEMBER STATES OF THE EEC (%)

	Multifiber agreement	*General system of preferences*
West Germany	28.5	27
United Kingdom	23.5	22
France	18.5	19
Italy	15.0	14
Benelux	10.5	10
Ireland	1.0	1
Denmark	3.5	7

lation). Problems arose as Germany and Denmark were much more liberal than some of the other member states. Germany, for example, wished to import large quantities of textiles to fight inflation.[155] While, on the surface, protectionist countries such as France could hardly object to this, they were extremely worried about the possibility of a diversion of goods from Germany to their markets as a result of free circulation in the EEC.

Unfortunately for the Commission, getting member states to agree to a unified position was only the first step; it also encountered major problems in the bilateral talks with LDCs. First, exporting countries were especially reluctant to agree to restraints. Since the United States had rapidly controlled its market access, the LDCs made a concerted effort to increase their exports to the Europeans.

Second, EEC countries bickered among themselves and even attacked the Commission once negotiations had begun. At one point, the German Wholesalers and Foreign Traders Association created a furor by calling on the German government to press for the replacement of Benedict Meynell, the EEC's chief textiles negotiator. The association argued that he had mishandled the negotiations with Korea and Hong Kong, and it was particularly upset about the ongoing Brazilian negotiations. The association accused him of being excessively protectionist and, although the German government never publicly said so, it appeared to sympathize with the association's view. Of course the accusations were not based solely on personality questions. As one observer commented:

Germany's motivations are thought to be two-fold: firstly, it probably has the most to lose were Brazil to implement the threats that it has been making privately of "coincidental" measures to restrict trade from Europe—say imports of steel—should it feel hard done by the terms of any agreement; with 50% of Brazilian industry government owned, it would be well placed to channel companies' orders elsewhere. Secondly, since industrial policy in Germany generally frowns on pampering lame ducks and its policy is generally liberal, it is less susceptible to pressure for protection from its textiles industry, than to the importers' and retailers' complaints that they are being prevented from supplying German consumers at the lowest possible cost.[156]

Meanwhile, Britain and France criticized Meynell for being too *liberal*.[157] Within a week—in an effort to ease matters—the commission issued a statement supporting Meynell and arguing that the "German authorities have let it be known that they regret these personal attacks."[158]

The negotiations continued to be difficult for the EEC. After India agreed to restraints, the EEC managed to secure agreements from Hong Kong and Taiwan in August and July 1975, respectively. Korea was not restrained until the end of December 1976.[159] In fact, the commission was still conducting negotiations with Hungary, the Philippines, and Thailand as late as 1981, when the MFA once again came up for renewal.

Other countries were also engaged in a wide variety of restrictive actions. Sweden eliminated some of its previous restraints and moved to Article 4 bilateral agreements after first using the provisions for unilateral controls under Article 3. In late 1976 the Textiles Surveillance Body commented: "There appears to have been some increase in access to the Swedish market."[160] Norway, while removing some of its previous restraints and replacing them with controls under the MFA, also moved to control a number of new suppliers such as Sri Lanka, India, Thailand, and Macao. On the whole their policies appeared to have become more protectionist. Finland negotiated a bilateral agreement with Hong Kong, whereas previously it had no restraints.

Australia and Canada both took actions somewhat inconsistent with the MFA. Although Australia did not have restrictions at the inception of the MFA, it concluded a number of one-year bilateral agreements in 1974 and then imposed unilateral restraints against a couple of countries in 1975. It subsequently dropped these actions and imposed tariff quotas on a wide variety of products, justifying these under the GATT rather than the MFA. In a similar vein, Canada, while first dropping many of its old quantitative restraints and replacing them with bilateral agreements, invoked Article 19 on a number of goods to restrain imports into its market. This created a major uproar since such actions were not to be used until all MFA remedies had been exhausted.

The governments of both Canada and Australia responded to pressure from domestic lobbies who reacted to the rapid influx of imports—resulting both from the difficulty that these smaller countries had in negotiating with the LDCs and diversion of exports from the United States. On the whole the smaller countries used Article 3, permitting unilateral action, much more often than the United States.[161]

Transactions. While the various trade controls by themselves do not account for the rate and total import growth in the various developed countries, they did have a major effect on the trade balances of these countries. Table 8 (for the year in which the MFA was negotiated and the subsequent three years before the year in which the MFA was renewed) indicates the problems that the EEC and other countries had in response to U.S. actions. As the figures indicate, all these countries experienced a sharp decline in their balance of trade in textiles and apparel products in the two years after the MFA—with the *exception* of the United States. While the net U.S. position worsened in 1976, that of the EEC deteriorated even more rapidly. These kinds of trends—readily perceived by EEC officials and leading to pressure from industry groups—led to the call for a revised MFA in 1977.

TABLE 8

Combined Net Trade in Textiles and Clothing, 1973-1976

| Country | Year | | | |
	1973	1974	1975	1976
United States	−1,795	−1,334	−1,408	−2,322
EEC	1,234	1,025	−29	−1,061
Sweden	−562	−702	−814	−968
Canada	−846	−1,111	−1,130	−1,509

Note: Amounts in U.S. dollars. Numbers exclude products not covered by the MFA. U.S. and Canadian imports F.O.B, all other C.I.F. Constructed from table 5, Com/Tex/W/63.

CONCLUSION

This chapter investigated the anomaly in what we might have expected based solely on an international system approach. The data suggest that an international regime regulating the actions of countries in man-made fiber and wool trade should have come into being in 1970 when the Americans first felt the need for such an agreement. Instead, as we saw in this chapter, no such regime came into being until 1973. How can we account for this delay?

The process-tracing analysis used here not only helps in explaining this delay but in actually providing further substantiation of the validity of the theory. As we saw, the United States originally sought to institute a regime when it was faced with problems in man-made fiber and wool textile and apparel trade. This action was unexpected: the theory suggested that bilateral agreements would have been the norm. What then accounts for the choice of regime?

It appears that American decision makers had learned from previous experience that bilaterals would not be sufficient to restrain imports. Their experience in the cotton textile and apparel areas with the first Japanese bilaterals and the subsequent entry of Hong Kong and other uncontrolled suppliers demonstrated to them that a regime would be needed sooner or later. Given the numerous countries entering into the production of these goods, there was already a need for a large number of bilaterals.

Moreover, the European countries and other industrialized states had been concluding bilaterals of their own and were instituting unilateral restraints. Therefore, American decision makers saw that it would be desirable to bring these various restraints into some kind of accord to prevent GATT from being undermined and to facilitate the negotiating process. And, of course, they also wished to control what the Europeans were doing. Learning from the past, American officials decided to develop a regime in wool and man-made fiber product trade.

They had problems, however, with the strategy they pursued: by first going to Europe, the United States raised the resistance level of these countries since it appeared that the United States wished to control their exports to its market. While U.S. decision makers had learned that a regime-type arrangement was preferable, they failed to learn from their experience in the mid-1960s in wool trade. As we saw in chapter 4, when the United States sought to impose restrictions on wool imports from the United Kingdom and Italy (as well as Japan and other wool product exporters), they failed. It was one thing to try to restrain LDCs and Japan, but quite another to restrain the United Kingdom and other developed countries. While the United States succeeded in restraining Italy in cotton velveteens, this was a very limited effort conducted originally in a highly surreptitious manner—open negotiations and across-the-board efforts were bound to fail.

By the time Stans backtracked a bit and tried to make it clear that the United States was interested in restraints from *Far Eastern* suppliers, the Europeans were in no mood to negotiate a global restraint. In packing Stans off to the Far East, however, the Europeans miscalculated: they failed to realize that the United States could use its power to alter the market situation (which was favorable to the Europeans at the time in the sense of officials feeling little pressure from their domestic industries) in a way that would make them want a regime. As we have seen, although the United States had to make numerous threats (and concessions) to Far Eastern suppliers, it did succeed in getting its desired bilaterals and creating a diversion to Europe. Further bilaterals with Macao and Singapore accelerated this process and, after some further bargaining, the Europeans went along with a regime in 1973. In the process-tracing, we saw that the United States recognized that it had the power to create a diversion and in going to the Far East, Stans and other U.S. officials expected that bilaterals with some countries would "help" the Europeans change their minds.

In summary, although poor strategy by both Americans and Europeans led to the delay we saw, the structural conditions were such that the deviation from the expected trend line was only relatively short. While the threat of U.S. textile and apparel power had been accurately perceived previously, in this instance it had to be demonstrated. In doing so, however, the United States lost its hegemonic position. The result was the near collapse of the textile regime when it came up for renewal in 1977.

6
Destruction: The Renewal of the Multi-Fiber Arrangement, 1977 and 1981

With the renewal of the MFA, in 1977 and again in 1981, the international regime in textile trade began to unravel. Protracted negotiations in both instances left a severely weakened regime that now does little to regulate national intervention in textile trade. Underlying this important change was a major shift in textile capabilities—away from the United States and in favor of the EEC.[1] Throughout the postwar period the United States had always taken the lead in trying to develop or modify international agreements in these products. Yet in 1977 and again in 1981, the EEC "took charge" and the United States became a follower. This change could have been anticipated by examining international factors.

Another distinctive aspect of this period was the length of the international negotiations preceding the two agreements. This extra time permitted domestic groups to muster their forces and participate transnationally in the renewal of the accords. Domestics politics, in these two instances, mixed much more than before with international politics.

THE RENEWAL OF THE MFA, 1977

The agreement renewing the MFA for the first time, in December 1977, marked the first step toward its destruction. Industry groups in the EEC member states, unhappy with increasing imports, and reacting in part to the recession of the 1975-1977 period, responded with a high-pitched campaign to directly press member governments for greater protection. They also used their pan-textile organization, Comitextil, to directly push the EEC Commission to revise the MFA in a more protectionist direction. The commission's decision to demand major changes in the MFA led to a long battle with the United States, resolved by an agree-

ment to tentatively weaken the regime. The EEC had proceeded to negotiate bilateral accords *prior* to signing the MFA, using its refusal to sign
as leverage in this process.

POLICY CHOICES

The wide variation in the time it took countries to decide on policy
positions was almost inversely related to a nation's capabilities in textile
trade. Whereas the LDCs, for the most part, had decided on realistic
negotiating positions by December 1976 (when most of them grudgingly
pushed for renewal of the MFA without changes),[2] the United States took
some time before recognizing that it would have to accept some modifications in the agreement. The EEC took the longest in developing a position—primary because of the long delay in resolving the conflict over
individual member state preferences.

The United States. For both international and domestic reasons, the
United States sought a simple renewal of the MFA. The U.S. government's bilateral deals had controlled imports from LDCs adequately
enough to satisfy domestic groups. Moreover, the agreement had forced
the EEC and other importing countries to take a larger share of LDC
exports than they had previously been taking before the advent of the
MFA.

As far as regime characteristics are concerned, the United States
pushed for a regime without changes. This may have been simply a bargaining ploy, however, since the United States recognized that it was no
longer a hegemon in textile trade. As one American negotiator noted,
"The EEC was considerably more powerful in the second MFA."[3] Another top American negotiator, explicitly perceiving the EEC capabilities,
argued: "The U.S. never conceived of going into the MFA alone. It was
not a credible threat to go it alone . . . by December 1976, everyone was
aware of the fact that 'How can you have an agreement with the biggest
guy [i.e., the EEC] out of it?'"[4] This recognition of the EEC's power
accounts for the position taken by the United States in March 1977. The
chief American textile negotiator said that while it wished to see the MFA
renewed as is, the United States is prepared "to listen to, and to join in
the discussion of, all proposals for improvements in the implementation
of the MFA."[5]

American success in rapidly concluding bilateral agreements with its
major suppliers of textile and apparel products encouraged even the traditionally protectionist ATMI to decide, in internal discussions, to
simply press for extension of the MFA.[6] Although the American textile
and apparel industries had decided they would be satisfied with a simple

renewal of the MFA, they continued to bargain with their government officials throughout the negotiations with cries for further restrictive measures.

In internal discussions, ATMI had decided on a fallback (or more accurately, a "fallforward" position)[7] if the MFA was opened to amendment. In this case, they argued:

the U.S. Government should press for a smaller growth rate conforming to actual market growth, the elimination of special treatment for cottage industries, and for defining market disruption in terms of total imports of the particular product for all countries.[8]

In addition, they suggested a number of other specific changes in the MFA (such as an eight-year extension of the agreement).

Subsequently, on March 10, 1977, they further specified their objectives. They argued that the

agreement should be extended for at least five years with the present 6% quota factor reduced to a level no greater than the domestic market growth, [and noted the need] for an exemption of textiles from the MTN and the need for a bilateral agreement with the PRC.[9]

Based on these points, the industry continued to lobby the U.S. government (after the December Textiles Committee meeting) directly and through Congress to institute changes in the MFA—even though they were willing to go along with simple extension.

Finally, in this case, previous American experience with the EEC in textile negotiations influenced the American perspective. Since the United States had almost always succeeded in securing its objectives (even though it occasionally had to struggle), American decision makers tended to be overly optimistic. As a result, the difficulty they encountered with the EEC in 1977 took them by surprise, with one negotiator commenting: "In early 1977, the view at that time was that the EEC would't go as far as they did."[10]

The EEC. The EEC Commission called for numerous changes in the MFA. It was in an unenviable position—torn between its international objectives and those espoused by member states and pan-European textile and apparel organizations.

An American negotiator commented that the EEC was worried about its international position since without the MFA, there would be confusion in the market and the EEC would no longer be a "legal good guy."[11] More pragmatically, if the EEC could conduct bilaterals under the guise of the MFA, there was no particular reason why it would not try to make some accommodation in the language of the MFA—rather than force its demise. Also, from the Commission's point of view, an agreement would bolster its authority over the member states of the EEC. The EEC therefore participated with the United States in developing a compromise position. The EEC pressed for a provision that would explicitly state that the EEC's signing of the MFA depended on its satisfactory completion of bilateral agreements with exporting countries.

The Commission found itself under fire from a number of internal sources. In May 1976, the pan-European textile organization (Comitextil) and the European Clothing Industries Association presented a paper to EEC officials warning of grave consequences if the MFA was not modified to permit further restrictions on imports of textiles and clothing. One of the most important elements in their demands was a call to differentiate between "genuinely developing countries and the other industrialized countries in the textile field"[12]—the latter being a euphemism for Hong Kong, Korea, Taiwan, and other highly competitive exporters.

The EEC was also beset with bickering among member states. Before presenting a position at the Textiles Committee in Geneva, the Commission had to secure a formal negotiating mandate from the Council of Ministers, hardly a simple task. The United Kingdom had moved from a traditional free trade position (or at least relatively liberal stance) to a highly protectionist position. It was joined in this view by the traditional protectionists, France and Ireland, and had some support from Italy. At the other end of the spectrum, Germany, supported by Denmark, wished to go along with a simple renewal of the MFA. The disdainful attitude of the member states toward the Commission further complicated matters. As *Europe* noted:

Not everyone believes either that the MFA is totally at fault. The Community had not always been a successful negotiator. In addition, its cumbersome internal procedures meant long delays in negotiating its agreements so that it is difficult to assess their real impact yet.[13]

The international constraints on the Commission and vigorous domestic pressure from industry associations and member states forced it to be vague at the December 1976 GATT Textiles Committee meeting. The Community representative, Meynell, stated that the "existing Agreement had proved inadequate to achieve the stated objectives of preventing market disruption and ensuring orderly and equitable development of trade."[14]

But since the Council of Ministers still had not given the Commission a mandate, Meynell was unable to propose specific changes in the arrangement. Instead, he simply indicated the five areas that concerned the EEC, and that in his view, needed to be addressed by the Textiles Committee: (1) the need to lower quota growth rates depending on import market penetration levels; (2) an examination of the cumulative impact of imports (akin to U.S. demands for a global quota rather than case-by-case treatment of countries); (3) the year to be used as a reference point in calculating allowable growth rate in imports; (4) attention not only to the *quantity* of imports from exporting countries but to regulation of *prices* as well (addressed in particular to low-priced goods from Eastern European countries); and (5) "forestalling"—that is, strategic delays by exporting countries during the negotiations to allow them to build up the level of their exports to a particular country before they concluded an agreement. Connected to the third point mentioned above, the LDCs could use this strategy to achieve a higher base level (or reference point)— thereby ensuring that they would have a higher subsequent quota.[15]

Japan. Like the United States, Japan was very concerned about the potential demise of the MFA. Because Japan recognized that the EEC was pushing for major changes that could be highly detrimental to its interests, it decided to follow the American lead, advocating only those changes in the agreement necessary to ensure EEC participation. A MITI official, referring to the difficult negotiations, argued:

At least we should avoid any confusion that may be brought out by such prolonged arguments or by an impasse. So we cooperate with, for example, Mr. Smith [the chief U.S. textile negotiator] and some other major partners in the MFA to achieve a very realistic solution to the question of extension of the MFA.[16]

Japan's position had undergone an important transformation by 1976-77. In contrast to the early 1970s, Japan concerned itself not only with facilitating textile exports but also with the possibility of using the MFA to restrict imports of textile and apparel imports from its low-wage neighbors.[17] In fact, Japan had already taken action to restrict silk imports from South Korea and China in the face of political pressure from its domestic industry.

Japanese decision makers, therefore, hoped to see some kind of multifiber agreement that would allow them to follow a middle road: that is, the strength and nature of the regime should permit Japan to avoid too many restrictions on its exports while at the same time offering it the possibility of eventually using such an agreement to control imports into its home market. The Japanese delegate to the Textiles Surveillance Body pointed out euphemistically that Japan's policy was currently "in transition."[18] Another Japanese official in the MITI noted:

In [the] future my view is that Japan's position in world textile trade will change year by year so we cannot fit our position at any particular posture or angle or viewpoint. It is necessary to be flexible in dealing with world textile trade, especially from Japan's viewpoint.[19]

The same official then warned, "I'm not sure how long we can maintain the existing free position in textile trade."[20] More explicitly, the Japanese TSB representative admitted, "As Japan moves to importing status in textiles, it is possible that it will negotiate bilaterals with exporters."[21] Contrasting with previous occasions, then, Japan's position was much more in tune with the desires of other developed countries.

LDCs. By and large, all LDCs recognized their relatively weak power position. They understood that the best they could hope to do would be to obtain a renewed MFA without modifications. Given the EEC's insistence on major changes toward protectionism, a more liberal agreement was out of the question. Moreover, they clearly recognized the new preeminence of the EEC. As early as the second week of the GATT Textiles Committee meeting of December 1976,

[it] was also tacitly understood . . . that the EEC was a power to be reckoned with in the textile world, that no MFA was possible without EEC involvement and that if the EEC were determined to wreck the MFA and to force through a renegotiation the developing countries could do little but go along with it.[22]

International and domestic factors affected LDC policy choices. Internationally, their choices were affected by their overall position in the international system and their dependence on foreign markets in textiles. LDCs which were highly dependent on the European and American markets favored a simple renewal of the MFA. For example, Hong Kong, which exported 90 percent of its production (two-thirds of which went to the EEC and United States),[23] stated that it "would also accept prolongation for a further period"[24] to prevent even severer protectionist actions.

Less dependent countries, such as India, asked that the agreement be extended but noted that if there were to be modifications in the arrangement they should be in the direction of greater liberalization. India then proceeded to list a number of desired changes. Similarly, Pakistan, with a larger domestic market and therefore less dependent than Hong Kong on the U.S. and EEC markets (as well as relatively less successful under the arrangement), called for a number of changes without supporting renewal of the arrangement. In the negotiations, Brazil and India were the most vocal critics of the EEC, as they were the two most powerful LDCs in overall terms and the ones which could most credibly threaten to retaliate. LDC views on the nature of the regime were most significantly afected by how decision makers viewed the competitive position of their textile industries. Three groups stand out: (1) highly competitive countries (Hong Kong, Korea, Taiwan, and Singapore); (2) countries competitive in some products due to comparative advantage and competitive in other products due to restrictions on the first group of countries (India, Brazil, Pakistan); and (3) uncompetitive countries from the standpoint of comparative advantage (or very small suppliers) who benefited from restrictions on the more competitive countries (Thailand, Sri Lanka, other Latin American countries).

The first group of countries preferred a free-for-all in textile trade since they would capture the markets of developed countries relatively easily.[25] The second group of LDCs had mixed preferences. In products in which they were highly competitive (cotton-based products), they wished to have no restrictions on trade whatsoever. On other products, they were not averse to seeing some kind of selective controls—particularly if they were not the intended victims. As a Pakistani official in Geneva noted with respect to the agreement on cotton: "The LTA was sold to LDCs as a means to restrain Japan. LDCs were given the impression that they need not fear this device as a restriction on their exports."[26]

Finally, the third group of countries—the small uncompetitive suppliers—wished to ensure that they would have some market access to the developed countries. This essentially meant two things: first, they were not adverse to bilateral agreements in principle, especially if they restricted the larger suppliers; and second, they were quite insistent on having the larger suppliers' quotas cut back in the face of developed country protectionism.

An LDC delegate commenting on the attempt by these southern countries to develop a unified position summed up the situation accurately, stating that prior to the MFA, the "LDCs were quite incoherent in their demands. They focussed on an individual assessment of the situation and on a maximization of their [individual] positions."[27]

THE NEGOTIATIONS

The Delay: Problems in EEC Policy Formulation. The EEC, a key actor in the 1977 negotiations, failed to develop a clear negotiating position for many months. As a result, serious international negotiations in the Textiles Committee did not begin until July 1977. In the meantime, however, informal bilateral and multilateral contacts took place between the participants. American actions to influence the development of the EEC position were particularly interesting. In January 1977, following the December Textiles Committee meeting, the Commission submitted a memorandum to the council outlining a number of changes to improve its ability to control imports under the MFA. Yet the German delegation, while

recognizing that the agreement should be improved, fear[ed] that the EEC might encounter serious difficulties in Geneva, since the United States had come out in favour of the renewal of the agreement as it stands, and that the developing countries would be prepared to negotiate alterations which would certainly not go in the direction which the Community wants.[28]

Other member states expressed more confidence in the EEC's capabilities to resist the United States, arguing,

The EEC in its capacity as the principal world importer of textiles has the right to make itself heard, whatever the position of the United States.[29]

As expected, the shift in textile capabilities appears to have influenced the development of the EEC's policy stance.

The United States was heavily involved in transatlantic talks to influence the development of EEC policy.[30] It sent representatives to individual member states, although as one negotiator put it:

It was not a question of breaking their unity, but of stating our view. We were trying to sell our position and pointed out that the idea of rewriting the MFA was a non-starter.[31]

Another high-level negotiator reported that in U.S.-EEC private sessions the Americans often threatened to join the LDCs against the EEC.[32] He also mentioned that Robert Strauss (the American special trade representative) would directly link textiles to the ongoing trade negotiations when negotiations appeared to be at an impasse, warning "no MFA, no MTN."[33] But in this negotiator's view, this was a hollow threat since the "Community didn't care if there was an MTN."[34]

The above examples illustrate the use of both within-issue and across-issue linkages in the negotiations. Still, the United States had great difficulty in accomplishing its ends through such linkages because of the shift in the distribution of capabilities in both textile and overall trade. As the negotiations proceeded, the United States was keenly aware that there would be no MFA without the EEC, and thus eventually capitulated to the Community's demands.

After protracted negotiations among the EEC member states, the Council of Ministers finally gave the Commission its negotiating mandate on June 21, 1977—a decision spurred by a French threat to invoke GATT Article 19 restrictions on a number of products.[35] The EEC's mandate emphasized bilateralism, rather than the multilateralism of a regime, stating that "the Community is concerned that its stabilization objectives be equitably attained by means of bilateral agreements."[36] The Council demonstrates its disregard for the utility of the MFA, stating that "should the bilateral negotiations not have been successfully completed by that date [the end of 1977] the Community will be obliged to take appropriate measures to ensure the attainment of its stabilization objectives."[37]

The EEC now felt strong enough to dictate the rules of the renewed regime. It called for exceptions in choosing the reference period that would be used in determining the quota base levels. This increase in latitude would allow the EEC to be more restrictionist. The EEC also sought to change the Textiles Surveillance Body, arguing that "a balance must be maintained between parties viewing trade problems as importers and those viewing them as exporters."[38] This attempt would shift the TSB's role further away from an impartial panel of experts that would judge cases of control imposition, to a more highly politicized body to "facilitate the settlement of disputes by means of conciliation between the parties."[39]

In addition, the EEC wished to differentiate between MFA participants who were party to the GATT and those who were not. This would give the EEC further latitude in conducting its negotiations—and also undermine the independent existence of the MFA apart from the GATT.

The EEC mandate also called for a number of changes in the nature of the arrangement. One of these, the possibility of a global quota, led to sharp dispute among the EEC member states. The United Kingdom, France, and Italy wished to have a maximum ceiling for all imports from Third World countries. In contrast, Germany, Denmark, and the European Commission opposed this. They argued that "the EEC could never obtain the inclusion of such a provision in the multifiber agreement, and that it could, consequently, lead to a breakdown in the Geneva negotiations."[40] In the end, the EEC countries decided to internally set the total level of imports that would be accepted by the Community; that is, rather than having an official external global quota, the EEC would decide on an unofficial internal quota that the Commission would strive to maintain in negotiations with the LDCs. While the net result was almost the same, an external global quota ran contrary to the MFA and would have created great furor. This path made the achievement of "globalization" dependent on the success of the Commission's bargaining effort.

The most important change the EEC sought in the nature of the MFA was a demand the U.S. industries had held dear for over twenty years— keying the growth rate of imports to the increase in the rate of consumption of the home market. As the EEC noted, "it is essential that the rate of penetration of imports by comparison with 1976 levels be stabilized."[41] It went on to explain that

such stabilization implies that the growth rate of all imports giving rise to disruption of the Community market will in no case exceed the growth rate of consumption for each of the products concerned.[42]

The EEC made it evident that it was quite serious about this demand, arguing that stabilization measures are "an absolute prerequisite to the

Community's continuing participation in a special arrangement for tex-tiles."[43] With respect to less "sensitive products," the Community allowed for the possibility of a higher level of growth.

The EEC also called for numerous other changes in the nature of the arrangement. It asked that the criteria used to determine market disruption be changed to take into account such things as low prices, cumulative effect of imports, the growth rate in domestic consumption, and the rate of penetration of imports from all sources in the market of the importing country—a change enabling the EEC to invoke market disruption with greater ease. To stop what the EEC labeled "forestalling," it demanded that the reference period used in determining quota levels be set prior to when the importing country called for consultations. This would aid in preventing the buildup of imports during the negotiation period. Finally, the EEC even argued for a modification in the arrangement's scope. Its position paper noted specifically that unless hand-loom products were properly certified they would not automatically be exempted from quotas.

Michael Smith, the chief American negotiator, responded to the EEC's July 1977 Textiles Committee statement by first welcoming the "fact that the EEC was prepared to move ahead with all deliberate speed on the renewal of the MFA."[44] Reiterating the previous American stance, he stated that "his delegation felt that MFA extension without change was not only desirable but entirely possible."[45] The United States argued that all the EEC's complaints could be handled under the current arrangement; what was needed was "the rational application of all its provisions."[46] For instance, the Americans pointed out that they had a number of bilateral agreements with a 1 percent growth rate in wool imports. They argued that this type of deviation was possible under Article 4 of the MFA. The commission responded by arguing that they were fearful of a lawsuit by importers and thus needed a formal cover—a position that does not seem very credible, given the propensity of American importers to take the U.S. government to court on every conceivable issue.[47]

The EEC persisted in its call for major changes in the MFA. In an obvious threat couched in the niceties of diplomatic language, Tran van Thinh, the chief EEC negotiator, "urged all parties to address themselves to this question in a spirit of moderation and realism."[48] By the end of the second meeting, however, the EEC demonstrated that it believed in the maxim, "actions speak louder than words." On June 23, 1977, the EEC announced that while it was not allowing France to invoke GATT Article XIX (allowing for the restriction of imports for reason of "injury"), it would "take appropriate safeguard measures against imports from countries with which it had bilateral textile agreements or general association agreements, and from the state trading countries."[49]

The EEC then tried the French tactic of calling for unilateral restraints as a spur to influence the deliberations of the Textiles Committee. On July 6, 1977—one day after presenting its demands for changes in the MFA—the commission announced numerous restrictions on imports of textile and apparel products. On the next day, with passions running high and no compromise in sight, Olivier Long, director general of GATT and chairman of the Textiles Committee, suspended the formal meetings to permit informal consultations among the participants.

Over the following two weeks the United States, the EEC, and Japan met to work out a compromise. Ironically, the U.S. position paper presented on July 24, when the Textile Committee meetings resumed, was based on a statement made by Peter Tsiao, the Hong Kong delegate to the talks. Tsiao had argued in a July 7 meeting on the negotiation of bilateral accords under the auspices of the MFA, that *"reasonable departure from particular elements"* of the MFA should be permitted as long as they were more liberal than actions taken under Article 3 (which allows for unilateral restraints).[50]

In its proposal, the United States seized on this notion of "reasonable departures" to allow importing countries to deviate from the terms of the MFA. Still, the EEC pushed for a statement that would note that its acceptance of the renewed MFA would be conditional on its satisfactory conclusion of bilateral accords with exporters. While protesting this "conditionality" at first, in the end the United States recognized that there would not be an MFA without the EEC and went along with the EEC's demands.

The EEC also clearly recognized its ability to sharply change the MFA. When asked why the United States came up with a compromise to "help the EEC," Tran stated:

Very simple, the Americans made an analysis. They need the MFA because it could provide an expansion of trade on a very reasonable basis and it can also provide them with a legal basis for the bilateral agreements for restraint of imports. So they need the MFA, not only for internal or domestic reasons but *also because of their responsibility world wide, and they know that we are the major market in the world* and if we don't join the MFA, if we walk out, they have no more MFA. So they had no choice in fact but to help us.[51]

A major struggle between the developed and less developed countries over the MFA's renewal took place at the July 24 meeting of the Textiles Committee. Though Hong Kong, Korea, and a number of other LDCs went along with the American-inspired compromise,[52] Brazil and India countered with a proposal that recognized the problems encountered by "one importer" but that argued that such problems could be handled under existing provisions of the MFA. Furthermore, the Brazilian delegate reacted to the discussion of the Textiles Committee, stating "his delegation would not associate itself [with a proposal] permitting importing countries to violate the very concept of the Arrangement."[53] The Indian delegate supported this response, arguing that the American-inspired compromise allowing for mutually agreed departures would strengthen the hand of the importing countries. The Brazilian and Indian position was supported by Colombia, Egypt, Guatemala, Hungary, Rumania, Spain, Sri Lanka, Uruguay, and Yugoslavia.

The United States responded by warning that "a failure in this regard [MFA extension] would lead to a lapse of the MFA at the end of the year. Failure would result in a calamitous situation, both for exporting and importing countries."[54] Moreover, the actions of the EEC had convinced a number of LDCs that the time had come to bite the bullet and go along with the "compromise." In addition to the developed importers and Japan, the reasonable departures clause was supported by Korea, the Philippines (on behalf of the ASEAN countries), Hong Kong, and Turkey. Most of these countries had fared extremely well under the MFA: in their view, a breakdown in the regime could only work against them. Hong Kong's delegate (on behalf of a number of LDCs) pointed out that "as they saw the situation the choice was between [a reasonable departures clause] and no MFA."[55] This, they felt, would hardly be in the interest of the developing countries—"especially those who were the weakest."[56]

The Bilateral Negotiations. Having secured wide latitude from the Textiles Committee to negotiate bilateral agreements with "reasonable departures," the Commission turned to the Council of Ministers for a mandate. But the internal decision-making procedure of the EEC was not conducive to quick decisions. As with the decision on renegotiation of the MFA, the EEC took a very long time in developing a negotiating mandate for bilateral agreements. First, Tran immediately went on a trip to discuss developments with Far Eastern exporters and warned them that they would have to be flexible in the forthcoming negotiations. In talks with a member of the Hong Kong Trade Department, Tran did not mince words. He pointed out that

while Hong Kong was in a very strong position legally speaking, it did not have the same pull as India, say. Should the EEC be forced therefore to act outside the framework of the MFA it would probably be more generous to India and some other countries.[57]

This was only a portent of the tactics the EEC would use to play off one developing country against another. Another action by the EEC served to bolster the credibility of its threat to use extra MFA measures. On August 12, the EEC Commission imposed additional unilateral restrictions against a number of countries to supplement the measures announced in early July. Commenting on the reasons for taking these measures, Tran said:

The behavior of the authorities in the EEC now is something which is quite special. More or less we have to invoke the state reason in French, *raison d'etat*, because we are all of us more or less in the sea under highly political pressure.[58]

Prior to the negotiations with the LDCs, Tran's comments to the press served as a warning. In classical mercantilist, zero-sum terminology, he noted that with regard to controlling exports from the ACP countries (the African, Caribbean, and Pacific countries—part of the Lome convention) as well as with regard to the Mediterranean countries (with whom the EEC had special arrangements), "we will set up a cake for each item, and this cake will of course be divided among the different suppliers."[59] In addition, he stated that to make room for the newly emerging countries and smaller suppliers, dominant suppliers such as Hong Kong and Korea will have "their present quota cut."[60] And once again, reiterating the EEC's threat to go outside the framework of MFA restrictions, Tran said:

If we fail in negotiating the 22 bilateral agreements, it was already agreed at the level of the Council of Ministers of the EEC that we have to invoke Article XIX.[61]

While Tran was on his surveying trip, the EEC member states were haggling over the terms of the mandate to be given to the EEC negotiating team. The Commission proposed a complicated scheme that distinguished not only among supplying countries but also among various products by degree of sensitivity (most often, *political* sensitivity). This scheme was submitted as a formal proposal to the Council of Ministers on September 7, 1977.

At the same time, the Commission was also busy preparing for the "possible introduction of a unilateral regime"[62] if the textile negotiations should fail—a fact not lost sight of by the exporting countries. On September 20, 1977, the Council of Ministers adopted the brief proposed by the Commission. Yet all problems had not been solved. While the negotiations were to begin in early October, the United Kingdom had continued to protest about some of the specific figures in the EEC proposals.[63] Thus, when the exporting countries arrived in Brussels for talks with the Commission representatives, they were faced with a team that did not have its official negotiating mandate.

There were two aspects to the EEC's negotiating mandate. First, the broad outlines of policy approved by the Council on September 20 called for:

(1) A new system of surveillance and control covering imports of all textiles from all sources and maintenance of complete information of imports.

(2) A new set of rules of origin to prevent circumvention of the agreements.

(3) Tariff reductions by exporting countries on a reciprocal basis.

(4) Control of imports from countries linked to the EEC by preferential arrangements.

(5) Improved General System of Preferences (GSP) concessions to especially cooperative countries in the bilateral arrangements.

(6) An EEC-wide industrial policy.[64]

At a more detailed level—in which much bickering took place—a number of complicated arrangements were developed. First, the Commission decided to use 1976 as the base year from which the quotas and their growth levels would be calculated, thus forcing countries who had been exporting large quantities of goods in 1977 to reduce their total exports. Second, all textile and apparel products were divided into six categories or groups based on their level of import penetration of the EEC market.[65] Third, to further ensure that imports would be controlled, the Commission was empowered to negotiate "basket extractor" arrangements—that is, consultation agreements that come into effect when imports from an exporting country reach a certain percentage of the EEC's total imports.[66]

The EEC summoned the developing countries to Brussels and, having finally gotten a mandate from the Council of Ministers on October 18, Tran formally began negotiating with the supplying countries. EEC threats to invoke unilateral restraints encouraged most LDCs to negotiate immediately, but some countries held out, feeling that the threat of unilateral restrictions was not the worse of two evils. In fact, some major suppliers actually resisted the EEC's call to come to Brussels in the hope that the EEC member states would disagree among themselves over unilateral measures. In such a case, countries such as Germany and Denmark might offer more liberal bilateral arrangements than would be forthcoming from any concerted EEC decision.[67]

To get the LDCs to bargain, Tran stated that countries which signed up first would get better bilateral agreements. Furthermore, he warned that the EEC's market was limited, and threatened unilateral action to hold imports within those limits. The negotiations were marked by much hard feeling and conflict, but by the end of October Tran's negotiating strategy had borne fruit. He had secured bilateral agreements with four countries (which he refused to name at that time for tactical reasons),[68] and Uruguay and some other Latin American countries joined soon thereafter. But while the strategy was succeeding with minor suppliers, major suppliers such as Hong Kong, India, Brazil, and South Korea continued to resist.[69] In response, Tran decided to take stronger action.

At a press conference in Brussels on November 4, 1977, Tran warned that "there is a danger that the share of the 'cake' proposed to [Hong Kong] might be reduced to the benefit of smaller suppliers."[70] Hong Kong did, however, have some bargaining power. As one high-level EEC negotiator noted, "In a way, Hong Kong is seen as a representative of China."[71] And a top Hong Kong negotiator argued that there is "pressure from the PRC [on their behalf] insofar as it has a vested interest in Hong Kong not being damaged. Hence DCs do not want to antagonize the PRC."[72] But these ties—both actual and presumed—were not always as effective for negotiating purposes as the bargaining power India and Brazil could muster as a result of their large markets available for DC exports and their leadership in the nonaligned movement.

The Commission criticized India for an "unrealistic approach to the negotiations which revealed a failure to understand what was going on or the efforts the Community has made in not actually asking for cuts in Indian exports."[73] But both India and Brazil continued to resist Tran's offers—even though his offers had gone beyond his mandate. As *Textile Asia* commented, Tran recognized that "Brazil had the power to retaliate against individual member states [of the EEC by restricting imports from the Community]."[74] In addition, India felt itself to be invulnerable to pressure since it "it could live with the unilateral measures, even if it meant a reduction in imports."[75]

In the talks, the LDCs were apparently misled by Tran. According to one LDC delegate in Geneva, Tran "had given hints and assurances that his only concerns were Hong Kong and Korea, while suggesting that other LDCs would do ok."[76] But once the negotiations started, Tran's fixed-pie warning had an effect. As this LDC delegate put it, "LDCs each had secret hopes of better deals."[77] This clearly contributed to their disunity in the negotiations.

On November 8, 1977, negotiations between the Commission and Hong Kong were suspended while negotiations with others continued to drag on. The United States, agitated by the delay and fearing that the MFA would not be renewed, "urged the Common Market to refrain from assuming 'too tough' a stance with the producing countries, lest a failure to come to terms jeopardizes approval later this year of a four year extension of the international fiber agreement."[78] Of course this warming was not solely motivated by altruism. The United States was worried that restrictive bilaterals "would inevitably lead to pressure from American manufacturers in Washington similarly to extend its protectionism."[79] The EEC retorted by warning the United States to "stop interfering in their bilateral negotiations with others, or the effort could backfire against the multifiber agreement."[80]

In any event, the EEC continued its negotiations with exporting countries. Its emphasis on a neomercantilist policy is best illustrated by the observation in a commentary in *Textile Asia* that

The projected transfer of quotas from Asian developing countries to some of the ACP countries seems to represent an extension of the Lome deal. Furthermore the EEC is planning to withdraw textile quotas from Asian suppliers and use them as levers to bargain for trade expansion with Rumania, Hungary, and Poland, an intention whose political motive seems obvious.[81]

By the end of November it looked as though no major agreements were likely to be concluded.[82]

This holdout appears to have been a tactical move on the part of the LDCs. Hong Kong and others were ready to go along with bilateral accords when it became clear that time was running out and that the alternative of unilateral actions would be worse for its trade. With the December deadline of the meeting of the Textile Committee approaching, the LDCs buckled under.

In comparison to the excitement and bickering characterizing the EEC's negotiations with exporters, the bargaining conducted between the United States and exporters was rather tame. On June 23, 1977, as part of its strategy to encourage a quick renewal of the MFA without changes, the United States concluded its first bilateral agreement with Hong Kong. Although the United States cut back the growth rate in quotas for the first year, for the most part no severe changes were made in the agreement as compared to those concluded under the original MFA.[83] This is not to say that there were no problems in the negotiations. The talks with Hong Kong were lengthy and the final round of negotiations lasted twenty-four days. But when Hong Kong complained about the restricted growth in the first year, the American negotiator responded by telling its delegation, "Wait till you talk to the EEC. Then you'll be surprised."[84]

After the Hong Kong agreement, the United States went on to negotiate with other exporting countries. Most American bilateral agreements extended into 1978, however, and were not subject to negotiation. The United States negotiated with about a dozen countries in 1977 but was quite careful to avoid antagonizing the LDCs since it wished to maintain their support for the extension of the MFA.

THE OUTCOME: SIGNING OF THE PROTOCOL

The negotiations in Geneva resumed on 5 December, with the United States having completed most of its bilateral agreements and the EEC satisfied with its commitments from exporting countries. At the time it looked as though there would be long negotiations over the content of the protocol of extension. As India, Brazil, Pakistan, and Egypt—four major participants—had still not concluded their bilateral agreements with the EEC, they were attempting to institute changes in the American-inspired protocol.

After some struggle, the LDCs managed to have two changes instituted in the protocol. The first bore heavily on the bilateral/multilateral aspect of the arrangements. The developing countries inserted a paragraph in the text dealing with the role of the Textiles Committee and the TSB. Paragraph 7 noted:

The Committee reaffirmed that the two organs of the Arrangement, the Textiles Committee and the Textiles Surveillance Body should continue to function effectively in their respective areas of competence.[85]

As might be expected, the exporting countries were trying their best to preserve the regime and avoid bilateralism in the arrangements. In a time of growing protectionism their only hope lay in having some rules that would regulate the restrictive behavior of states in textile and apparel trade.

But while giving with one hand, the EEC proceeded to take with the other: they furnished their own interpretation of the rules adopted in the protocol of the MFA. As the EEC negotiator argued in the Textile Committee meeting of December 14 (when Com/Tex/W/47, the protocol opened for signature, was issued) discussing the TSB:

for the Community it was an organ of *conciliation,* as distinguished from arbitral or judicial bodies. [But] the Community would not accept that such actions included putting into question the bilateral agreements concluded by any importing participants with any exporting countries.[86]

The EEC clearly indicated that the bilaterals were to be the real arrangement. If there were any doubts regarding the EEC's intentions, these were laid to rest in the discussions held by the Council of Ministers. A Common Market spokesman reiterated: "It should be absolutely clear that any MFA is subordinated to the enforcement of the negotiated agreements."[87]

In a vain attempt at strengthening the regime, the LDCs secured a second change in the protocol indicating that "reasonable departures" were only to be used temporarily. The Indians went on to argue that

the bilateral agreements that might be concluded with a major importing participant, in terms of the understandings arrived at, would not be considered a precedent available to other importing countries.[88]

The importers quickly challenged this idea. The Canadians in particular were worried, as they had not yet concluded their own bilaterals. At the December meeting, they argued that "no paragraph in the agreement would apply to any single country."[89] The United States tried to convince the Canadians that if they continued to make an issue of the mutually agreed departure clause in the Textile Committee meeting, a "disaster would occur" since the MFA would collapse.[90] As a result, the issue was not discussed further in the meeting of the Textiles Committee and the fight was postponed for the future.[91]

With respect to the nature and scope of the regime, we have already seen that the EEC did not have to obtain changes in the MFA formally. Simply by *weakening* the agreement by the relatively innocuous language of "mutually agreed departures," both the issues of nature and scope were taken care of. In the bilateral negotiations—which in an important sense became the real arrangement—the nature of the controls used by states became more protectionist and the scope of protection was enlarged to include hand-loom products and even products of flax and ramie,[92] leading a Hong Kong delegate to the Textiles Committee meeting in December to comment:

The concept of reasonable departures was not used as conceived by Hong Kong, and in fact under pressure, Hong Kong had to accept departures which, in its view, were not within the scope of the concept expounded in July.[93]

BEHAVIOR OF COUNTRIES AND TRANSACTIONS

Controls. Two major incidents after the conclusion of multilateral negotiations were quite important and have had a significant effect on discussions leading to the next renewal of the MFA in 1981. First, domestic American textile and apparel producers pushed for and succeeded in forcing the U.S. government to renegotiate a number of its bilateral accords. Second, MFA participants fought over which countries would be allowed to use the reasonable departures clause.

In 1978 textile and apparel groups increased their pressure on the U.S. government since they thought that the EEC had done "better" than the

United States in restricting imports through bilateral agreements. Moreover, they were concerned about the absence of bilateral accords or unilateral restraints to restrict the rapid growth of Chinese exports. Bolstered by the obvious leverage point of the ongoing Tokyo Round negotiations, the industries set out to do battle.

In April 1978, William Klopman, chairman of the ATMI Foreign Trade Committee,

emphasized the need for the Committee and the industry to stick together and not let the Government 'divide and conquer.' Stressing that the industry approved policy was to keep all textile products off the tariff table, he warned that attempts to make cases for particular products would only play into the hands of Ambassador Strauss and others.[94]

The industry staged a press conference in June 1978 with George Meany, president of the AFL-CIO, and Irving Shapiro, chairman of Dupont Corporation. They called for an exemption of textiles from tariff cutting as well as tighter administration of trade agreements, an import accord with China, and a renegotiation of agreements with Asian countries to freeze imports.[95] Meany argued, "The U.S. cannot allow any industry . . . to be destroyed by unfair trade competition," and Shapiro concurred, "A change in this disastrous import trend must be made and it must be made immediately."[96] To give meat to their demands, the industry pressured Congress to pass a bill exempting textiles from the prospective tariff cutbacks.[97]

Their efforts had the desired effect. A Senate amendment to an authorization bill for the Export-Import Bank sponsored by Senator Ernest Hollings (D-S.C.), which exempted textiles from the Tokyo Round, passed by a Senate vote of 56 to 21 in early October. While it was subsequently removed from the Export-Import Bank authorization bill in conference, the move to exempt textiles found its way into the Carson City Dollar Bill (H.R. 9937). This bill, sponsored by Representative Ken Holland and Hollings, was passed in late October 1978.

If the Carson City Dollar Bill would have been accepted by the president, it would have created major problems and possibly prevented a successful conclusion of the Multilateral Trade Negotiations. The LDCs and the Europeans were both fighting to have the United States lower its textile tariffs. Thus, President Carter was forced to veto this bill. Recognizing that the industries' allies would continue to pass similar legislation in the future, Carter pledged that "we will review existing bilateral agreements to be sure they really work, and if there are harmful surges we will work promptly to remedy them."[98] Moreover, among others, he also promised to restrain uncontrolled suppliers where needed. To ensure that

Carter would honor his commitments, the industries then proceeded to hold up passage of a bill to extend a waiver on countervailing duties—an essential component in the ongoing negotiations with the Europeans.[99]

In quick response to this pressure, Strauss proposed a comprehensive program to address some of the industries' complaints—a plan that came to be known as the "White Paper." Along with measures providing for global import monitoring, better enforcement, a "snapback clause,"[100] and improvement of the competitiveness of the U.S. textile and apparel industries, the White Paper promised to control import surges.[101]

To implement the portion of the program on surges, the United States renegotiated the flexibility provisions in its bilateral agreements with Hong Kong, South Korea, and Taiwan. In its agreement with Hong Kong, the United States eliminated carry forward and borrowing from the forthcoming year and also cut the amount of swing (intercategory switching); these measures were to take effect in the last remaining year of the agreement. Moreover, when it conducted new negotiations with China and Sri Lanka, it gave them reduced flexibility in the bilateral accords as well.

In July 1979, a mini-crisis developed in the Textiles Surveillance Body. When an agreement between Canada and the Philippines (concluded in April 1979) came up for discussion, the delegate from Colombia argued that Canada should not have been permitted to use the provision for reasonable departures in its agreement with the Philippines.[102] In response to his protest, Canada threatened to pull out of the MFA unless it was agreed that all countries would have a right to invoke the reasonable departures clause.[103] The United States supported Canada and followed with a similar threat to leave the MFA. While the United States was motivated in part by concern for consistent, nondiscriminatory application of the MFA, it also worried about industry pressure and, more important, that "textiles kept out of the Community will flood U.S. markets."[104] As before, fears of diversion from one market to another persisted. The conflict in the TSB was resolved by a footnote to its report approving the Canadian agreement but noting, "While Mr. Suarez did not join the consensus . . . he nevertheless did not oppose it."[105]

The TSB reported to the Textiles Committee in 1980 on its examination of bilateral and unilateral actions.[106] In general—and this caused severe criticism by the LDCs—only departures from the base level from which future import growth would be determined were seen as "departures" by the TSB. Other measures that appeared to the LDCs to be departures from the agreement were cataloged without specifically being classed as such. For example, rates of growth lower than 6 percent in particular cases were seen as being justifiable under Annex B of the MFA which states that "in exceptional cases where there are clear grounds for holding that the situation of market disruption will recur if the above [6%] growth rate is implemented, a lower positive rate may be decided upon."[107] Thus the TSB felt that the United States was justified in concluding bilaterals restricting growth in wool products to only 1 percent because of the American "declaration that this lower growth rate reflected the continuing chronic state of disruption of the United States wool textiles and apparel market."[108]

The TSB commented on only a few other aspects of the American bilaterals; in no case did it report that the United States was engaging in "departures." For example, it mentioned, but did not criticize the U.S. for the inclusion of flexibility provisions directly in the growth rates and the absence of growth in one year in its agreement with Singapore. With respect to the renegotiation of the bilaterals with the Far Eastern countries, in one case (Hong Kong's agreement) the TSB merely took note of the elimination of carryover and carry forward but stated that given the "limited duration of the reduction in flexibility, the impact of the modifications on trade flow did not appear seriously to affect Hong Kong's continued access to the United States market."[109]

The bilaterals negotiated by the EEC came in for considerably more criticism. The TSB disapproved of the "basket extractor" mechanism used by the EEC to bring new categories of goods under restraint and argued that a "real risk of market disruption . . . must be deemed to exist before such consultations are initiated."[110] The EEC was found to have used the departures clause in its action which "rolled back" countries to base levels other than 1977.

The TSB went on to state that the EEC had allowed a growth rate lower than 6 percent in many of its bilateral agreements with countries; yet these were seen as being justified under Annex B of the MFA in "exceptional circumstances." Finally, the TSB criticized the EEC and other developed countries for not formally justifying the absence of or lower rates of swing and carry over/carry forward in many of its bilateral accords. Yet in this instance as well the TSB did not refer to these deviations as a "departure"; it merely stated that "the low swing and those other aspects might have been agreed to in return for certain other considerations in the bilateral agreement."[111] This was a farcical statement in light of the obvious pressure the DCs put on the LDCs in the negotiations.

Among the other developed countries, Australia for one refused to sign the renewed MFA and imposed its own quotas and high tariffs on imports. Canada joined the agreement late after finally negotiating bilateral agreements, many of which were criticized by the TSB. By contrast, Sweden and Finland made all sorts of changes in their bilaterals which were overtly inconsistent with the MFA but which they tried to justify on a blanket basis using the "minimum viable production" (MVP) clause.[112] Though the use of lower growth rates would appear to be justifiable under the MVP clause, these countries had made changes in base levels, carry forward/carry over, swing, and in one case, even the coverage of products to include goods not covered by the MFA. Sweden subsequently modified its agreements increasing product coverage (concluded with South Korea, Pakistan, and the Philippines) in response to the TSB's criticism. Summing up its view of Sweden and Finland's agreements, the TSB noted that paragraph 6 of the Understanding in the protocol (reiterating the need to protect a country's minimum viable production) could "not be invoked as a general waiver of particular obligations under the Arrangement."[113]

Transactions. The restrictions pursued by countries under the 1977 MFA led to an important development (which the LDCs severely criticized): a growth in developed country exports to the markets of the EEC

TABLE 9

Overall Import Growth in Selected Countries and Percentage

	Year			
Country	*1976*	*1977*	*1978*	*1979*
European Community				
Value				
Textiles	4064	4600	5591	7581
Clothing	4459	4999	5964	8081
Percent from Developed				
Textiles	37.3	36.7	37.8	38.7
Clothing	12.1	12.9	13.3	13.5
Percent from LDCs (members)				
Textiles	31.1	30.8	28.2	28.6
Clothing	59.3	55.9	53.6	53.0
United States				
Value				
Textiles	1444	1558	1832	1824
Clothing	3258	3696	4911	5162
Percent from Developed				
Textiles	53.8	57.1	56.7	51.7
Clothing	16.1	16.4	15.0	11.9
Percent from LDCs (members)				
Textiles	33.4	32.3	31.4	35.0
Clothing	63.3	62.3	63.0	64.1

Source: GATT document, Com/Tex/W/78, 29 September 1980.

TABLE 10

EEC IMPORTS OF MFA PRODUCTS FROM SELECTED COUNTRIES

	Imports				Percentage change
Source	1976	1977	1978	1979	1979 from 1976
	1,000 metric tons				
Hong Kong	144.6	114.8	125.8	134.9	-7
Korea	65.2	81.7	83.1	79.7	22
India	76.5	70.9	53.9	74.5	-3
Taiwan	56.8	56.1	57.6	60.7	7
Brazil	48.4	50.9	47.6	58.2	20
China	36.5	27.8	30.9	40.9	12
Yugoslavia	42.1	30.7	30.2	38.8	-8
Romania	39.8	28.6	35.4	36.0	-10
Pakistan	31.7	23.3	28.2	35.1	10
Hungary	22.6	22.7	21.0	24.2	7
Thailand	19.1	19.9	22.2	24.0	26
Poland	19.8	19.0	17.6	20.9	6
Egypt	11.1	11.7	11.0	20.3	83
Greece	82.9	79.0	92.1	101.5	22
Turkey	84.8	60.8	80.4	90.8	7
Portugal	54.8	47.7	65.6	81.3	48
Spain	47.1	49.0	60.6	58.2	24
Subtotal	883.8	794.6	863.2	980.0	11
Japan	25.4	30.9	27.2	29.8	17
United States	150.7	127.3	128.1	212.6	41
Subtotal	176.1	158.2	155.3	242.4	38
Total	1,059.9	952.8	1,018.5	1,277.4	15

SOURCE: EEC statistical reports.

at the expense of the member LDCs.[114] In other cases, state-trading countries gained significantly more than the LDCs party to the MFA. Table 9 illustrates some of the trends. Because of upgrading by the LDCs to increase the value of their exports, the figures do not fully reflect the quantitative restraints these countries have faced.

Table 10 depicts the growth of exports of selected countries to the EEC's market and indicates the kind of cutbacks the LDCs experienced and the beneficiaries of their restraints. Of course variations in demand must be considered in evaluating import changes, but comparisons with developed countries give at least some indication of the effect of restraints. As can be seen from this table, the United States and preferential countries have gained more rapidly in their share of EEC imports than the countries regulated by the MFA. This can be seen in that part of the table comparing rates of import growth from 1976 to 1979. To a large extent, the developed countries have taken over market shares of LDCs restrained by the MFA. Although imports into the DCs declined from 1976 to 1977 as a result of the recession, the LDCs have not fared well with renewed world economic growth either. After intensive analysis of the effects of the renewed MFA, Keesing and Wolf concur with this assessment: they note that there has been a decline in the rate at which textile and apparel exports from the LDCs to developed countries' markets have grown and that this decline is due to increasing protection.[115]

CONCLUSION

Consistent with the hegemonic stability thesis, the major shift in the distribution of capabilities—from an asymmetry favoring the United States to a more bipolar situation in textile trade—led to the near collapse of the MFA. Unlike previous instances in which the United States was the "mover and shaker," in 1977 the EEC took the lead and fought for and secured many of the changes it desired. In this instance, the role of international factors appears to be strongly supported by the changes we see: all countries reacted to the power of the EEC. While the EEC could clearly not get everything it wanted and went along with the Americans' suggested compromise (inspired by Hong Kong), it was still able to secure the majority of its demands.

In part as a consequence of bipolarity in textile trade power and in part the EEC's cumbersome internal negotiation procedures, the negotiations were quite different in this instance than in previous cases. The United States participated in trying to modify the EEC's position before it came to the negotiating table with a full mandate.

Clearly demonstrating the weakness of the regime, the clause on "jointly agreed departures" led to a situation where the regime served basically only as a cover for the EEC's bilateral agreements. This change led to discrimination against particular supplying countries. As in the 1950s, then, countries having ties to the EEC or to the United States were able to exert their political pull to secure better agreements. Some LDCs lose; others gain. But international discipline in imposing restraints clearly eroded.

THE SECOND RENEWAL OF THE MFA, 1981[116]

The renewal of the 1977 MFA did little to placate the EEC and U.S. industries. Overall trade balances fell,[117] particularly in the apparel area, which now accounted for most LDC exports.[118]

TABLE 11

TRADE BALANCES: EEC AND U.S. (MILLION DOLLARS)

	EEC			U.S.		
	1977	1979	Change	1976	1979	Change
Textiles						
Non-MFA LDCs	+783	+422	−361	+110	+315	+205
MFA LDCs	−762	−1195	−433	−213	−82	+131
Clothing						
Non-MFA LDCs	−439	−1119	−680	−573	−845	−272
MFA LDCs	−2629	−4030	−1401	−2112	−3060	−948
Total: (all LDCs)	−3047	−5922	−2875	−2788	−3672	−884

SOURCE: Computed from GATT CT/W/78, September 1980, tables 1A and 1C (for the EEC) and 2A and 2C (for the United States).

NOTE: Data for U.S. and EEC are not strictly comparable because all figures are F.O.B. with the exception of EEC imports, which are C.I.F.

Textile interests in the EEC now pressed for a strong protectionist regime. This option, while not as potentially restrictive as a unilateral quota, would be more politically feasible. The EEC Commission and the U.S. government, with broader trading interests in mind, initially simply preferred to renew the weak protectionist regime of 1977. The battle that ensued, with domestic interests pushing for increased protection on one side and with the LDCs pushing for a more liberal approach on the other side, was particularly ferocious. The position of the Commission and the U.S. government in the middle of this fracas was not an enviable one.

FORMATION OF POLICY CHOICES: OCTOBER 1980 TO JUNE 1981

The United States. The initial U.S. policy choice on the MFA renewal was to maintain the weak international regime of 1977 without major changes. As long as the regime permitted sharp limits on the growth of imports from the "Big Three" countries, the U.S. government was indifferent to the exact language.[119] In late 1980 and early 1981 the United States was still working on developing a proposal; by July 1981, Peter Murphy, the chief American textiles negotiator, was stating the U.S. desire to "negotiate, as appropriate, a protocol that would provide with some certainty for the negotiation of bilateral agreements with minimal growth for the major suppliers in large quotas on import-sensitive categories."[120]

The U.S. preference for a regime rather than simple bilateral accords was influenced by both international and domestic structure. Murphy recognized that the textile and apparel issue nested within the broader trading and economic system. In a U.S. position paper, he pointed out that the American regime proposal "minimizes the likelihood of the meeting deteriorating into strong north/south dialogue that could spill over to other fora."[121] Other discussions of the U.S. position expressed similar concerns shortly before the October 1981 Cancun meeting between North and South.

American officials also expressed concern about controlling the behavior of other countries. For example, Murphy stressed that a regime had to include the EEC; otherwise the "EC could leave us high and dry by doing a lot of fast deals."[122] Murphy argued that the protocol amending the MFA should "give further latitude of approach to address particular importing [countries'] concerns, but also [should be] one that *provides discipline and certainty* in order to accommodate exporting country concerns."[123] A regime would also control the LDCs: at one point in the discussions to formulate American policy, Murphy felt it would be helpful to have language in the MFA that would "push countries like Taiwan and Brazil to open up more to exports."[124] This was often raised in the negotiations and served at times as a bargaining point.

Finally, a renewed arrangement seemed desirable to avoid what Murphy described privately as the alternative of a "chaotic period" without the MFA.[125] Moreover, one major textile newspaper, reporting on a meeting attended by Deputy Special Trade Representative Smith (in which he called for urgent action on the MFA's renewal), commented that the "consensus was that there would be chaos in world textile and apparel trade without it."[126] While not phrased in terms of information and organization costs, these statements imply high uncertainty costs in the absence of the MFA.

Domestic structure affected the U.S. decision to pursue a regime. In preparing the U.S. position, the government pressed for a multilateral arrangement that would allow the United States to legally restrict imports under Section 204 of the Agricultural Act.[127] If a multilateral accord was not reached, American officials feared that the government might be sued or the industry might press for a solution through Congress. As Murphy wrote, there was a need to move forward quickly on a multilateral accord since it would "make the Administration less vulnerable to dangers of serious efforts being attempted at reaching a legislative solution to the issue."[128] A legislative solution would undoubtedly be extremely protectionist and undermine the Reagan administration's espoused free trade stance.

The powerful domestic textile and apparel coalition would have liked to restrict all imports into the United States. As this was not politically feasible, the coalition pressed for a unilateral global quota as a bargaining ploy to secure a strong protectionist international regime. Bilateral agreements were not thought to be adequate because they would not prevent new suppliers from entering the market. The American Textile Manufacturers Institute argued for a global quota to restrict imports. Although the American Importers Association and consumer groups opposed such a quota, they had little effect on the final American proposals for the MFA's renewal.

The American policy choice concerning the strength and nature of the regime was affected by American decision makers' perceptions of international and domestic factors. With respect to international power considerations, Murphy noted that

other importing countries are expected to pursue a far more restrictive approach than that being contemplated by the United States. . . . It is highly unlikely that an international arrangement for textiles would be likely or viable without the participation of key importing countries, *particularly the EEC*. Therefore any satisfactory arrangement will have to strike a balance of importer and exporter country interests.[129]

Recognition of the EEC's textile power extended to other internal discussions. Specifically, Murphy urged that a new protocol be developed quickly since it would "not be in U.S. interest to have exports from the EEC diverted here."[130]

With respect to the nature of the regime, domestic groups sought greater protection, arguing that low-cost imports undermined their production. As one official of the Knitted Wear Association noted in discussing the increasing number of entrants in apparel exports:

[No] matter how hard we run, the gap in wage costs between the U.S. and these new developing countries is so great that there will always be vulnerability in certain sectors to devastating import competition from extra low cost countries.[131]

The low-wage argument was often used as a scapegoat for technological changes and general softness in the market; still, congressional supporters of the industries and labor unions continued to raise the issue of growing imports from LDCs.

When combined with the weakness of the U.S. state, these demands led to a more protectionist U.S. position. American government officials also perceived a growing movement toward protectionism by the Europeans. Commenting on the growth of U.S. exports to Europe and the general displeasure in Europe with increasing imports, U.S. Special Trade Representative William Brock argued: "They're very concerned in Europe, and this is going to mean a very delicate process to renew the

MFA."[132] Rather than the strong protectionist regime advocated by the EEC, however, the United States preferred a weak regime to temper protectionist pressures and to avoid undermining its international objectives.

Domestically, the 1980 U.S. presidential election had given the textile and apparel industries a further opportunity to work toward their long sought goal of more complete protection. As candidates had done previously, Ronald Reagan offered the industries a carrot to secure their support in the election. In a letter to Senator Strom Thurmond (R-S.C.) he promised to renew the MFA, stating that it "needs to be strengthened by relating import growth from all sources to domestic market growth. I shall work to achieve that goal."[133] While the industries had managed to extract a White Paper on textiles from the Carter administration in exchange for a pledge not to disrupt the Tokyo Round GATT negotiations, they had not secured an import growth rate keyed to the domestic market's growth.[134] Thus, they greeted Reagan's election with satisfaction.

The textiles lobby used its influence in Congress to pressure Brock and various government agencies to negotiate a strong protectionist regime. Senators Hollings and Thurmond (both of South Carolina) continuously attacked U.S. officials. In a letter to Brock, Hollings criticized a statement by the chairman of the Council of Economic Advisers, Murray Weidenbaum. Weidenbaum had said that President Reagan had pledged to "explore the possibility" of global quotas. As Hollings tersely noted, the president had never used the word "explore" but, on the contrary, had made a commitment to institute global quotas keyed to the domestic growth rate. In his letter, he even called for *negative* growth rates for the Big Three in some categories. In another letter to Brock, members of the Textile Caucus of the U.S. House of Representatives expressed their pleasure at his proposal to "isolate [the Big Three] and severely limit their exports to [the U.S.]."[135] In sum, domestic pressure was directed toward securing a more protectionist regime.

The EEC. The Commission was initially disposed toward simple renewal of the MFA. There were some splits among the various Directorates, but, for the most part, the MFA was seen as placing policymaking firmly in the hands of the Commission, thereby promoting greater supranationalism. Pressures for major changes came, however, for both international and domestic reasons.

The Commission's original objective was to reduce the major suppliers' growth rates; it felt this was possible under the existing reasonable departures clause of the MFA. In the first meeting to discuss renewal of the MFA in October 1980, the Commission took a low-key approach and, while not offering specifics, appeared to favor renewal. By April 1981, however, the Commission buckled under severe pressure from various industrial groups and from protectionist member states. It submitted a proposal to the Council of Ministers which called for a lower growth rate for imports; differentiation among suppliers; greater control of cheating; reduction in swing and flexibility; and increase in the number of sensitive products subject to highly restrictive quotas; and a five-year extension of the MFA. A number of other ideas were also suggested, such as greater reciprocity by LDCs, more "burden sharing" of imports by the United States and Japan, and some accord on outward processing to ensure that LDCs would buy from European textile producers.

With regard to the development of a regime rather than bilateral agreements or unilateral measures, the EEC was not concerned with maintaining a multilateral approach to achieve consistency with GATT norms (at least until the end of negotiations in November 1981). While favoring renewal of the MFA, the EEC continued to focus on the negotiation of bilateral accords. On a number of occasions the Commission made it clear that it wanted "bilateral textile agreements negotiated at the same time as the Multi-Fiber Arrangement."[136] Nesting considerations influenced the EEC in its desire for multilateral accord to some extent but primarily it was a legal cover. The EEC's view of the larger trade system in which textiles are nested accounts for this approach: in the GATT itself the EEC was pushing for selective safeguards. Thus the notion of keeping the textile accord consistent with the GATT norms of multilateralism and nondiscrimination was not important.[137]

The desire to control countries through a regime proved to be a weak constraint on policy formation. The EEC wanted to allow for different accords for different groups of countries. It wished to be more liberal toward the Mediterranean countries with which it had various kinds of preferential agreements. The Lome countries also demanded preferential treatment. Furthermore, some EEC member states had certain interests in giving their "client" states better accords (the United Kingdom for Hong Kong, the French for some African nations, etc.). Since the MFA was premised on nondiscrimination against specific LDCs, the EEC showed more interest in bilateral accords. Information and organization costs were not a factor.

Domestically, the member states of the EEC were clearly split into two factions: the United Kingdom, France, and Italy on the one hand, and West Germany, the Netherlands, and Denmark on the other. Highly protectionist, the first group was not terribly concerned about maintaining a regime since they were under severe pressure from their domestic industries. They were willing to press for unilateral controls if they did not receive satisfaction through a strong protectionist regime. The French even threatened to impose unilateral restraints on imports unless they were satisfied with the new arrangement—a credible threat, since they had done so during discussions for the 1977 renewal of the MFA. In fact, the U.S. position paper noted that the Commission was under pressure to use "non-MFA type remedies" in textile trade.[138] The second faction was much more liberal. Since their industries were more competitive, they were under less pressure from domestic interest groups and sought a more liberal international regime.

With respect to strength and nature, the Commission initially pressed for a weak protectionist regime. Unlike the United States, it persisted in calling for a continuation of the reasonable departures clause (added in 1977), which weakened the MFA by allowing deviations from the 1974 terms of the original MFA.

The EEC clearly saw itself as a powerhouse (as the United States and the LDCs recognized).[139] Repeatedly, the chief textiles negotiator for the Commission, Horst Krenzler, reminded the other participants that the EEC was "the world's leading importer of textile products"[140] and stressed that "the EEC imported more from developing countries than any other country."[141] While moving toward a dominant position in textile trade, however, the EEC still did not have the capability to institute a strong protectionist regime on its own (and the Commission wished to prevent protectionist member states from doing so). The United States still retained a significant share of the import market and was a credible counter to the Community.

The EEC was reluctant to move to a much more protectionist regime, "for the sake of maintaining good relations with the Third World."[142] Since the Commission was Interested in broader trading objectives with the LDCs, it worried about "a possible threat of retaliation by developing countries."[143] In addition, as the *Financial Times* commented, the EEC was willing to ease its stance on "cutbacks" and "negative growth rates" because of a "fear that inflammatory language would ensure the talks' immediate collapse in a year expected to see the important resumption of the North-South dialogue between the industrialized West and the developing world."[144] Although these factors led the Commission to be somewhat liberal and press for ambiguity in the agreement to give it more leeway in the bilateral negotiations, it was under heavy domestic pressure for a more protectionist accord. Groups such as Comitextil (and protectionist member states) argued that "intervention is widespread in the Third World, where such policies as fiscal measures, exchange control, and aids to exports 'all contribute to imbalance in the condition of trade.'"[145]

Comitextil pressed the Community to lower the growth rate of imports and also demanded a global quota. Similarly, the pan-European clothing association argued that such a quota should be introduced category by category and that imports should be allowed only if the EEC were given reciprocity through open markets in the LDCs. With a relatively weak competitive position, the textile and apparel interests preferred unilateral closure; as a fallback, they preferred a strong protectionist regime.

The protectionist and liberal factions of member states fought over the nature of the regime. While the Germans argued that there was a need to "defend EEC consumers,"[146] the increasingly protectionist British argued that "the 6% growth for quotas included in the original M-FA is highly unrealistic in today's conditions. We must now seek some closer linking of growth rates to the estimated growth of consumption in the Community."[147] Such sentiments were also voiced repeatedly by French officials.

The case of Italy is particularly interesting. While superficially there was little reason for it to be protectionist as it was competitive with the LDCs, Italy saw a regime that controlled LDC imports into the Common Market as useful. Since it was one of the more competitive EEC producers, it would be able to take advantage of other countries' protection to sell its own goods in the Common Market.

In addition to member states, trade unions and industrial interests all exerted pressure on the Commission. For instance, trade union representatives walked out of a meeting in Brussels in October 1980 because the Commission would not make a commitment to a ten-year, highly protectionist regime. In sum, then, the Commission found itself in a tug of war between liberal and protectionist interests. This delayed the formulation of a detailed position for the meetings of the international textile committee.

The LDCs. While the LDCs on the whole sought a strong liberal regime, there were differences among the same three groups participating in the negotiation of the MFA: (1) highly competitive countries (Hong Kong, Korea, Taiwan, Singapore); (2) countries competitive in some products due to comparative advantage and competitive in other products due to restrictions on the first group of countries (India, Brazil, Pakistan); and (3) uncompetitive countries from the standpoint of comparative advantage who benefited from restrictions on the more competitive countries (Thailand, Sri Lanka, other Latin American countries).

In spite of these sharp differences in competitive positions, the LDCs managed to take a unified position through most of the negotiations—in contrast to their disarray at the 1977 renewal of the MFA. A recognition of weakness led to a unified policy choice even though the interests of all countries would not necessarily be fully met.

While several LDCs preferred no restraints whatsoever on textile trade, their policy choice was moderated by international systemic constraints. They recognized that their only feasible option was a textile regime, preferably a strong and liberal one. When asked if it was useful to renew the MFA, Ambassador Felipe Jaramillo of Colombia, the representative of the coordinated LDC group, remarked: "With an MFA there is this discrimination, but we know what the situation is through the bilaterals. Without an MFA we don't know."[148] And in another interview, Jaramillo noted, "An MFA is better than the law of the jungle."[149] For the LDCs, the most important benefit of the regime was its role in controlling the protectionist behavior of the developed countries.

Another benefit from the regime, however, was the possibility of sharing information on bilateral accords to ensure that no one country suffered discrimination. As a GATT official commented on part of the negotiations leading up to the MFA's renewal, "the LDCs agreed to exchange information on bilaterals to prevent being knocked off one by one."[150]

While preferring a regime over simple bilateral accords, the LDCs also strove to secure a strong regime (and, of course, a liberal one). In their early discussions, they noted the need for "redress[ing] their lack of bargaining power by seeking to inject some discipline into Article 4 [which permitted negotiation of bilateral accords under the auspices of the MFA]."[151] Furthermore, they called for a stronger Textiles Surveillance Body, "because one cannot expect the TSB to correct violations of the MFA, unless it possesses the requisite powers."[152] And, even more directly, they argued "what is required is a stronger MFA, because the interpretation or application of ambiguous law tends commonly to be made against the interests of the weaker party."[153]

The LDCs were greatly concerned with EEC capabilities. As one U.S. official noted, these exporters feared that the EEC might use its power to negotiate restrictive bilateral accords before renewing the MFA—just as it had done in 1977.[154] In addition, the LDCs wanted some kind of arrangement because they recognized the "enormous size [of the EEC] as a buyer."[155]

Finally, with respect to the nature of the regime, the LDCs pressed for a "gradual return to free trade in conformity with normal GATT rules and practices." They also asked that such ideas as "Cumulative Market Disruption" be eliminated.[156] This concept, supported by the United States, asserted that importers should be allowed to impose restraints merely because imports were at a high level, *without* forcing firms to demonstrate that they were being harmed by imports. While LDCs differed in their competitive positions, they pressed for a larger market with the expectation that they would all gain.[157] Since there was little question of reciprocity being granted, the LDCs were supported by their domestic industries.

The International Negotiations: October 1980 to November 1981

Although discussion regarding renewal of the MFA took place at the October 1980 meeting of GATT, little progress was made toward a consensus on renewing the arrangement. Subsequently, meetings were held in December 1980, and in May, July, September, and November-December 1981.

At the December 1980 meeting of the Textiles Committee, the LDCs presented their bargaining stance; it was based on consultations they had held with one another in Bogota, Colombia, in November 1980. Among other demands, the LDCs called for free trade and an eventual end to the MFA. More realistically, in the actual bargaining they pressed for the removal of the reasonable departures clause inserted in the protocol renewing the MFA in 1977.

They found the response by the developed countries, as they would for many months, extremely disappointing. The American delegate, Peter Murphy, simply indicated that the rate of growth in the domestic market had fallen considerably in recent years and that the "arrangement had to address the issues of the years ahead and they [the United States] would work constructively with other members of the Committee to achieve that end."[158] The EEC position was similarly vague: "The Community's position regarding the nature of such a regime had still to be defined."[159]

At the May 1981 meeting, the United States continued to favor a protocol extension of the MFA allowing differentiation between small and large suppliers to its market. Because of internal conflict, the EEC did not submit a draft protocol but made it clear that it wished to see lower import growth. In response, the LDCs attacked the developed countries for allowing the "short-term interests of limited sectors" to prevail.[160] The May meeting ended with a clear indication that a return to the first MFA was out of the question. Debate had narrowed to how the larger suppliers would be cut back and the extent to which smaller suppliers might also suffer.

Before the Textiles Committee meeting on July 14 the policy positions stood as follows: the United States was ready to present a proposal at the forthcoming meeting; the LDCs were meeting in Hong Kong to develop their own position; and the EEC was still debating numerous issues and had yet to develop a single coherent set of demands. At the July meeting the LDCs once again took the offensive and presented their unified demands. They asked for a modification in the concept of MVP[161] on a nondiscriminatory basis to ensure that if developed countries were the largest suppliers to a particular market, they would be cut back first; further specifications of when "market disruption" was taking place to prevent its misuse by developed countries; a program of industrial adjustment by the developed countries; special treatment (i.e., more favorable treatment) for new entrants, small suppliers, and exporters of cotton products; a phasing out of restrictions on exports from the developing countries; the strengthening of the Textiles Surveillance Body and improved dispute settlement procedures; and elimination of the reasonable departures clause.[162]

In contrast to the May meeting, the EEC Commission now presented more specific points, though the Council of Ministers continued to be sharply divided between protectionist and liberal factions. France was pressing for cutbacks in the quotas to be given to developing countries and also asked for "negative" growth rates, but opposition by West Germany and the Netherlands prevented the Commission from presenting this as its position. Demonstrating its concern with information and organization costs, the Commission seemed keen on the continuation of a regime to "prevent chaotic conditions in trade" and wished to differentiate among exporting countries. While some saw this differentiation as a cynical move to divide the LDCs, others saw the Commission as being motivated by a genuine desire to help the poorer LDCs.[163] At the July meeting, the EEC chief textile negotiator reemphasized the preeminent position of the EEC as an importer of textile and apparel products and argued that "cheap textile imports were among the factors which had placed the EEC's own textile industry in its present difficulties."[164] He went on to state that the EEC would only agree to a renewed MFA if there were changes in the growth rate of imports, a five-year extension, differentiation among suppliers, changes in flexibility, and some solution to the cheating problem. Significantly, he argued there was "a vital and necessary link between the satisfactory conclusion of bilateral agreements and the renewal for the MFA."[165]

The development of the U.S. bargaining position for the July meeting was quite complicated. Originally, the United States had planned to submit a highly restrictive draft protocol as a bargaining ploy; it would have included the "reasonable departures" language with further specification of the conditions under which this clause could be used.[166] Unfortunately for the U.S. delegation, strong pressure from Congress forced the United States to withdraw even its "protectionist" bargaining proposal. Responding to a briefing given by Murphy, a number of congressmen argued that "the government should be taking the toughest possible stance at the outset of the negotiations, rather than a weak initial position."[167]

Murphy was thus forced to talk in generalities at the July meeting; he simply criticized proposals put forth by the EEC and the LDCs as possibly leading to a breakdown in negotiations. The response from the

LDCs was sharp. They condemned both the EEC and the United States—the former for its restrictive proposals, the latter for inadequate preparation and the lack of concrete proposals.

The acrimonious debate between the U.S. industries and the government over the nature of the U.S. proposal continued throughout August. In addition, Murphy and Paul O'Day, top textile officials in the Commerce Department, went to the Far East for discussions with the ASEAN countries. Reporting on his efforts to gather international support for the U.S. position, Murphy noted that such countries as Singapore, Malaysia, and Thailand could be convinced to agree to cuts to Hong Kong, South Korea, and Taiwan since they would gain by taking over the trade. Discussing strategy, Murphy argued that the U.S. position in September would be to present the previously agreed proposal with some modifications and then "jam it down the industry's throat."[168]

Supported by Brock, who argued that even the "present protocol, if renewed, would be acceptable to the White House,"[169] Murphy prevailed in the internal discussions. To counter protectionist sentiments, he argued, the United States had to put "something on the table that ruled out rollbacks in trade" since this would allow the United States to break the exporters' coalition.

At the September 22 meeting of the Textiles Committee, the United States finally presented a proposal (almost identical to the original July proposal that had been blocked). Specifically, Murphy argued that the decline in the growth rate of per capita textile consumption and the impact of large quotas on market shares in sensitive products necessitated changes. The latter implicit reference to the Big Three exporters was accompanied by a statement calling for the possible elimination of swing and flexibility in "exceptional cases or circumstances"—the language replaced the 1977 protocol's reasonable departure clause. But Murphy did promise that the United States would not seek "reductions or negative growth rates" in imports.[170]

The EEC Commission wished to secure a weak regime—allowing it to handle the LDCs on a bilateral basis without regime constraints. This represented a delicate balance. While the commission felt that a weak regime would allow it more leeway to contend with protectionist member states, the protectionists planned to use a weak regime to press for restrictive bilaterals if they failed to secure a strong protectionist regime. The LDCs were incensed; Jaramillo saw the MFA as "setting the maximum limits of protectionist measures permitted to importing countries."[171] He attacked the EEC, stating, "It is difficult to discuss the so-called proposals put forward by the Community with any measure of seriousness."[172] The September meeting closed with much ill feeling and few results.

The LDCs' concern with a strong regime may have been misguided. While a strong *liberal* regime was clearly desirable from their perspective, a strong protectionist regime would prove the worst of all possible worlds. As one adviser to the ASEAN countries argued in a brief outlining trade-offs between strength and nature in the regime:

The relatively broad and general formulation does not offer a high degree of protection from abuse to the exporting countries. Nevertheless, a more precise definition could well cause greater problems, for then the developed importing countries would most likely want to express the lowest common denominator. With today's political and economic climate an attempt [to secure greater precision] would be more severely restrictive.[173]

Simply put, a weak protectionist regime might give some LDCs a better chance than a strong protectionist regime. Several LDCs would follow this advice in the final negotiations.

Throughout October and early November 1981, the EEC member states fought over the proposal to be presented at the final negotiating session, which was to start on 18 November. They argued fiercely about three key issues: the type of global ceilings for imports; the rate of growth of imports; and whether base levels should be cut. As the EEC discussions dragged on into November, France threatened once again to "apply unilateral measures if no MFA mandate could be thrashed out in time for the discussions in Geneva."[174]

Anxious to develop consensus, the Commission suggested a compromise. Rather than a global ceiling on imports, which would be imposed externally, similar to the 1977 decision, the Commission would negotiate on the basis of an "internal" global ceiling. Focusing on bilateral accords to meet the ceiling, rather than on a strong protectionist regime, placated the liberal Germans who did not want harsh language in the accord.[175]

With respect to the weak regime's proposed nature, the idea of negative growth rates was rejected; instead, the Commission would press for rates of between zero and one percent in the most sensitive categories and at least one percent overall. Furthermore, rather than institute base-level cutbacks, it would propose an elaborate "surge mechanism" to prevent sudden surges: if exporters did not fill their quota in a particular year, they would lose their right to the full quota in the next year. But they would be able to recoup their right to the negotiated quotas over the remaining life of the MFA.

The major suppliers would also be asked to reduce their quotas in exchange for outward processing quotas. Finally, the Commission agreed to seek reductions in flexibility for the major suppliers in sensitive products, and to avoid transfers of quotas from one category to another and carry overs to other years. Having secured member states' agreement, the Commission presented these demands on 20 November.

ASEAN countries attacked the EEC for the "ambiguities and incertitudes" in its proposal, while Mexico and Brazil asked the EEC to display "more understanding and flexibility."[176] The United States, which had maintained its September proposal, joined in the criticism. The root cause of American displeasure was the EEC's proposal to give LDCs outward processing quotas in exchange for quota cutbacks, which would have obligated exporting countries to buy cloth from the EEC. Moreover, the United States did not want cutbacks specified in the MFA since this would increase domestic pressure on the U.S. government to match the EEC's cuts to suppliers.

The LDCs' unity began to break down as negotiations dragged on. Small suppliers worked to develop a strong regime by arguing for "as much rigidity as possible to ensure that importing countries are locked into making concessions."[177] At the same time, they indicated privately to the United States that they would be "prepared to accept cutbacks on dominant suppliers [in return] for more favorable treatment [by importers]." Meanwhile, Hong Kong, South Korea, and the ASEAN countries, seeing the writing on the wall, began to argue for "an ambiguous formulation" with respect to flexibility provisions. This would possibly allow them greater success through bilateral negotiations.[178]

Meanwhile, domestic lobbying by the U.S. industries increased. In support of the textile and apparel industries, the congressional House Textile Caucus members threatened to withhold support from President Reagan's foreign aid bill in early December. Recognizing that the caucus could obstruct his legislative efforts, Reagan had an aide notify Rep. Carroll Campbell, a key member, that "the President has instructed the U.S. negotiators in Geneva to strengthen the U.S. proposal in Geneva on the renewal of the MFA." Further, Reagan pledged, "This Administration will make every effort to conclude an M-FA that will allow us to relate total import growth to the growth in the domestic textile and apparel market."[179]

Murphy was in a delicate position. Domestic interests and the EEC were clamoring for a rigid protectionist MFA, while the LDCs were still pressing for liberal provisions. Without agreement and with only two weeks left before the expiration of the MFA, Murphy cabled Washington with his analysis of the situation and presented the available options. Briefly, these were an MFA without the EEC, continued efforts to seek consensus with a short extension of the MFA as a fallback, an MFA that allowed the EEC its objectives, and simply letting the MFA expire without replacement.

Murphy argued that an MFA without the EEC would meet domestic legislative needs and gain the support of LDCs (even though the agreement would have to be more protectionist to meet the new presidential directive) but exacerbate tensions with the EEC and possibly lead to intense pressure from the U.S. industries as the EEC pursued protectionist measures. Moreover, the LDCs would not favor an agreement without the largest importer.

The second option (which Murphy supported) of seeking consensus language with a simple one-year extension as a fallback would allow the United States more time to pressure the EEC and permit trade to continue, but might lead to a more protectionist EEC position and greater domestic pressure during the extension.

The third option, a protectionist MFA, would resolve the conflict between the EEC and the United States but hurt the latter among the LDCs and lead the American industries to demand that every EEC protectionist move be matched. Finally, simply letting the MFA expire would put the industry on the spot and allow the United States to maintain goodwill with the LDCs. But Murphy saw this as being unrealistic: Congress would undoubtedly press for highly protectionist measures, and the option might lead to problems with the use of GATT Article 19 on a selective basis.[180]

Authorized by the government to follow option two with extension as a fallback, Murphy pressed for consensus language in the MFA. He was supported by Secretary of State Alexander Haig and Ambassador Brock of the Special Trade Representative's office, both of whom were in Brussels on other business. They told the EEC that the United States was determined to have the MFA renewed and would do so even without the EEC. The tactic appeared to work. Not wanting to bear the brunt of LDC displeasure, the EEC agreed to extremely vague language to get around U.S. objections.

THE AGREEMENT: DECEMBER 1981

The international negotiations came to an end on December 22, 1981. American and EEC demands were met in four key paragraphs of the final protocol. Paragraph 6 noted the

goodwill expressed by certain exporting countries now predominant in the exporting of textile products in all three fibres . . . in contributing to mutually acceptable solutions to particular problems relative to particularly large restraint levels.[181]

This paragraph satisfied the EEC's demands for authority to impose cutbacks on major suppliers and met U.S. demands for vague language.

To ensure that the major exporters would actually show "goodwill" in the negotiations, the EEC exchanged letters with Hong Kong and Macao stating its intentions to seek reductions in access. While the United States recognized that this paragraph could be used for cutbacks not only in quotas but in trade, it pledged not to cut trade levels. But the Americans saw the paragraph as a potential source of power with which to threaten the Big Three if they did not cut growth rates in quotas and flexibility to American satisfaction.

Paragraph 9 met American demands to cut back the Big Three by allowing differential treatment of suppliers. It allowed for the negotiation of lower positive growth rates and any "mutually acceptable arrangement with regard to flexibility" for major exporters who accounted for a large share of the market of an importing country.[182]

Paragraphs 10 and 13 addressed two problems raised by the EEC— underutilized quotas and outward processing quotas to replace cutbacks. The medium-size exporters strongly opposed the surge mechanism of paragraph 10. Since dominant suppliers generally filled their quotas, cuts due to underutilization would mainly harm the medium-size suppliers. Paragraph 13, intended by the EEC as an "outward processing clause," was watered down in the text due to opposition by exporters and U.S. pressure, but the EEC clearly intended to force major exporters to buy its fabric for outward processing.

Thus, the EEC met the import "problem" in three ways: outright cuts for big suppliers, some compensation in the form of outward processing quotas, and a surge mechanism directed primarily at the medium-size exporters. And the United States achieved its goals through the differentiation contained in paragraph 9. No country was able to simply impose its will, and the weak protectionist MFA 3 is the result.

CONCLUSION

The international regime that regulates intervention by countries in textile trade is unraveling. Developed in the early 1960s, the regime has become weaker in strength and increasingly protectionist in nature since 1977. This trend continued in 1981.

The bargaining that led to the 1981 renewal of the MFA provides evidence for the role of international and domestic factors in influencing the development and change of international regimes. The international factors are nesting, control of others, and information and organization costs. Nesting proved to be an important factor: American and EEC Commission decision makers recognized that constraints arose from the broader international system and the trading system.

All countries wished to employ a regime to regulate others' behavior, although for different purposes. American decision makers, for example, wished to prevent the EEC from being unduly protectionist in order to avoid a diversion of goods to the American market. They also hoped to use the regime as a device to control LDCs from exporting too much and to force them to open up their own markets. Since the LDCs were weak relative to the developed countries, their hope in securing market access lay in a strong regime that would constrain the behavior of developed countries. Finally, all actors recognized the advantages of a regime in minimizing informational and organization costs, though such advantages served as an inducement in varying degrees.

Domestic structure, in terms of the relationship between state and society and between the Commission and member states, proved to be a significant constraint on the choice of a regime. For legal reasons, the United States preferred a regime to the likely alternative, a unilateral quota advocated by textile and apparel interests. The Commission was particularly constrained by member states who in some cases were quite willing to see the end of the regime and its replacement by unilateral measures. Internationally, changes in the strength and nature of the regime appear to be caused by a shift in the distribution of capabilities and increasing competition from newly industrializing countries in the textile and apparel trade.

In the matter of regime strength, the absence of a hegemon to impose or cajole others into subscribing to an international regime led to an accord that was of necessity a product of compromise between two key actors—the EEC and the United States. Concerning regime nature, the MFA in 1981 became somewhat more protectionist as developed countries faced increasing competition from the LDCs across a wide range of textile and apparel products. Domestic textile and apparel industries in the developed countries responded to this competition with increased lobbying. In the EEC's case, however, LDC and U.S. pressure tempered protectionist demands.

Domestically, the U.S. government and EEC Commission were faced with numerous groups wanting a strong *protectionist* regime. The American textile and apparel industries lobbied hard and managed to force the United States to move in a more protectionist direction, especially toward the end of the negotiations. They repeatedly demonstrated the weakness of the U.S. government to resist strong protectionist pressures. The United States did manage, however, to develop a weak regime and prevent a strong protectionist accord. Similarly, the Commission was forced by its member states and pan-European lobbies to move away from its initial position of maintaining the regime without major changes.

PART III
WEAVING A NEW REGIME?

Markets are like parachutes—they only function when open.

—Helmut Schmidt, *The Economist,*
February 26, 1983

7
Conclusion

We have now come full circle—from the unregulated intervention of the 1950s to the increasingly unregulated trade intervention of the 1980s. The next incarnation may well see an international regime promoting organized protection.

It is now possible to answer some of the following questions: How and why have modes of collaboration in international trade in textiles and apparel varied? What implications does this study have for the development of theory about international regime transformation and protectionism? What are the prospects for the LDCs and DCs in textile trade? And finally, does the demise of organized textile trade cast doubt on the possibilities of managed trade in general?

COLLABORATION IN TEXTILE TRADE

In the face of increased LDC competition in textile and apparel trade, the developed countries have relied on a variety of protectionist measures in support of their domestic industries. The ensuing conflict over markets between both developed and less developed countries—and among the developed countries themselves—created numerous problems. Such problems have been common to a number of other products such as steel, electronics, and autos, to name some of the most salient conflicts. In the increasingly anarchic world of unregulated intervention, the international regimes in textile trade have been seen by some as a bastion of stability, introducing order where only chaos reigned before, and serving to moderate protectionist impulses.

This study has emphasized the role of international system level factors in explaining international regime transformation. I have applied this perspective to the pre-regime period in textile trade and then to the origin, maintenance, and destruction of the regime of this area. My focus on the decision-making process and consideration of the extent to which government officials perceived the various structural constraints and incentives of the international systemic forces provided the basis for this analysis.

To reiterate, why do regimes change? First, a distinction I have drawn to distinguish various aspects of regimes is helpful. A regime can be analyzed on at least three dimensions, namely, strength, nature, and scope. Coding historical events in textile and apparel trade using these categories enabled us to specify more clearly what a theory of regime change should explain.

An international systemic approach to regime transformation based on the structure of the overall political, trade, and textile systems argues that countries will prefer international regimes over other possible arrangements to regulate national behavior for the following reasons. First, regimes may be preferred in subsystems if higher-level system arrangements are undermined by particular national actions (e.g., when national actions in textiles undermine the overall trade regime). In such a case, a regime that is at least partially in accord with rule systems at higher levels will be preferred to unrestrained national actions, a phenomenon I have termed "nesting." Second, regimes provide a simple mechanism for regulating the behavior of other countries: if a country finds that others are engaging in behavior that is undesirable, a system of rules constraining other actors may be more desirable than activating power resources to secure national objectives. Finally, regimes minimize the organizational costs involved in monitoring and regulating the actions of a variety of states. They also lower the costs of obtaining information; this concern was particularly significant for LDCs, since regimes provided them with easy access to market information as well as data about what kinds of agreements other countries had been concluding.

Hegemonic stability theory proved to be particularly relevant in accounting for the strength of textile regimes. This theory argues that regimes will be strong when there is a unipolarity in the distribution of capabilities in a system. With oligopsony power (the power to demand) being the relevant capability in textile trade, I argued that regimes will be strong when one country has preponderant market power (as indicated by a large market for textiles and apparel as well as a high level of imports). In such cases, the theory suggests that the hegemon will be able and willing to use its capabilities to set up a rule system it desires. The rationale for this assertion is based on collective goods theory, which argues that a large power is needed to provide such goods. In textile trade, this implied that when the United States (the former hegemon) underwent a decline in capabilities as the EEC became a significant power, the regime would also decline in strength.

With regard to the nature and scope of regimes, I have argued that these characteristics would be a function of changing competition in trade. As developed countries faced growing import competition in an increasing number of products, the regime became more protectionist and wider in scope. The nature and scope of the regime is also based on the meta-regime; agreement on principles and norms to regulate an issue-area affects the characteristics of the regime.

Regime change is also affected by domestic politics and individuals' beliefs. In particular, as hegemony waned, one might expect domestic politics to become a more potent force and beliefs to make more of a difference in bargaining. Depending on the power relationship between state and societal groups, one would expect different degrees of pressure to change international regimes. With respect to individuals, lessons learned from experience and existing political beliefs affect the objectives and strategies pursued in bargaining.

These factors served as a guide for a process-tracing of the decision making in the pre-regime period, and the origin, maintenance, and destruction of the regime. This empirical analysis allowed us to examine the anomalies from the perspective of what we might expect if we only focused on international variables; and it provided a way to validate the expectations arising from the model developed in Part I of this work. The absence of a sufficient number of cases, combined with the fact that the cases were not totally independent, did not permit us to empirically examine the validity of the theory using statistical tests of significance. Observing how decision makers act and interact, however, and examining the logic in their choice of actions, provides a powerful substitute for such statistical analysis. As we saw, a number of anomalies from the perspective of an international structural model could be readily explained by taking domestic and individual level factors into account. And with respect to the validation process, evidence of the influence of structural configurations entering the calculations of decision makers could usually be found.

IMPLICATIONS FOR THEORY

Thus far I have argued that an international system level approach appears to have a high degree of utility. On the whole, decision makers responded to international factors in the manner postulated. This was sometimes not the case, however. This section examines what might be considered "anomalies" if we only focused on international-level factors in an effort to gauge the extent to which such factors by themselves are necessary and/or sufficient to explain the events we have seen. Once we have some idea about how good the international structural model is, we can assess the relative importance of domestic and individual level variables identified in the study in contrast to international factors in the international regime transformation process.

What does it mean to say that a factor was "necessary" and/or "sufficient"? "If an event will never occur in whatever the circumstances" without a particular condition(s), then it can be said that these conditions are *necessary.* And if we have a "set of conditions given which an event will always occur whatever the circumstances," then this set is *sufficient* to explain the outcome.[1] Alexander George draws a further distinction. In some cases, he argues, it is not possible to gauge the necessity and/or sufficiency of a particular set of independent variables in determining outcomes. In such a situation, a weaker variant of the importance of specific conditions can be asserted, namely, that "an independent variable merely 'favors' the occurrence of (an) outcome."[2]

While self-evident to some extent, there has been some confusion in the usage of the terms "necessary" and "sufficient." Scholars often try to find explanations that are "sufficient" to predict an outcome; but an independent variable can be sufficient to explain an outcome without being necessary. In fact, it may often be easier to find sufficient conditions without being able to determine if they are in fact necessary for an outcome.[3]

The familiar problem in the social sciences with models that are "overdetermined" clearly illustrates this. While we know that the model is *sufficient* to explain the outcome in question, we may be unable to determine which elements in our model are *necessary.* Another possibility is that we might in some cases find that our model is "underdetermined." That is, while we find factors that are necessary to explain an outcome, we still do not have a satisfactory explanation since additional factors must be introduced to achieve sufficiency. The ideal model is one whose independent variables are both necessary *and* sufficient.

In the pre-regime period from 1950 to 1960 discussed in chapter 3, I have argued that the development of a regime in textiles would have been an unlikely result. Bilateral accords or unilateral controls could be employed to handle any problem that arose as long as the problem stayed limited. One unexpected event during this period was the failure of the United States to conclude an agreement with Hong Kong to have it restrict its exports. Though the international factors clearly *favored* the development of bilateral arrangements, by themselves international factors are clearly not *sufficient* to explain the outcome. An international structural approach would suggest that Hong Kong and the United States should have come to a successful bilateral agreement. Yet we saw that domestic politics in both countries served to undermine a possible accord.

Moreover, it appears that in this particular situation, the United States bargained poorly and did not utilize its considerable asymmetrical capabilities to full advantage.

Given that exporting countries do not simply accept bilateral controls after a simple request by exporting countries, and given the intense diplomatic maneuvering and pressure applied by the United States and the United Kingdom in their various bilateral accords, there seems to be some evidence for structural factors being *necessary* for the conclusion of such agreements. In this case, we can specify some of the conditions that affect the efficacy of an international structural approach in accounting for outcomes. I would argue that if there is overwhelming asymmetry in a relationship (e.g., U.S.-Japan in the 1950s), then other factors such as poor bargaining, domestic politics, or learning the wrong lessons from history may not be enough to prevent a particular outcome; when the asymmetry is less pronounced, however, as in the U.S.-Hong Kong case, these other factors may be enough to prevent the outcome expected from focusing solely on international factors. Domestic and individual level factors have been important in a number of cases; the analyst who focuses only on international level factors might thus find anomalies if only this level is considered.

The negotiations leading to the first textile regime, the STA, and its successor, the LTA, were consistent with what a focus on international factors would lead us to expect. The nesting effects of higher-level interests, the need to control other countries' behavior, and the desire to reduce information and organization costs led the United States, the overall trade and textile hegemon at the time, to develop an international textile regime. Moreover, the characteristics of the regime were also of the type we expected *and* for the reasons I asserted.

While international factors appear to be necessary and sufficient in the development of the textile regime, other factors proved to be quite important in the maintenance of the LTA and its expansion into the MFA. The evidence that an emphasis on international systemic factors was *necessary* is supported by the views of different decision makers. LDC and European negotiators clearly perceived that the United States was putting pressure on them, and American decision makers anticipated that they would succeed in their efforts. Moreover, as before, officials of most countries did *not* secure their policy preferences in the final outcomes. The fight between India and the United States is particularly significant: throughout the negotiations, the United States held to its position that the LTA should be renewed before it would grant any further liberalization; in the end India was forced to accede to American wishes. Structure clearly mattered.

As far as sufficiency is concerned, the evidence is not quite as strong. American power was not always an overwhelming factor in outcomes. The American effort in the early 1960s to develop a regime in wool products before concluding bilateral agreements illustrates this. The importance of learning by decision makers was particularly significant. As we saw, the United States tried to develop a regime in this area—rather than simply conclude bilateral agreements with the offending countries. This effort proved to be a failure; although the U.S. had "learned" that bilaterals by themselves would not be effective in restraining imports and would create problems with diversion from one country to another, the U.S. decision to seek restraint by other developed countries was poorly conceived. Dealing with DCs was obviously a problem of a different type from negotiating with LDCs, and it was clearly more difficult to use U.S. capabilities against relatively powerful countries. The next step that the United States pursued—trying to have Japan restrain its exports—also seems to have been adversely affected by previous experience. In this case, Japanese officials were unhappy about the fact that restraints had been forced on them in cotton goods and hoped to secure an open market in wool (and MMF) products. Moreover, domestic politics played a significant role in the negotiations as Japanese and American business groups became involved in the negotiations.

International systemic explanations appear weakest (at least on the surface) in accounting for the development of the MFA. From an international systemic perspective, a regime governing the behavior of countries in MMF and wool products should have been developed at this time. In addition, the United States should have negotiated bilateral agreements as a first step when faced with import problems instead of trying to develop a regime. Let us first consider necessary and sufficient conditions before reviewing these efforts to account for the anomaly.

Considering only international factors, it is obvious that these are not *sufficient* to explain the developments at this time. The United States clearly had the motivation to develop a regime and the capabilities to do so. But although other factors intervened, as I note below, a focus on international constraints and incentives is clearly *necessary* to account for the events we saw.

The reversal in U.S. strategy clearly stems from a perception on the part of U.S. decision makers that regimes were better than simple bilateral accords. They realized that new suppliers would enter the market and were also concerned that uncoordinated national policies of various countries would create a partial diversion of goods into the American market. Instituting a unilateral quota was ruled out for reasons of undermining the GATT (the nesting argument). But although the motivation to pursue a regime was understandable, their strategy was incorrect. Although the United States was powerful, American decision makers failed to learn from their previous experience during the Johnson administration about the problems of trying to secure restraints on the export of wool products by developed countries. Even though the American concern was with Far Eastern suppliers, the decision to send Stans to Europe first was disastrous: it merely served to increase their resistance by provoking fears that such an accord would be used against them.

There was also misperception on the part of the Europeans: they failed to recognize that the United States had the capability to use its market power to eventually force through the development of a regime—although one that only dealt with restraints on LDCs and Japan. This misperception was responsible for the subsequent efforts and success of the United States in creating a diversion of goods into the EEC's market, which led EEC member states to change their position to favor a regime.

Why is it essential to focus on international structure? The analysis of the perceptions of decision makers makes it quite clear that the asymmetrical distribution of capabilities in textile trade (as well as constraints and incentives arising from the overall political and trade systems) and the American decision to utilize these capabilities had the desired effect. Without knowledge of international factors, we cannot explain the development of a regime. What this suggests is that structure may constrain outcomes—even when it is inaccurately perceived initially. In this case, the existence of U.S. capabilities was insufficient: it had to be used. And the result was the MFA agreement of 1973.

The two renewals of the MFA in 1977 and 1981 marked a shift away from American dominance and a rise in EEC capabilities in textile trade. The result was disastrous for the regime: for the most part bilateralism replaced the regime, and the regime itself has been reduced to a cover for these bilaterally negotiated accords. As we saw in chapter 6, the phrase, "jointly agreed reasonable departures from particular elements in particular cases," resulting from the 1977 renewal, was used to justify a variety of deviations from the terms of the agreement.

The importance of domestic politics emerges clearly here: international structural changes provide a necessary, but by no means sufficient, explanation of the evolution in the regime and national behavior. The U.S. textile and apparel industries, observing the success the EEC had had in its bilateral agreements, demanded revisions in the accords controlling imports into their respective countries. In the United States, the industries' threat to hold up the GATT Tokyo Round accords led the U.S. government to abrogate existing agreements and seek downward revisions in flexibility and carry over/carry forward in its agreements with Hong Kong, Korea, and Taiwan. Moreover, although the United States never formally referred to "jointly agreed departures" in its bilateral agreements, it supported Canada in its fight in the Textiles Surveillance Body to assert its right to use this clause if need be. While the LDCs opposed this notion and argued that only the EEC (which had fought for such a right in 1977) should be allowed to use it, they lost this battle.

How well did the international structural theory predict and explain what we have seen? As expected, the move toward bipolarity in textile trade would result in the collapse of the agreement. Yet because of the prior existence of a regime (the old MFA), the inertia has led to the continuation of a regime—although a severely weakened one that permits growing protectionism. In chapter 2, I identified the changing position of the United States vis-à-vis the EEC after 1974. The importance of this shift was substantiated in chapter 6: we saw that the United States and the LDCs were cognizant of the EEC's new power. Of course the EEC was not powerful enough to obtain all the changes it initially desired in the MFA. But it was able to utilize the Hong Kong suggestion for a compromise permitting "jointly agreed departures" to convince LDCs that they should go along with the kind of bilateral agreements they were being offered. While the structural asymmetries in the EEC's position versus the LDCs were evident, this still does not detract from the astute bargaining strategy employed by the EEC's chief textile negotiator, Tran van Thinh. By making the EEC's position extremely clear, he left no room for misperception: the EEC's protectionist intentions could and would be fulfilled.

In the case of the MFA's first renewal, one could have anticipated the problems that would arise in renewing the MFA based on our knowledge of international factors. Still, the exact nature of the agreement and the process leading to the accord is usefully supplemented by an analysis of domestic politics, something we would anticipate in the absence of a hegemon to provide international stability. As far as the question of "necessity," it is difficult to explain the sharp change in the MFA without recourse to the growth in the EEC's capabilities and the increasing competition from LDCs in textile trade. These two factors, in combination with the fact that a regime previously existed, appear to be critical in accounting for what has taken place. When supplemented by domestic politics, one gains a clear understanding of the reasons behind the severe weakening of the regime.

The second renewal of the MFA in 1981 is also consistent with an international structural account, particularly one that concentrates on the structure of the textile trading system. The situation remained bipolar, and, as anticipated, the negotiations were prolonged and difficult and resulted in further weakening of the regime. This last renewal has been an important step in bringing about the destruction of the MFA as a significant constraint on national actions.

In the analysis of the 1981 renewal, many of the factors previously identified as potentially significant in the decision to continue with a regime format, and with a particular strength, nature, and scope, appeared to be perceived by decision makers in the negotiations. Moreover, my argument on the growing role of domestic politics under conditions of bipolarity was also borne out. When taken together, the international and domestic factors I pointed to appear to be both necessary and sufficient to explain the type of renewal of the MFA which took place in 1981.

To sum up, in light of the process-tracing analysis of the various cases, the international and domestic factors I pointed to (and occasionally, individual-level variables) appear to be both necessary and generally sufficient to predict and explain regime transformation in textile trade over the last thirty years. A regime never arose in textiles without a hegemonic power backing its development. And when the situation moved away from unipolarity, the regime nearly collapsed. But this simple matching is further substantiated by the process-tracing analysis of decision making: government officials appear to respond to changes in structure and act accordingly. Moreover, misperceptions of structure do not last for very long, as structure (to be anthropomorphic for a moment) asserts itself.

A critical point in this context is the mode of analysis pursued here. The model used for predicting and explaining change was not developed using simple induction. It was based on a number of theories relating to various facets of the regime transformation process. This is quite important. A model based on a deductive theory allows one to understand anomalies much better than a theory that simply generalized on existing cases. This kind of theory development is essential if we are to move beyond analysis of a single issue-area.

A focus on the international factors I have discussed is often sufficient by itself in explaining regime change. The evidence for this assertion derives from this method's success in predicting and explaining what is likely to take place, and its ability to provide reasons for these assertions with only occasional recourse to other factors. Such factors as learning by decision makers and domestic politics do make a difference. But they are by no means preponderant, and the lack of learning and the occurrence of mislearning are striking. On the whole, while such factors lead to deviations from the trend line predicted from an international structural focus, these deviations are only temporary. As a parsimonious model, then, the international structural systemic analysis provides a way of predicting *and* explaining the changes we see.

Two important benefits can be derived from pursuing the theoretical ideas developed here in other areas of study. First, studies of other issue-areas would help to further validate some of the hypotheses on regime transformation considered in this study, and would assist in establishing the conditions of necessity and sufficiency of the theory. Second, in many cases analysts have failed to develop a well-specified theory of regime transformation, and existing analyses of other issue-areas are often little more than correlational exercises.

An analysis of other issue-areas, with an emphasis on the question of necessary and sufficient conditions, would help support my assertion that the variables identified here appear to be necessary and often sufficient to explain regime change. Moreover, such work would establish whether the model is valid for the *class* of events of regime transformation and not just for textile regimes. If a regime was developed without the underlying factors identified as being of critical significance, then the factors would obviously not be necessary. And if the theory always needed to be supplemented by other variables, then doubt would be cast on the sufficiency of the argument. The clearer the operationalization and specification of variables in other areas, the easier it would be to judge if in fact either of these two possibilities were the case. With respect to meta-regimes, a focus on other areas would help in addressing my argument that a cognitive approach is best suited to an analysis of principles and norms, while structural theories are better for examining changes in rules and procedures.

PROSPECTS FOR TEXTILE TRADE

In many ways it is difficult to be optimistic about the likelihood of smooth transitions favorable to cooperation in textile and apparel trade. In fact the international systemic analysis, which proved highly successful in explaining regime change in this issue-area, would cast doubt on the prospects for organized trade in general. There is now increasing pressure to institute severe protectionist measures on a unilateral basis in this area. How can this study contribute to better policymaking?

From a U.S. perspective, an understanding of the process of regime transformation is clearly essential. American decision makers have failed to learn how to negotiate in the textile and apparel area—in part, no doubt, a result of continual changes in personnel. Thus, in the most recent negotiations in 1981, the United States chose the tactic of starting out with a protectionist position, which it then planned to change in response to demands from the LDCs. Only after preliminary negotiations and conflict did the United States realize that the key "opponent" was the EEC—not the LDCs. Organized trade in textiles will succeed or fail depending on whether or not a compromise can be reached between the two major powers in this area—the United States and the EEC. When the EEC came out with a highly protectionist position of its own, this merely supported protectionist elements in the United States and has led to much more protectionism than key U.S. policymakers would like. Understanding collaborative processes is clearly more important when one is no longer a hegemon.

What can the LDCs do when faced with protectionism and a regime that is used to justify increasing protectionism rather than to constrain it? These problems faced by LDCs are important to the industrialized world, as it is only through increasing manufactured exports (given the instability in commodity markets) that LDCs will be able to grow rapidly and service their huge debts owed to Western banks. As Barry Sullivan, chairman of the First National Bank of Chicago, recently argued, "a principal condition for stabilizing the international financial situation" is the containment of protectionist forces.[4]

Although better bargaining in bilaterals and efforts to collaborate in the international negotiations have been tried by the LDCs, such efforts only work under very specific conditions.[5] The United States—as we have seen—was willing throughout the 1960s and part of the 1970s to give LDCs flexibility in their bilateral agreements (and other concessions) in exchange for comprehensive agreements with the minimum mandated growth rate. But the few remaining elements in the U.S. government willing to have such policies now find themselves besieged with protectionist pressures from the domestic industries. Elsewhere, I have suggested that the LDCs and the U.S. government must learn to play on the potential splits between the textile and apparel industries in the United States.[6] A similar split can be fostered in other developed countries.

What are the LDCs to do? The prospects for LDC collaboration are not very good in the face of attempts by developed countries to play off certain LDCs against others in the negotiations. While certain changes can be made at the margin, on the whole it is unpleasant to play a mercantilist game when one is weak.

THE CYCLE REPEATS?

Are the arrangements in textile and apparel trade the wave of the future? Will the cycle of (1) increasing import competition; (2) voluntary export restraints in the face of threatened unilateral controls; (3) new producers taking the place of those under restraint; (4) organized liberal protectionism; (5) evasion and widening scope of regimes; and (6) eventual collapse followed by a system of organized protection, repeat itself in autos, steel, semiconductors, and personal computers?[7] For illustrative purposes, let us take a brief look at trade in steel, color televisions, and autos.

In the case of these three industries, import competition in these politically significant sectors has led to voluntary export restraints or unilateral controls. Japan voluntarily restrained its steel exports to the United States in 1969, agreed to an Orderly Marketing Agreement (OMA) in color televisions with the United States in 1977, and a VER to the United States in autos in 1981. It also has restraints on its exports of autos, steel, televisions, and videotape recorders to the EEC countries.

Surging imports led the United States to push a VER on Japanese color television producers in 1977. Yet as this is an industry with comparatively low barriers to entry, new producers sprang up to fill the gap left by the Japanese restraint. Taiwan doubled its color television exports and the South Koreans quadrupled theirs from 1977 to 1978. As a consequence, the United States moved to control exports with OMAs from these countries in 1978. These OMAs, renewed in 1980, were allowed to expire in 1982 as major U.S. companies producing color televisions (Zenith excepted) moved offshore to produce in the Far East and Mexico.

Although costs of entry are high, governments have subsidized domestic steel for national security reasons and also to develop backward linkages as part of an imports substitution industrialization strategy. In response to growing steel imports—which increased their proportion of the U.S. market from 5 percent of consumption 1961 to 16.7 percent in 1968—the United States threatened both the Europeans and Japanese with quotas unless they agreed to "voluntary" export restraints.[8] Under this pressure, both Japan and the EEC agreed to limit their exports to the United States. As Curtis and Vastine note, "Central to the arrangement was the fiction that the Japanese and European producers 'offered' the arrangement to the U.S. State Department."[9] Obviously, the United States did not wish to appear to be violating GATT. With European and Japanese producers adhering to the VERs, unrestrained producers took up most of the slack; their exports increased by 70 percent in just two years.[10]

In 1976, the U.S. International Trade Commission ruled that stainless steel and alloy tool steel were being subsidized by Canada, Sweden, Japan, and the EEC. President Ford then attempted to negotiate OMAs with these countries; when only Japan acquiesced, he imposed a three-year quota against the other producers. A Japanese VER to the EEC led to a call by the American Iron and Steel Institute (AISI) for the United

States to control the diversion of all types of Japanese steel from the European to the American market. With the EEC negotiating with Brazil, South Africa, South Korea, Spain, Australia, and COMECON producers, French President Giscard D'Estaing echoed the 1975 position of the AISI and called for "organized free trade" in steel.[11]

Subsequently, in return for U.S. Steel dropping its antidumping petitions, the EEC and Japan agreed to an American trigger price system in late 1977. This program set a minimum price level based on Japanese production costs below which there would be an automatic presumption of dumping with a threat of countervailing duties. While this proved satisfactory at first, as numerous producers sold steel just above the trigger price, U.S. producers once again filed antidumping actions. In 1980 the trigger price was raised 12 percent.[12] When the industry once again filed a massive antidumping case in 1982, however, the Reagan administration dropped the trigger price system. It instead chose to pressure the EEC into a VER agreement.

After a ten-month battle, the EEC agreed to limit its shipments in products covering some 90 percent of European exports to the United States to 5.44 percent on average of the American market. In return, European steel makers were exempted from antidumping prosecution (which thus allowed them to subsidize their exports and slash prices as needed to ensure that they would fill their quota).[13] Now, however, other exporters wanted the same kind of deal. But, as one source reported, "The Reagan Administration, however, has been reluctant to duplicate the U.S.-Europe pact for fear of moving further toward dividing the world steel market among a series of cartels."[14]

On July 5, 1983, President Reagan, under pressure from specialty steel producers, adopted an ITC recommendation to impose a four-year tariff increase on these products. This move infuriated the Europeans and on January 16, 1984, the EEC retaliated by imposing quotas on American chemicals and sporting goods. During the fall, the United States negotiated OMAs with many exporting countries. The election year exhibited a marked increase in protectionist pressure. In November, the American Iron and Steel Institute (AISI) had called for legislative quotas for the first time. On January 24, Bethlehem Steel filed a complaint with the ITC requesting that the Reagan administration limit carbon-steel imports to 15 percent from the current 22 percent of the U.S. market for five years. On July 11, the ITC ruled in Bethlehem's favor, giving Reagan until September 24 to act on the ITC's action. As this book goes to press, the administration is attempting to negotiate new OMAs with the Europeans to quell the domestic political uproar that could develop should he choose not to implement the quota plan.

Now that more and more producers are entering the world steel market,[15] efforts to develop a global marketing arrangement should increase.

Protectionist developments in the auto industry are still unfolding. In 1980, with a slackening demand for oversize U.S. cars and with Japanese exports (which comprised almost 80 percent of U.S. auto imports) having doubled in just two years,[16] the United States shifted its emphasis from encouraging Japan to allow more U.S. imports to pushing them to limit exports. In November, the U.S. ITC rejected a United Auto Workers plea for restrictions, arguing that imports resulted from a failure of U.S. auto manufacturers to produce small cars. Congress then entered the picture, urging Reagan to impose import restraints. The administration was able to head off cries from a protectionist Congress by getting the Japanese to agree to a VER in May 1981 (an accord the Japanese have since renewed repeatedly). While domestic pressure for lower quotas and local content requirements continues, higher profits for American producers appear to have diminished the intensity of protectionist demands.

We see that in the cases of steel and color televisions, developments have reached step three of our hypothesized progression of protectionism. Increasing imports have led to VERs and new producers have entered the picture. In autos, step three has not yet occurred. Yet in none of these sectors has step four been reached—that of organized liberal protectionism with an international regime. To understand why, the theory developed in this study is helpful. When the United States was confronted with textile competition in the late 1950s, it was still an overall trade hegemon with a strong interest in preserving the GATT. The STA and LTA were designed, therefore, to restrain unilateral controls from undermining the GATT, a factor I have referred to as nesting constraints. However, the problem of import competition in steel, color televisions, and autos manifested itself during a period of eroding overall trade hegemony, and therefore, even though the United States was still a hegemonic steel and auto importer, decision makers no longer felt the need to keep arrangements in these sectors from eroding the GATT.

With respect to the desire to form a regime, there are two factors in connection with controlling the behavior of other countries. One is to prevent new producers from jumping into the importer's market when other exporters are restrained. We saw this happen in textiles, steel, and color televisions, but the problem was handled in color televisions by the U.S. government seeking restraints from other producers. The fact that U.S. manufacturers in this industry moved offshore also diminished protectionist pressures. High barriers to entry in automobile production have prevented other countries from filling the void created by Japanese auto restraints to the United States and Europe. In steel, however, while high costs of entry served to restrain new producers in the past, increasing investment supported by governments and advancing technology has led to a variety of new entrants (Argentina, Brazil, Mexico, India, Taiwan, Spain) into the market.

The second factor connected with controlling the behavior of other countries is diversion. When one importer restrains certain producers, they seek export markets elsewhere. In the late 1950s, the EEC's textile barriers led to a diversion to the U.S. market and thus U.S. policymakers sought to develop a regime to control European behavior. This process was reversed in the early 1970s when U.S. controls on Far Eastern producers led to flooding of the European market. This phenomenon has repeated itself in steel as American producers repeatedly complained that the EEC's restrictive actions against the Japanese have led to diversion of steel to the American market. Finally, in autos, no new producers have entered the market (South Korea is currently preparing to significantly increase exports) because of the constraints on entering production discussed above. This contributes to the lack of incentive for government officials to seek an international regime.

Finally, from an organization and information cost perspective, VERs are a low-cost solution in the auto and steel cases as there are still relatively few exporters of these products. However, even this has changed as more and more LDCs are entering the steel markets. After the 1982 U.S.-EEC accord, new entrants clamored for guaranteed quota shares for the U.S. market. The ensuing negotiations have proved costly, both in time and in the acrimony they have generated. Of the sectors besides textiles discussed here, the demand for a regime appears to be the highest in steel trade.

We have reviewed the three structural factors that would encourage the demand for a regime, but cognitive factors affecting the development of a meta-regime may also play a role. When textile trade was seen to be a problem in the late 1950s and early 1960s, there was a widespread hope shared by almost all countries that a sector-specific international regime could be a solution to the problem of competition over market shares. Although the LDCs were never enthusiastic about trade restrictions, they did recognize that a "reasonable" rate of export growth might facilitate the industrial adjustment process in developed countries. But the increasingly protectionist turn of the MFA has led to cognitive dissensus about the prospects of orderly trade, both in textiles and in other sectors, and has undermined the GATT. The recent Tokyo Round negotiations reflect the erosion of GATT norms in the face of increasing sector-specific conflict.[17] With structural and cognitive factors running against the development of a regime, the textile regime is likely to be both unique and short-lived.

In whatever areas the LDCs have developed the capacity to export manufactures that are highly competitive with the products of developed countries, the response has been toward protectionism. From color televisions to autos and steel, increased LDC competition has been met with protection. In the absence of a hegemonic power to police a system of organized trade, domestic special interests in the DCs have had the freedom to run rampant. Whether we are on a slippery slope or merely a staircase that might allow us to climb back toward greater liberalism, the movement from postwar liberalism to posthegemonic protectionism is readily evident and increasing its thrust. In light of international systemic configurations and protectionist domestic coalitions, the prospects for organized international trade are dismal at best. In fact, efforts to pursue organized trade may actually *facilitate* protectionist actions since the mechanisms for restraining trade already exist. In such a situation, domestic protectionist interests can focus their efforts on seeking protection through existing arrangements. For example, if we are to move to a strong protectionist regime (and there are some signs that we are moving in that direction), then the LDCs might actually find themselves to be better off without any international multilateral accord whatsoever.

The most important postwar experiment in organized trade is coming to an end. Rather than a stable equilibrium point, liberal protectionism now appears to be merely a temporary phase between liberalism and protectionism. If the slide toward protectionism is to be reversed, the key trading powers in the world today, the United States and the EEC, must learn to collaborate positively. Faced with an international debt crisis, decision makers must take the link between trade and finance seriously: if the LDCs are to finance their debts, they must export to the developed countries. Although it is difficult to be optimistic, we must hope that government officials will make efforts to build countercoalitions of consumers, bankers, exporters, and enlightened individuals to resist accelerating protectionist pressures and generate pressures for liberal trade policies. In fact, Robert Samuelson noted in a September 12, 1984, *Washington Post* commentary:

In the past few months, steel users, copper users, major retailers and farm groups have all vigorously protested proposed new trade restrictions. Their energetic opposition is new and could change the politics of trade protection. It belies the conventional wisdom that victims of protectionism won't organize against workers and firms whose jobs and survival are jeopardized.[18]

This study has examined efforts at collaboration and sought to develop and test a theory of international regime transformation. For the most part, the approach I used was successful in explaining changes in textile trade. Although an understanding of change in this area is helpful for scientific purposes and may help policymakers in the long run, in the short run knowledge may lead to frustration for policymakers rather than to power, as the variables we examined cannot be easily manipulated. In the long run, understanding how the whole system works and knowing where intervention can and cannot take place may be the best way of developing policy advice. As we contemplate weaving new regimes, every thread of knowledge helps.

Chronology of Events

1955 September   Fourteen countries invoke GATT Article XXXV against Japan.

       December   Japan announces first restraint action on cotton textile and apparel goods to the U.S. commencing January 1956.

1956 September   Japan restrains exports of cotton textile and apparel goods to the U.S. for five years beginning January 1957.

1957 November   U.K. restricts imports of cotton textile and apparel products from China.

1958 May   Noordwijk Agreement on reexport of cotton textiles to other members signed by trade associations of Austria, Belgium, France, Italy, Netherlands, Norway, Switzerland, and West Germany.

1958 December   Hong Kong agrees to restrict cotton textile and apparel goods to the U.K. starting January 1959.

1959 February   U.S. makes effort to have Hong Kong restrain its cotton textile and apparel exports. Effort comes to an end without success in early 1960.

       September   India and Pakistan agree to restrain cotton textile and apparel exports to the U.K.

1958 to 1960   Europeans employ a variety of illegal restrictions on cotton textile and apparel imports from LDCs.

1960 November   GATT members agree on a definition of "Market Disruption."

1961 July   Short-Term Arrangement on Cotton Textiles agreed to commencing October 1, 1961.

1962	February	Long-Term Arrangement on Cotton Textiles agreed to commencing October 1, 1962.
1962 to 1967		Various bilateral agreements concluded and unilateral restraints imposed under the LTA.
1963	(December) to 1964	U.S. tries and fails to secure an international agreement in the area of wool textiles and apparel.
1965	June	U.S. fails to obtain restraints on Japanese wool product exports.
1966	June	U.K. implements global quota scheme in violation of the LTA.
1967	April	LTA renewed for three years commencing October 1967.
1969	April	U.S. attempts unsuccessfully to have the Europeans agree to a regime covering actions by countries in the area of wool and man-made fiber trade.
1970	October	LTA renewed again.
1969 to 1971		U.S. tries and eventually succeeds in having Far Eastern suppliers restrain exports of wool and man-made fiber products to the American market.
1973	December	Multi-Fiber Arrangement agreed to commencing January 1, 1974.
1977	July to December	EEC and the U.S. negotiate bilateral agreements with LDCs prior to agreeing to renewal of MFA.
1977	December	MFA renewed for four years with clause allowing "jointly agreed reasonable departures."
1981	December	MFA renewed a second time for four years and seven months. Numerous clauses further weaken the MFA and allow greater protectionist action.

Appendixes

Appendix A
Short-Term Arrangement on Cotton Textiles

ANNEX   PR 531

GENERAL AGREEMENT ON TARIFFS AND TRADE
21 July 1961

TEXT OF ARRANGEMENTS REGARDING INTERNATIONAL TRADE IN COTTON TEXTILES

THE PARTICIPATING COUNTRIES recognize the need to take cooperative and constructive action with a view to the development of world trade and that such action should be designed to facilitate economic expansion and in particular to promote the development of the less-developed countries by providing increasing access for their exports of manufactured products.

They take note, however, that in some countries situations have arisen which, in the view of these countries, cause or threaten to cause "disruption" of the market for cotton textiles. In using the expression "disruption" the countries concerned have in mind situations of the kind described in the Decision of the CONTRACTING PARTIES of 19 November 1960 the relevant extract from which is annexed as Appendix A to this Agreement.

The participating countries desire to deal with these problems in such a way as to provide growing opportunities for exports of these products provided that the development of this trade proceeds in a reasonable and orderly manner so as to avoid disruptive effects in individual markets and on individual lines of production.

I. SHORT-TERM ARRANGEMENT

Pending a long-term solution the participating countries agree to deal with immediate problems relating to cotton textiles through international action designed, at the same time:

   (i) to significantly increase access to markets where imports are at present subject to restriction;
  (ii) to maintain orderly access to markets where restrictions are not at present maintained; and
 (iii) to secure from exporting countries, where necessary, a measure of restraint in their export policy so as to avoid disruptive effects in import markets.

Accordingly the participating countries agree to adopt the following short-term arrangement for the twelve-month period beginning 1 October 1961.

A. A participating country, if unrestricted imports of cotton textiles are causing or threatening to cause disruption of its domestic market, may request any participating country to restrain, at a specified level not lower than the level prevailing for the twelve-month period ending 30 June 1961, its total exports of any category (see Appendix B) of cotton textiles causing or threatening to cause such disruption, and failing agreement within thirty days, the requesting country may decline to accept imports at a level higher than the specified level.* In critical circumstances, action may be taken provisionally by either country involved while the request is under discussion. Nothing in this arrangement shall prevent the negotiation of mutually acceptable bilateral arrangements on other terms.

It is intended by the participating countries that this procedure will be used sparingly, with full regard for their agreed objective of attaining and safeguarding maximum freedom of trade, and only to avoid disruption of domestic industry resulting from an abnormal increase in imports.

---

*In Canada, there is no legislation whereby imports may be limited in a precise quantitative manner as envisaged in this paragraph. The provision available for limiting imports in order to avoid injury or a threat of injury to a domestic industry is contained in Section 40 A(7)(c) of the Customs Act which authorizes the application of special values for duty purposes. These special values cannot be used to achieve a precise level of imports. Accordingly, the participating countries recognize that, should Canada find it necessary to take action to limit imports pursuant to this arrangement, it would not be in a position to ensure that imports would not fall below the minimum level as defined in this paragraph.

B. A country requested to restrain its exports to a specified level may exceed the specified level for any category by 5 per cent provided that its total exports to the requesting country of the categories of products subject to restraint do not exceed the aggregate for all the categories.

C. If a requesting country determines that a shift in the pattern of imports within any category is producing undue concentration of imports of any particular item and that such concentration is causing or threatening disruption, the requesting country may, under the procedure set forth in paragraph A above, request the producing country to restrain its total exports of the said item during the 12 months beginning 1 October 1961 to a prescribed level not lower than that which prevailed during the year ending 30 June 1961.

D. Participants agree to take action to prevent circumvention or frustration of this short-term arrangement by non-participants, or by transshipment, or by substitution of directly competitive textiles. In particular, if the purposes of this arrangement are being frustrated or are in danger of being frustrated through the substitution of directly competitive textiles, the provisions of paragraph A above shall apply to such goods, to the extent necessary to prevent such frustration.

E. Participating countries presently maintaining quantitative restrictions on cotton textile imports shall, as from 1 January 1962, significantly increase access to their markets by countries the exports from which are now restricted. A specific statement of the new access will be forthcoming.

F. This short-term arrangement shall be valid for a period of 12 months, beginning on 1 October 1961: however, the provisions of section E above shall enter into force not later than 1 January 1962.

G. In accordance with GATT provisions for joint consultations the parties to this arrangement shall meet as necessary to consider any problems arising out of the application of this Agreement. Such consultations could, in particular, take place in the event that a country, the exports of which are under restraint as a result of action taken under paragraph A above, considers that experience shows that the level of restraint is inequitable.

II. *LONG-TERM ARRANGEMENT*

A. Participating countries agree to create a Provisional Cotton Textile Committee and to request the CONTRACTING PARTIES to confirm the establishment of the Committee at the nineteenth session.

The Committee shall:

1. undertake work looking toward a long-term solution to the problems in the field of cotton textiles on the basis of the guiding principles set out in the Preamble to this Agreement.
2. Collect all useful data for this purpose.
3. At an early date, not later than 30 April 1962, make recommendations for such long-term solution.

B. The discussions and consultations to be undertaken by the Committee on the long-term problem shall be of the kind provided for by the Market Disruption Committee at the seventeenth session of the CONTRACTING PARTIES. The Committee shall, as appropriate, from time to time report to this Committee and to Committee III of the Expansion of Trade Programme on progress made and on its findings.

C. The Provisional Cotton Textile Committee referred to in this article shall meet on 9 October 1961 to initiate consideration of this long-term problem.

Appendix B
Definition of Market Disruption

PR 531

A

Extract from the CONTRACTING PARTIES'
Decision of 19 November 1960

"These situations [market disruption] generally contain the following elements in combination:

  (i) a sharp and substantial increase or potential increase of imports of particular products from particular sources;
 (ii) these products are offered at prices which are substantially below those prevailing for similar goods of comparable quality in the market of the importing country;
(iii) there is serious damage to domestic producers or threat thereof;
 (iv) the price differentials referred to in paragraph (ii) above do not arise from governmental intervention in the fixing or formation of prices or from dumping practices.

In some situations other elements are also present and the enumeration above is not, therefore, intended as an exhaustive definition of market disruption."

B

Cotton Textile Categories

List of Categories	*Unit*
1. Cotton yarn, carded, singles, not ornamented, etc.	lb.
2. Cotton yarn, plied, carded, not ornamented, etc.	
3. Cotton yarn, singles, combed, not ornamented, etc.	
4. Cotton yard, plied, combed, not ornamented, etc.	
5. Ginghams, carded yarn	Sq. yds.
6. Ginghams, combed yarn	
7. Velveteens	
8. Corduroy	
9. Sheeting, carded yarn	
10. Sheeting, combed yarn	
11. Lawns, carded yarn	
12. Lawns, combed yarn	
13. Voiles, carded yarn	
14. Voiles, combed yarn	
15. Poplin and broadcloth, carded yarn	
16. Poplin and broadcloth, combed yarn	
17. Typewriter ribbon cloth	
18. Print cloth type shirting, 80 x 80 type, carded yarn	
19. Print cloth type shirting, other than 80 x 80 type, carded yarn	
20. Shirting, carded yarn	
21. Shirting, combed yarn	
22. Twill and sateen, carded yarn	
23. Twill and sateen, combed yarn	
24. Yarn-dyed fabrics, except ginghams, carded yarn	
25. Yarn-dyed fabrics, except ginghams, combed yarn	
26. Fabrics, n.o.s., carded yarn	
27. Fabrics, n.o.s., combed yarn	
28. Pillowcases, plain, carded yarn	Numbers
29. Pillowcases, plain, combed yarn	
30. Dish towels	
31. Towels, other than dish towels	
32. Handkerchiefs	Dozen
33. Table damasks and manufactures of	lb.
34. Sheets, carded yarn	Numbers
35. Sheets, combed yarn	

List of Categories (cont.)	*Unit*
36. Bedspreads	Numbers
37. Braided and woven elastics	lb.
38. Fishing nets	
39. Gloves and mittens	Doz.
40. Hose and half hose	Doz. prs.
41. Men's and boys' all white T. shirts, knit or crocheted	Doz.
42. Other T. shirts	Doz.
43. Knitshirts, other than T. shirts and sweatshirts (including infants)	Doz.
44. Sweaters and cardigans	Doz.
45. Men's and boys' shirts, dress, not knit or crocheted	Doz.
46. Men's and boys' shirts, sport, not knit or crocheted	Doz.
47. Men's and boys' shirts, work, not knit or crocheted	Doz.
48. Maincoats, 3/4 length or over	Doz.
49. All other coats	Doz.
50. Men's and boys' trousers, slacks and shorts (outer), not knit or crocheted	Doz.
51. Women's, misses' and children's trousers, slacks and shorts (outer), not knit or crocheted	Doz.
52. Blouses, and blouses combined with skirts, trousers, or shorts	Doz.
53. Women's, misses', children's and infants' dresses (including nurses' and other uniform dresses), not knit or crocheted	Doz.
54. Playsuits, sunsuits, washsuits, croopers, rompers, etc. (except blouse and shorts; blouse and trouser; or blouse, shorts and skirt sets)	Doz.
55. Dressing gowns, including bathrobes and beach-robes, lounging gowns, dusters and housecoats, not knit or crocheted	Doz.
56. Men's and boys' undershirts (not T. shirts)	Doz.
57. Men's and boys' briefs and undershorts	Doz.
58. Drawers, shorts and briefs (except men's and boys' briefs), knit or crocheted	Doz.
59. All other underwear, not knit or crocheted	Doz.
60. Nightwear and pyjamas	Doz.
61. Brassieres and other body supporting garments	Doz.
62. Other knitted or crocheted clothing	Units or lbs.

List of Categories (cont.)   Unit

63. Other clothing, not knit or crocheted   Units or lbs.
64. All other cotton textile items   Units or lbs.

To whatever extent this List of Categories may present questions in the light of established listing practices of any participating country, such questions shall be resolved by consultation between the countries concerned or by the process of joint consultation referred to in Paragraph G of the Short-term Arrangement.

*   *   *

State—RD, Wash., D.C.

Appendix C
Text of the Long-Term Arrangement on Cotton Textiles*

RECOGNIZING the need to take co-operative and constructive action with a view to the development of world trade;

RECOGNIZING further that such action should be designed to facilitate economic expansion and promote the development of less-developed countries possessing the necessary resources, such as raw materials and technical skills, by providing larger opportunities for increasing their exchange earnings from the sale in world markets of products which they can efficiently manufacture;

NOTING, however, that in some countries situations have arisen which, in the view of these countries, cause or threaten to cause "disruption" of the market for cotton textiles;

DESIRING to deal with these problems in such a way as to provide growing opportunities for exports of these products, provided that the development of this trade proceeds in a reasonable and orderly manner so as to avoid disruptive effects in individual markets and on individual lines of production in both importing and exporting countries;

DETERMINED, in carrying out these objectives, to have regard to the Declaration on Promotion of the Trade of Less-developed Countries

*The negotiation of this arrangement was concluded in Geneva on an *ad referendum* basis on February 9, 1962 by representatives of the following governments: Australia, Austria, Canada, Denmark, India, Japan, Norway, Pakistan, Portugal, Spain, Sweden, United Kingdom (also representing Hong Kong), United States, and the member states of European Economic Community (Belgium, France, Federal Republic of Germany, Italy, Luxembourg, and Netherlands).

adopted by Ministers at their meeting during the nineteenth session of the CONTRACTING PARTIES in November 1961;

The PARTICIPATING COUNTRIES have agreed as follows:

Article 1

In order to assist in the solution of the problems referred to in the Preamble to this Arrangement, the participating countries are of the opinion that it may be desirable to apply, during the next few years, special practical measures of international co-operation which will assist in any adjustment that may be required by changes in the pattern of world trade in cotton textiles. They recognize, however, that the measures referred to above do not affect their rights and obligations under the General Agreement on Tariffs and Trade (hereinafter referred to as the GATT). They also recognize that, since these measures are intended to deal with the special problems of cotton textiles, they are not to be considered as lending themselves to application in other fields.

Article 2

1. Those participating countries still maintaining restrictions inconsistent with the provisions of the GATT on imports of cotton textiles from other participating countries agree to relax those restrictions progressively each year with a view to their elimination as soon as possible.

2. Without prejudice to the provisions of paragraphs 2 and 3 of Article 3, no participating country shall introduce new import restrictions, or intensify existing import restrictions, on cotton textiles, insofar as this would be inconsistent with its obligations under the GATT.

3. The participating countries at present applying import restrictions to cotton textiles imported from other participating countries undertake to expand access to their markets for such cotton textiles so as to reach, by the end of the period of validity of the present Arrangement, for the products remaining subject to restrictions at that date, taken as a whole, a level corresponding to the quotas opened in 1962, for such products, as increased by the percentage mentioned in Annex A.

Where bilateral arrangements exist, annual increases shall be determined within the framework of bilateral negotiations. It would, however, be desirable that each annual increase should correspond as closely as possible to one fifth of the overall increase.

4. The participating countries concerned shall administer their remaining restrictions on imports of cotton textiles from participating countries

in an equitable manner and with due regard to the special needs and situation of the less-developed countries.

5. Notwithstanding the provisions of paragraph 3 above, if, during the licensing period preceding the entry into force of this Arrangement, a specific basic quota is nil or negligible, the quota for the succeeding licensing period will be established at a reasonable level by the participating importing country concerned in consultation with the participating exporting country or countries concerned. Such consultation would normally take place within the framework of the bilateral negotiations referred to in paragraph 3 above.

6. Participating countries shall, as far as possible, eliminate import restrictions on the importation, under a system of temporary importation for re-export after processing, of cotton textiles originating in other participating countries.

7. The participating countries shall notify the Cotton Textiles Committee as early as possible, and in any case not less than one month before the beginning of the licensing period, of the details of any quota or import restriction referred to in this Article.

Article 3

1. If imports from a participating country or countries into another participating country of certain cotton textile products not subject to import restrictions should cause or threaten to cause disruption in the market of the importing country, that country may request the participating country or countries whose exports of such products are, in the judgment of the importing country, causing or threatening to cause market disruption to consult with a view to removing or avoiding such disruption. In its request the importing country will, at its discretion, indicate the specific level at which it considers that exports of such products should be restrained, a level which shall not be lower than the one indicated in Annex B. The request shall be accompanied by a detailed, factual statement of the reasons and justification for the request; the requesting country shall communicate the same information to the Cotton Textiles Committee at the same time.

2. In critical circumstances, where an undue concentration of imports during the period specified in paragraph 3 below would cause damage difficult to repair, the requesting participating country may, until the end of the period, take the necessary temporary measures to limit the imports referred to in paragraph 1 above from the country or countries concerned.

3. If, within a period of sixty days after the request has been received

by the participating exporting country or countries, there has been no agreement either on the request for export restraint or on any alternative solution, the requesting participating country may decline to accept imports for retention from the participating country or countries referred to in paragraph 1 above of the cotton textile products causing or threatening to cause market disruption, at a level higher than that specified in Annex B, in respect of the period starting on the day when the request was received by the participating exporting country.

4. In order to avoid administrative difficulties in enforcing a given level of restraint on cotton textiles subject to measures taken under this article, the participating countries agree that there should be a reasonable degree of flexibility in the administration of these measures. Where restraint is exercised for more than one product the participating countries agree that the agreed level for any one product may be exceeded by 5 per cent provided that the total exports subject to restraint do not exceed the aggregate level for all products so restrained on the basis of a common unit of measurement to be determined by the participating countries concerned.

5. If participating countries have recourse to the measures envisaged in this Article, they shall, in introducing such measures, seek to avoid damage to the production and marketing of the exporting country and shall co-operate with a view to agreeing on suitable procedures, particularly as regards goods which have been, or which are about to be, shipped.

6. A participating country having recourse to the provisions of this Article shall keep under review the measures taken under this Article with a view to their relaxation and elimination as soon as possible. It will report from time to time, and in any case once a year, to the Cotton Textiles Committee on the progress made in the relaxation or elimination of such measures. Any participating country maintaining measures under this Article shall afford adequate opportunity for consultation to any participating country or countries affected by such measures.

7. Participating importing countries may report the groups or categories to be used for statistical purposes to the Cotton Textiles Committee. The participating countries agree that measures envisaged in this Article should only be resorted to sparingly, and should be limited to the precise products or precise groups or categories of products causing or threatening to cause market disruption, taking full account of the agreed objectives set out in the Preamble to this Arrangement. Participating countries shall seek to preserve a proper measure of equity where market disruption is caused or threatened by imports from more than one participating country and when resort to the measures envisaged in this Article is unavoidable.

Article 4

Nothing in this Arrangement shall prevent the application of mutually acceptable arrangements on other terms not inconsistent with the basic objectives of this Arrangement. The participating countries shall keep the Cotton Textiles Committee fully informed on such arrangements, or the parts thereof, which have a bearing on the operation of this Arrangement.

Article 5

The participating countries shall take steps to ensure, by the exchange of information, including statistics on imports and exports when requested, and by other practical means, the effective operation of this Arrangement.

Article 6

The participating countries agree to avoid circumvention of this Arrangement by trans-shipment or re-routing, substitution of directly competitive textiles and action by non participants. In particular, they agree on the following measures.

(a) *Trans-shipment*
    The participating importing and exporting countries agree to collaborate with a view to preventing circumvention of this Arrangement by trans-shipment or re-routing and to take appropriate administrative action to avoid such circumvention. In cases where a participating country has reason to believe that imports shipped to it from another participating country and purporting to have originated in that country did not originate there, it may request that country to consult with it with a view to assisting in the determination of the real origin of the goods.

(b) *Substitution of directly competitive textiles*
    It is not the intention of the participating countries to broaden the scope of this Arrangement beyond cotton textiles but, when there exists a situation or threat of market disruption in an importing country in terms of Article 3, to prevent the circumvention of this Arrangement by the deliberate substitution for cotton of directly competitive fibers. Accordingly, if the importing participating country concerned has reason to believe that imports of products in which this substitution has taken place have increased abnormally, that is that this substitution has taken place solely in order to circumvent that provision of this Arrangement,

that country may request the exporting country concerned to investigate the matter and to consult with it with a view to reaching agreement upon measures designed to prevent such circumvention. Such request shall be accompanied by a detailed, factual statement of the reasons and justification for the request. Failing agreement in the consultation within 60 days of such request, the importing participating country may decline to accept imports of the products concerned as provided for in Article 3 and, at the same time, any of the participating countries concerned may refer the matter to the Cotton Textiles Committee which shall make such recommendations to the parties concerned as may be appropriate.

(c) *Non-participants*

The participating countries agree that, if it proves necessary to resort to the measures envisaged in Article 3 above, the participating importing country or countries concerned shall take steps to ensure that the participating country's exports against which such measures are taken shall not be restrained more severely than the exports of any country not participating in this Arrangement which are causing, or threatening to cause, market disruption. The participating importing country or countries concerned will give sympathetic consideration to any representations from participating exporting countries to the effect that this principle is not being adhered to or that the operation of this Arrangement is frustrated by trade with countries not party to this Arrangement. If such trade is frustrating the operation of this Arrangement, the participating countries shall consider taking such action as may be consistent with their law to prevent such frustration.

Article 7

1. In view of the safeguards provided for in this Arrangement the participating countries shall, as far as possible, refrain from taking measures which may have the effect of nullifying the objectives of this Arrangement.

2. If a participating country finds that its interests are being seriously affected by any such measure taken by another participating country, that country may request the country applying such measure to consult with a view to remedying the situation.

3. If the participating country so requested fails to take appropriate remedial action within a reasonable length of time, the requesting participating country may refer the matter to the Cotton Textiles Committee which shall promptly discuss such matter and make such comments to the participating countries as it considers appropriate. Such comments

would be taken into account should the matter subsequently be brought before the CONTRACTING PARTIES under the procedures of Article XXIII of the GATT.

Article 8

The Cotton Textiles Committee, as established by the CONTRACTING PARTIES at their nineteenth session, shall be composed of representatives of the countries party to this Arrangement and shall fulfill the responsibilities provided for it in this Arrangement.

(a) The Committee shall meet from time to time to discharge its functions. It will undertake studies on trade in cotton textiles as the participating countries may decide. It will collect the statistical and other information necessary for the discharge of its functions and will be empowered to request the participating countries to furnish such information.
(b) Any case of divergence of view between the participating countries as to the interpretation or application of this Arrangement may be referred to the Committee for discussion.
(c) The Committee shall review the operation of this Arrangement once a year and report to the CONTRACTING PARTIES. The review during the third year shall be a major review of the Arrangement in the light of its operation in the preceding years.
(d) The Committee shall meet not later than one year before the expiry of this Arrangement, in order to consider whether the Arrangement should be extended, modified or discontinued.

Article 9

For purposes of this Arrangement the expression "cotton textiles" includes yarns, piece-goods, made-up articles, garments, and other textile manufactured products, in which cotton represents more than 50 per cent (by weight) of the fiber content, with the exception of handloom fabrics of the cottage industry.

Article 10

For purposes of this Arrangement, the term "disruption" refers to situations of the kind described in the Decision of the CONTRACTING PARTIES of 19 November 1960, the relevant extract from which is reproduced in Annex C.

Article 11

1. This Arrangement is open for acceptance, by signature or otherwise, to governments parties to the GATT or having provisionally acceded to that Agreement, provided that if any such government maintains restrictions on the import of cotton textiles from other participating countries, that government shall, prior to its accepting this Arrangement, agree with the Cotton Textiles Committee on the percentage by which it will undertake to increase the quotas other than those maintained under Article XII or Article XVIII of the GATT.

2. Any government which is not party to the GATT or has not acceded provisionally to the GATT may accede to that arrangement on terms to be agreed between that government and the participating countries. These terms would include a provision that any government which is not a party to the GATT must undertake, on acceding to this Arrangement, not to introduce new import restrictions or intensify existing import restrictions, on cotton textiles, insofar as such action would, if that government had been a party to the GATT, be inconsistent with its obligations thereunder.

Article 12

1. This Arrangement shall enter into force on 1 October 1962 subject to the provisions of paragraph 2 below.

2. The countries which have accepted this Arrangement shall, upon the request of one or more of them, meet within one week prior to 1 October 1962 and, at that meeting, if a majority of these countries so decide, the provisions of paragraph 1 above may be modified.

Article 13

Any participating country may withdraw from this Arrangement upon the expiration of sixty days from the day on which written notice of such withdrawal is received by the Executive Secretary of GATT.

Article 14

This Arrangement shall remain in force for five years.

Article 15

The Annexes to this Arrangement constitute an integral part of this Arrangement.

ANNEXES

ANNEX A

For purposes of Article 2 the percentages referred to in paragraph 3 thereof shall be:

For Austria	95 percent
For Denmark	15 percent
For European Economic Community	88 percent
For Norway	15 percent
For Sweden	15 percent

ANNEX B

1. (a) The level below which imports or exports of cotton textile products causing or threatening to cause market disruption may not be restrained under the provisions of Article 3 shall be the level of actual imports or exports of such products during the twelve-month period terminating three months preceding the month in which the request for consultation is made.

(b) Where a bilateral agreement on the yearly level of restraint exists between participating countries concerned covering the twelve-month period referred to in paragraph (a), the level below which imports of cotton textile products causing or threatening to cause market disruption may not be restrained under the provisions of Article 3 shall be the level provided for in the bilateral agreement in lieu of the level of actual imports or exports during the twelve-month period referred to in paragraph (a).

Where the twelve-month period referred to in paragraph (a) overlaps in part with the period covered by the bilateral agreement, the level shall be:

(i) the level provided for in the bilateral agreement, or the level of actual imports or exports, whichever is higher, for the months where the period covered by the bilateral agreement and the twelve-month period referred to in paragraph (a) overlap; and

(ii) the level of actual imports or exports for the months where no overlap occurs.

2. Should the restraint measures remain in force for another twelve-month period, the level for that period shall not be lower than the level specified for the preceding twelve-month period, increased by 5 per cent.

In exceptional cases, where it is extremely difficult to apply the level referred to above, a percentage between 5 and 0 may be applied in the light of market conditions in the importing country and other relevant factors after consultation with the exporting country concerned.

3. Should the restraining measures remain in force for further periods, the level for each subsequent twelve-month period shall not be lower than the level specified for the preceding twelve-month period, increased by 5 per cent.

ANNEX C

Extract from the CONTRACTING PARTIES' Decision of 19 November 1960

"These situations [market disruption] generally contain the following elements in combination:

(i) a sharp and substantial increase or potential increase of imports of particular products from particular sources;
(ii) these products are offered at prices which are substantially below those prevailing for similar goods of comparable quality in the market of the importing country;
(iii) there is serious damage to domestic producers or threat thereof;
(iv) the price differentials referred to in paragraph (ii) above do not arise from governmental intervention in the fixing or formation of prices or from dumping practices.

In some situations other elements are also present and the enumeration above is not, therefore, intended as an exhaustive definition of market disruption."

ANNEX D

For the purposes of applying Article 9, the following list of the groups or sub-groups of the S.I.T.C. is suggested. This list is illustrative and should not be considered as being exhaustive.

	SITC Rev.	BTN
I Cotton yarns and fabrics	651.3	55.05
	.4	.06
	652	.07
		.08
		.09
		58.04A
II Cotton made-up articles and special fabrics	ex 653.7	ex 46.02
	ex 654	ex 58.01-03
	ex 655	ex 58.05-10
	ex 656	ex 59.01-17
	ex 657	ex 60.01
		ex 62.01-05
		ex 65.01-02
III Cotton Clothing	ex 841	ex 60.02-06
		ex 61.01-11
		ex 65.03-07

ANNEX E

Interpretative Notes

1. Ad. Article 3, paragraph 3

In Canada, there is no legislation whereby imports may be limited in a precise quantitative manner as envisaged in this paragraph. The provision available for limiting imports in order to avoid injury or a threat of injury to a domestic industry is contained in Section 40 A(7)(c) of the Customs Act which authorizes the application of special values for duty purposes. These special values cannot be used to achieve a precise level of imports. Accordingly, the participating countries recognize that, should Canada find it necessary to take action to limit imports pursuant to this arrangement, it would not be in a position to ensure that imports would not fall below the minimum level as defined in this paragraph.

2. Ad. Article 9

Notwithstanding the provisions of Article 9, any country which is applying a criterion based on value will be free to continue to use that criterion for the purposes of Article 9.

Appendix D
Text of the MFA

ARRANGEMENT REGARDING INTERNATIONAL
TRADE IN TEXTILES

PREAMBLE

Recognizing the great importance of production and trade in textile products of wool, man-made fibres and cotton for the economies of many countries, and their particular importance for the economic and social development of developing countries and for the expansion and diversification of their export earnings, and conscious also of the special importance of trade in textile products of cotton for many developing countries;

Recognizing further the tendency for an unsatisfactory situation to exist in world trade in textile products and that this situation, if not satisfactorily dealt with, could work to the detriment of countries participating in trade in textile products, whether as importers or exporters, or both, adversely affect prospects for international co-operation in the trade field, and have unfortunate repercussions on trade relations generally;

Noting that this unsatisfactory situation is characterized by the proliferation of restrictive measures, including discriminatory measures, that are inconsistent with the principles of the General Agreement on Tariffs and Trade and also that, in some importing countries, situations have arisen which, in the view of these countries, cause or threaten to cause disruption of their domestic markets;

Desiring to take co-operative and constructive action, within a multi-lateral framework, so as to deal with the situation in such a way as to promote on a sound basis the development of production and expansion of trade in textile products and progressively to achieve the reduction of trade barriers and the liberalization of world trade in these products;

Recognizing that, in pursuit of such action, the volatile and continually evolving nature of production and trade in textile products should be constantly borne in mind and the fullest account taken of such serious economic and social problems as exist in this field in both importing and exporting countries, and particularly in the developing countries;

Recognizing further that such action should be designed to facilitate economic expansion and to promote the development of developing countries possessing the necessary resources, such as materials and technical skills, by providing larger opportunities for such countries, including countries that are, or that may shortly become, new entrants in the field of textile exports to increase their exchange earnings from the sale in world markets of products which they can efficiently produce;

Recognizing that future harmonious development of trade in textiles particularly having regard to the needs of developing countries, also depends importantly upon matters outside the scope of this Arrangement, and that such factors in this respect include progress leading both to the reduction of tariffs and to the maintenance and improvement of schemes of generalized preferences, in accordance with the Tokyo Declaration;

Determined to have full regard to the principles and objectives of the General Agreement on Tariffs and Trade (hereinafter referred to as the GATT) and, in carrying out the aims of this Arrangement, effectively to implement the principles and objectives agreed upon in the Tokyo Declaration of Ministers dated 14 September 1973 concerning the Multilateral Trade Negotiations;

THE PARTIES TO THIS ARRANGEMENT have agreed as follows:

Article 1

1. It may be desirable during the next few years for special practical measures of international co-operation to be applied by the participating

countries* in the field of textiles with the aim of eliminating the difficulties that exist in this field.

2. The basic objectives shall be to achieve the expansion of trade, the reduction of barriers to such trade and the progressive liberalization of world trade in textile products, while at the same time ensuring the orderly and equitable development of this trade and avoidance of disruptive effects in individual markets and on individual lines of production in both importing and exporting countries. In the case of those countries having small markets, an exceptionally high level of imports and a correspondingly low level of domestic production, account should be taken of the avoidance of damage to those countries' minimum viable production of textiles.

3. A principal aim in the implementation of this Arrangement shall be to further the economic and social development of developing countries and secure a substantial increase in their export earnings from textile products and to provide scope for a great share for them in world trade in these products.

4. Actions taken under this Arrangement shall not interrupt or discourage the autonomous industrial adjustment processes of participating countries. Furthermore, actions taken under this Arrangement should be accompanied by the pursuit of appropriate economic and social policies, in a manner consistent with national laws and systems, required by changes in the pattern of trade in textiles and in the comparative advantage of participating countries, which policies would encourage businesses which are less competitive internationally to move progressively into more viable lines of production or into other sectors of the economy and provide increased access to their markets for textile products from developing countries.

5. The application of safeguard measures under this Arrangement, subject to recognized conditions and criteria and under the surveillance of an international body set up for that purpose, and in conformity with the principles and objectives of this Arrangement, may in exceptional circumstances become necessary in the field of trade in textile products, and should assist any process of adjustment which would be required by the changes in the pattern of world trade in textile products. The parties to this Arrangement undertake not to apply such measures except in accordance with the provisions of this Arrangement with full regard to the impact of such measures on other parties.

---

*The expressions "participating country," "participating exporting country" and "participating importing country," wherever they appear in this Arrangement, shall be deemed to include the European Economic Community.

6. The provisions of this Arrangement shall not affect the rights and obligations of the participating countries under the GATT.

7. The participating countries recognize that, since measures taken under this Arrangement are intended to deal with the special problems of textile products, such measures should be considered as exceptional, and not lending themselves to application in other fields.

Article 2

1. All existing unilateral quantitative restrictions, bilateral agreements and any other quantitative measures in force which have a restrictive effect shall be notified in detail by the restraining participating country, upon acceptance of or accession to this Arrangement, to the Textiles Surveillance Body, which shall circulate the notifications to the other participating countries for their information. Measures or agreements which are not notified by a participating country within sixty days of its acceptance of, or accession to, this Arrangement shall be considered to be contrary to this Arrangement and shall be terminated forthwith.

2. Unless they are justified under the provisions of the GATT (including its Annexes and Protocols), all unilateral quantitative restrictions and any other quantitative measures which have a restrictive effect and which are notified in accordance with paragraph 1 above shall be terminated within one year of the entry into force of this Arrangement, unless they are the subject of one of the following procedures to bring them into conformity with the provisions of this Arrangement:

(i) inclusion in a programme, which should be adopted and notified to the Textiles Surveillance Body within one year from the date of coming into force of this Arrangement, designed to eliminate existing restrictions in stages within a maximum period of three years from the entry into force of this Arrangement and taking account of any bilateral agreement either concluded or in course of being negotiated as provided for in (ii) below; it being understood that a major effort will be made in the first year, covering both a substantial elimination of restrictions and a substantial increase in the remaining quotas;

(ii) inclusion, within a period of one year from the entry into force of this Arrangement, in bilateral agreements negotiated, or in course of negotiation, pursuant to the provisions of Article 4; if, for exceptional reasons, any such bilateral agreement is not concluded within the period of one year, this period, following consultations by the participating countries concerned and with the concurrence

of the Textiles Surveillance Body, may be extended by not more
than one year;
(iii) inclusion in agreements negotiated or measures adopted pursuant
to the provisions of Article 3.

3. Unless justified under the provisions of the GATT (including its
Annexes and Protocols) all existing bilateral agreements notified in accordance with paragraph 1 of this Article shall, within one year of the
entry into force of this Arrangement, either be terminated or justified
under the provisions of this Arrangement or modified to conform there-
with.

4. For the purposes of paragraphs 2 and 3 above the participating
countries shall afford full opportunity for bilateral consultation and
negotiation aimed at arriving at mutually acceptable solutions in accordance with Articles 3 and 4 of this Arrangement and permitting from the
first year of the acceptance of this Arrangement the elimination as complete as possible of the existing restrictions. They shall report specifically
to the Textiles Surveillance Body within one year of the entry into force
of this Arrangement on the status of any such actions taken or negotiations undertaken pursuant to this Article.

5. The Textiles Surveillance Body shall complete its review of such
reports within ninety days of their receipt. In its review it shall consider
whether all the actions taken are in conformity with this Arrangement. It
may make appropriate recommendations to the participating countries
directly concerned so as to facilitate the implementation of this Article.

Article 3

1. Unless they are justified under the provisions of the GATT (including its Annexes and Protocols) no new restrictions on trade in textile
products shall be introduced by participating countries nor shall existing
restrictions be intensified, unless such action is justified under the provisions of this Article.

2. The participating countries agree that this Article should only be
resorted to sparingly and its application shall be limited to the precise
products and to countries whose exports of such products are causing
market disruption as defined in Annex A taking full account of the agreed
principles and objectives set out in this Arrangement and having full regard to the interests of both importing and exporting countries. Participating countries shall take into account imports from all countries and
shall seek to preserve a proper measure of equity. They shall endeavour
to avoid discriminatory measures where market disruption is caused by

imports from more than one participating country and when resort to the application of this Article is unavoidable, bearing in mind the provisions of Article 6.

3. If, in the opinion of any participating importing country, its market in terms of the definition of market disruption in Annex A is being disrupted by imports of a certain textile product not already subject to restraint, it shall seek consultations with the participating exporting country or countries concerned with a view to removing such disruption. In its request the importing country may indicate the specific level at which it considers that exports of such products should be restrained, a level which shall not be lower than the general level indicated in Annex B. The exporting country or countries concerned shall respond promptly to such request for consultations. The importing country's request for consultations shall be accompanied by a detailed factual statement of the reasons and justification for the request, including the latest data concerning elements of market disruption, this information being communicated at the same time by the requesting country to the Chairman of the Textiles Surveillance Body.

4. If, in the consultation, there is mutual understanding that the situation calls for restrictions on trade in the textile product concerned, the level of restriction shall be fixed at a level not lower than the level indicated in Annex B. Details of the agreement reached shall be communicated to the Textile Surveillance Body which shall determine whether the agreement is justified in accordance with the provisions of this Arrangement.

5. (i) If, however, after a period of sixty days from the date on which the request has been received by the participating exporting country or countries, there has been no agreement either on the request for export restraint or on any alternative solution, the requesting participating country may decline to accept imports for retention from the participating country or countries referred to in paragraph 3 above of the textiles and textile products causing market disruption (as defined in Annex A) at a level for the twelve-month period beginning on the day when the request was received by the participating exporting country or countries not less than the level provided for in Annex B. Such level may be adjusted upwards to avoid undue hardships to the commercial participants in the trade involved to the extent possible consistent with the purposes of this Article. At the same time the matter shall be brought for immediate attention to the Textiles Surveillance Body.

(ii) However, it shall be open for either party to refer the matter to the Textiles Surveillance Body before the expiry of the period of sixty days.

(iii) In either case the Textiles Surveillance Body shall promptly conduct the examination of the matter and make appropriate recommendations to the parties directly concerned within thirty days from the date on which the matter is referred to it. Such recommendations shall also be forwarded to the Textiles Committee and to the GATT Council for their information. Upon receipt of such recommendations the participating countries concerned should review the measures taken or contemplated with regard to their institution, continuation, modification or discontinuation.

6. In highly unusual and critical circumstances, where imports of a textile product or products during the period of sixty days referred to in paragraph 5 above would cause serious market disruption giving rise to damage difficult to repair, the importing country shall request the exporting country concerned to co-operate immediately on a bilateral emergency basis to avoid such damage, and shall, at the same time, immediately communicate to the Textiles Surveillance Body the full details of the situation. The countries concerned may make any mutually acceptable interim arrangement they deem necessary to deal with the situation without prejudice to consultations regarding the matter under paragraph 3 of this Article. In the event that such interim arrangement is not reached, temporary restraint measures may be applied at a level higher than that indicated in Annex B with a view, in particular, to avoiding undue hardship to the commercial participants in the trade involved. The importing country shall give, except where possibility exists of quick delivery which would undermine the purpose of such measure at least one week's prior notification of such action to the participating exporting country or countries and enter into, or continue, consultations under paragraph 3 of this Article. When a measure is taken under this paragraph either party may refer the matter to the Textiles Surveillance Body. The Textiles Surveillance Body shall conduct its work in the manner provided for in paragraph 5 above. Upon receipt of recommendations from the Textiles Surveillance Body the participating importing country shall review the measures taken, and report thereon to the Textiles Surveillance Body.

7. If recourse is had to measures under this Article, participating countries shall, in introducing such measures, seek to avoid damage to the production and marketing of the exporting countries, and particularly of the developing countries, and shall avoid any such measures taking a

form that could result in the establishment of additional non-tariff barriers to trade in textile products. They shall, through prompt consultations, provide for suitable procedures, particularly as regards goods which have been, or which are about to be, shipped. In the absence of agreement, the matter may be referred to the Textiles Surveillance Body, which shall make the appropriate recommendations.

8. Measures taken under this Article may be introduced for limited periods not exceeding one year, subject to renewal or extension for additional periods of one year, provided that agreement is reached between the participating countries directly concerned on such renewal or extension. In such cases, the provisions of Annex B shall apply. Proposals for renewal or extension, or modification or elimination or any disagreement thereon shall be submitted to the Textiles Surveillance Body, which shall make the appropriate recommendations. However, bilateral restraint agreements under this Article may be concluded for periods in excess of one year in accordance with the provisions of Annex B.

9. Participating countries shall keep under review any measures they have taken under this Article and shall afford any participating country or countries affected by such measures, adequate opportunity for consultation with a view to the elimination of the measures as soon as possible. They shall report from time to time, and in any case once a year, to the Textiles Surveillance Body on the progress made in the elimination of such measures.

Article 4

1. The participating countries shall fully bear in mind, in the conduct of their trade policies in the field of textiles, that they are, through the acceptance of, or accession to, this Arrangement, committed to a multilateral approach in the search for solutions to the difficulties that arise in this field.

2. However, participating countries may, consistently with the basic objectives and principles of this Arrangement, conclude bilateral agreements on mutually acceptable terms in order, on the one hand, to eliminate real risks of market disruption (as defined in Annex A) in importing countries and disruption to the textile trade of exporting countries, and on the other hand to ensure the expansion and orderly development of trade in textiles and the equitable treatment of participating countries.

3. Bilateral agreements maintained under this Article shall, on overall terms, including base levels and growth rates, be more liberal than measures provided for in Article 3 of this Arrangement. Such bilateral agreements shall be designed and administered to facilitate the export in full of

the levels provided for under such agreements and shall include provisions assuring substantial flexibility for the conduct of trade thereunder, consistent with the need for orderly expansion of such trade and conditions in the domestic market of the importing country concerned. Such provisions should encompass areas of base levels, growth, recognition of the increasing interchangeability of natural, artificial and synthetic fibres, carry forward, carryover, transfers from one product grouping to another and such other arrangements as may be mutually satisfactory to the parties to such bilateral agreements.

4. The participating countries shall communicate to the Textiles Surveillance Body full details of agreements entered into in terms of this Article within thirty days of their effective date. The Textiles Surveillance Body shall be informed promptly when any such agreements are modified or discontinued. The Textiles Surveillance Body may make such recommendations as it deems appropriate to the parties concerned.

Article 5

Restrictions on imports of textile products under the provisions of Article 3 and 4 shall be administered in a flexible and equitable manner and over-categorization shall be avoided. Participating countries shall, in consultation, provide for arrangements for the administration of the quotas and restraint levels, including the proper arrangement for allocation of quotas among the exporters, in such a way as to facilitate full utilization of such quotas. The participating importing country should take full account of such factors as established tariff classification and quantitative units based on normal commercial practices in export and import transactions, both as regards fibre composition and in terms of competing for the same segment of its domestic market.

Article 6

1. Recognizing the obligations of the participating countries to pay special attention to the needs of the developing countries, it shall be considered appropriate and consistent with equity obligations for those importing countries which apply restrictions under this Arrangement affecting the trade of developing countries to provide more favourable terms with regard to such restrictions, including elements such as base level and growth rates, than for other countries. In the case of developing countries whose exports are already subject to restrictions and if the restrictions are maintained under this Arrangement, provisions should be made for higher quotas and liberal growth rates. It shall, however, be

borne in mind that there should be no undue prejudice to the interests of established suppliers or serious distortion in existing patterns of trade.

2. In recognition of the need for special treatment for exports of textile products from developing countries, the criterion of past performance shall not be applied in the establishment of quotas for their exports of products from those textile sectors in respect of which they are new entrants, in the markets concerned and a higher growth rate shall be accorded to such exports, having in mind that this special treatment should not cause undue prejudice to the interests of established suppliers or create serious distortions in existing patterns of trade.

3. Restraints on exports from participating countries whose total volume of textile exports is small in comparison with the total volume of exports of other countries should normally be avoided if the exports from such countries represent a small percentage of the total imports of textiles covered by this Arrangement of the importing country concerned.

4. Where restrictions are applied to trade in cotton textiles in terms of this Arrangement, special consideration will be given to the importance of this trade to the developing countries concerned in determining the size of quotas and the growth element.

5. Participating countries shall not, as far as possible, maintain restraints on trade in textile products originating in other participating countries which are imported under a system of temporary importation for re-export after processing, subject to a satisfactory system of control and certification.

6. Consideration shall be given to special and differential treatment to re-imports into a participating country of textile products which that country has exported to another participating country for processing and subsequent re-importation, in the light of the special nature of such trade without prejudice to the provisions of Article 3.

Article 7

The participating countries shall take steps to ensure, by the exchange of information, including statistics on imports and exports when requested, and by other practical means, the effective operation of this Arrangement.

Article 8

1. The participating countries agree to avoid circumvention of this Arrangement by trans-shipment, re-routing, or action by non-participants. In particular, they agree on the measures provided for in this Article.

2. The participating countries agree to collaborate with a view to taking appropriate administrative action to avoid such circumvention. Should any participating country believe that the Arrangement is being circumvented and that no appropriate administrative measures are being applied to avoid such circumvention, that country should consult with the exporting country of origin and with other countries involved in the circumvention with a view to seeking promptly a mutually satisfactory solution. If such a solution is not reached the matter shall be referred to the Textiles Surveillance Body.

3. The participating countries agree that if resort is had to the measures envisaged in Article 3 and 4, the participating importing country or countries concerned shall take steps to ensure that the participating country's exports against which such measures are taken shall not be restrained more severely than the exports of similar goods of any country not party to this Arrangement which are causing, or actually threatening, market disruption. The participating importing country or countries concerned will give sympathetic consideration to any representations from participating exporting countries to the effect that this principle is not being adhered to or that the operation of this Arrangement is frustrated by trade with countries not party to this Arrangement. If such trade is frustrating the operation of this Arrangement, the participating countries shall consider taking such actions as may be consistent with their law to prevent such frustrations.

4. The participating countries concerned shall communicate to the Textiles Surveillance Body full details of any measures or arrangements taken under this Article or any disagreement and, when so requested, the Textiles Surveillance Body shall make reports or recommendations as appropriate.

Article 9

1. In view of the safeguards provided for in this Arrangement the participating countries shall, as far as possible, refrain from taking additional trade measures which may have the effect of nullifying the objectives of this Arrangement.

2. If a participating country finds that its interests are being seriously affected by any such measure taken by another participating country, that country may request the country applying such measure to consult with a view to remedying the situation.

3. If the consultation fails to achieve a mutually satisfactory solution within a period of sixty days the requesting participating country may refer the matter to the Textiles Surveillance Body which shall promptly

discuss such matter, the participating country concerned being free to refer the matter to that body before the expiry of the period of sixty days if it considers that there are justifiable grounds for so doing. The Textiles Surveillance Body shall make such recommendations to the participating countries as it considers appropriate.

Article 10

1. There is established within the framework of GATT a Textiles Committee consisting of representatives of the parties to this Arrangement. The Committee shall carry out the responsibilities ascribed to it under this Arrangement.

2. The Committee shall meet from time to time and at least once a year to discharge its functions and to deal with those matters specifically referred to it by the Textiles Surveillance Body. It shall prepare such studies as the participating countries may decide. It shall undertake an analysis of the current state of world production and trade in textile products, including any measures to facilitate adjustment and it shall present its views regarding means of furthering the expansion and liberalization of trade in textile products. It will collect the statistical and other information necessary for the discharge of its functions and will be empowered to request the participating countries to furnish such information.

3. Any case of divergence of view between the participating countries as to the interpretation or application of this Arrangement may be referred to the Committee for its opinion.

4. The Committee shall once a year review the operation of this Arrangement and report thereon to the GATT Council. To assist in this review, the Committee shall have before it a report from the Textiles Surveillance Body, a copy of which will also be transmitted to the Council. The review during the third year shall be a major review of this Arrangement in the light of its operation in the preceding years.

5. The Committee shall meet not later than one year before the expiry of this Arrangement in order to consider whether the Arrangement should be extended, modified or discontinued.

Article 11

1. The Textiles Committee shall establish a Textiles Surveillance Body to supervise the implementation of this Arrangement. It shall consist of a Chairman and eight members to be appointed by the parties to this Arrangement on a basis to be determined by the Textiles Committee so as

to ensure its efficient operation. In order to keep its membership balanced and broadly representative of the parties to this Arrangement provision shall be made for rotation of the members as appropriate.

2. The Textiles Surveillance Body shall be considered as a standing body and shall meet as necessary to carry out the functions required of it under this Arrangement. It shall rely on information to be supplied by the participating countries, supplemented by any necessary details and clarification it may decide to seek from them or from other sources. Further, it may rely for technical assistance on the services of the GATT secretariat and may also hear technical experts proposed by one or more of its members.

3. The Textiles Surveillance Body shall take the action specifically required of it in articles of this Arrangement.

4. In the absence of any mutually agreed solution in bilateral negotiations or consultations between participating countries provided for in this Arrangement, the Textiles Surveillance Body at the request of either party, and following a thorough and prompt consideration of the matter, shall make recommendations to the parties concerned.

5. The Textiles Surveillance Body shall, at the request of any participating country, review promptly any particular measures or arrangements which that country considers to be detrimental to its interests where consultations between it and the participating countries directly concerned have failed to produce a satisfactory solution. It shall make recommendations as appropriate to the participating country or countries concerned.

6. Before formulating its recommendations on any particular matter referred to it, the Textiles Surveillance Body shall invite participation of such participating countries as may be directly affected by the matter in question.

7. When the Textiles Surveillance Body is called upon to make recommendations or findings it shall do so, except when otherwise provided in this Arrangement, within a period of thirty days whenever practicable. All such recommendations or findings shall be communicated to the Textiles Committee for the information of its members.

8. Participating countries shall endeavour to accept in full the recommendations of the Textiles Surveillance Body. Whenever they consider themselves unable to follow any such recommendations, they shall forthwith inform the Textiles Surveillance Body of the reasons therefor and of the extent, if any, to which they are able to follow the recommendations.

9. If, following recommendations by the Textiles Surveillance Body, problems continue to exist between the parties, these may be brought

before the Textiles Committee or before the GATT Council through the normal GATT procedures.

10. Any recommendations and observations of the Textiles Surveillance Body would be taken into account should the matters related to such recommendations and observations subsequently be brought before the CONTRACTING PARTIES to the GATT, particularly under the procedures of Article XXIII of the GATT.

11. The Textiles Surveillance Body shall, within fifteen months of the coming into force of this Arrangement, and at least annually thereafter, review all restrictions on textile products maintained by participating countries at the commencement of this Arrangement, and submit its findings to the Textiles Committee.

12. The Textiles Surveillance Body shall annually review all restrictions introduced or bilateral agreements entered into by participating countries concerning trade in textile products since the coming into force of this Arrangement, and required to be reported to it under the provisions of this Arrangement, and report annually its findings to the Textiles Committee.

Article 12

1. For the purposes of this Arrangement, the expression "textiles" is limited to tops, yarns, piece-goods, made-up articles, garments and other textile manufactured products (being products which derive their chief characteristics from their textile components) of cotton, wool, man-made fibres, or blend thereof, in which any or all of those fibres in combination represent either the chief value of the fibres or 50 per cent or more by weight (or 17 per cent or more by weight of wool) of the product.

2. Artificial and synthetic staple fibre, tow, waste, simple mono- and multi-filaments, are not covered by paragraph 1 above. However, should conditions of market disruption (as defined in Annex A) be found to exist for such products, the provisions of Article 3 of this Arrangement (and other provisions of this Arrangement directly relevant thereto) and paragraph 1 of Article 2 shall apply.

3. This Arrangement shall not apply to developing country exports of handloom fabrics of the cottage industry, or hand-made cottage industry products made of such handloom fabrics, or to traditional folklore handicraft textiles products, provided that such products are properly certified under arrangements established between the importing and exporting participating countries concerned.

4. Problems of interpretation of the provisions of this Article should be resolved by bilateral consultation between the parties concerned and any difficulties may be referred to the Textiles Surveillance Body.

Article 13

1. This Arrangement shall be deposited with the Director-General to the CONTRACTING PARTIES to the GATT. It shall be open for acceptance, by signature or otherwise, by governments contracting parties to the GATT or having provisionally acceded to the GATT and by the European Economic Community.

2. Any government which is not a contracting party to the GATT, or has not acceded provisionally to the GATT, may accede to this Arrangement on terms to be agreed between that government and the participating countries. These terms would include a provision that any government which is not a contracting party to the GATT must undertake, on acceding to this Arrangement, not to introduce new import restrictions or intensify existing import restrictions, on textile products, in so far as such action would, if that government had been a contracting party to the GATT, be inconsistent with its obligations thereunder.

Article 14

1. This Arrangement shall enter into force on 1 January 1974.

2. Notwithstanding the provisions of paragraph 1 of this Article, for the application of the provisions of Article 2, paragraphs 2, 3 and 4 the date of entry into force shall be 1 April 1974.

3. Upon request of one or more parties which have accepted or acceded to this Arrangement a meeting shall be held within one week prior to 1 April 1974. Parties which at the time of the meeting have accepted or acceded to the Arrangements may agree on any modification of the date envisaged in paragraph 2 of this Article which may appear necessary and is consistent with the provisions of Article 16.

Article 15

Any participating country may withdraw from this Arrangement upon the expiration of sixty days from the day on which written notice of such withdrawal is received by the Director-General to the CONTRACTING PARTIES to the GATT.

Article 16

This Arrangement shall remain in force for four years.

Article 17

The Annexes to this Arrangement constitute an integral part of this Arrangement.

Done at Geneva this twentieth day of December one thousand nine hundred and seventy-three, in a single copy in the English, French and Spanish languages, each text being authentic.

ANNEX A

I. The determination of a situation of "market disruption," as referred to in this Arrangement, shall be based on the existence of serious damage to domestic producers or actual threat thereof. Such damage must demonstrably be caused by the factors set out in paragraph II below and not by factors such as technological changes or changes in consumer preference which are instrumental in switches to like and/or directly competitive products made by the same industry, or similar factors. The existence of damage shall be determined on the basis of an examination of the appropriate factors having a bearing on the evolution of the state of the industry in question such as: turnover, market share, profits, export performance, employment, volume of disruptive and other imports, production, utilization of capacity, productivity and investments. No one or several of these factors can necessarily give decisive guidance.

II. The factors causing market disruption referred to in paragraph I above and which generally appear in combination are as follows:

(i) a sharp and substantial increase or imminent increase of imports of particular products from particular sources. Such an imminent increase shall be a measurable one and shall not be determined to exist on the basis of allegation, conjecture or mere possibility arising, for example, from the existence of production capacity in the exporting countries;

(ii) these products are offered at prices which are substantially below those prevailing for similar goods of comparable quality in the market of the importing country. Such prices shall be compared both with the price for the domestic product at comparable stage of commercial transaction, and with the prices which normally prevail for such products sold in the ordinary course of trade and under open market conditions by other exporting countries in the importing country.

III. In considering questions of "market disruption" account shall be taken of the interests of the exporting country, especially in regard to its stage of development, the importance of the textile sector to the economy, the employment situation, overall balance of trade in textiles, trade balance with the importing country concerned and overall balance of payments.

ANNEX B

1. (*a*) The level below which imports or exports of textile products may not be restrained under the provisions of Article 3 shall be the level of actual imports or exports of such products during the twelve-month period terminating two months or, where data are not available, three months preceding the month in which the request for consultation is made, or, where applicable, the date of institution of such domestic procedure relating to market disruption in textiles as may be required by national legislation, or two months or, where data are not available, three months prior to the month in which the request for consultation is made as a result of such domestic procedure, whichever period is the later.

(*b*) Where a restraint on the yearly level of exports or imports exists between participating countries concerned, whether provided for under Article 2, 3 or 4, covering the twelve-month period referred to in paragraph (*a*), the level below which imports of textile products causing market disruption may not be restrained under the provisions of Article 3 shall be the level provided for in the restraint in lieu of the level of actual imports or exports during the twelve-month period referred to in paragraph (*a*).

Where the twelve-month period referred to in paragraph (*a*) overlaps in part with the period covered by the restraint, the level shall be:

(i) the level provided for in the restraint, or the level of actual imports or exports, whichever is higher, except in case of overshipment, for the months where the period covered by the restraint and the twelve-month period referred to in paragraph (*a*) overlap; and

(ii) the level of actual imports or exports for the months where no overlap occurs.

(*c*) If the period referred to in paragraph (*a*) is specially adverse for a particular exporting country due to abnormal circumstances, the past performance of imports from that country over a period of years should be taken into account.

(*d*) Where imports or exports of textile products subject to restraints were nil or negligible during the twelve-month period referred to in paragraph (*a*), a reasonable import level to take account of future possibilities of the exporting country shall be established through consultation between the participating countries concerned.

2. Should the restraint measures remain in force for another twelve-month period, the level for that period shall not be lower than the level specified for the preceding twelve-month period, increased by not less than 6 per cent for products under restraint. In exceptional cases where there are clear grounds for holding that the situation of market disruption will recur if the above growth rate is implemented, a lower positive growth rate may be decided upon after consultation with the exporting country or countries concerned. In exceptional cases where participating importing countries have small markets, an exceptionally high level of imports and a correspondingly low level of domestic production and where the implementation of the above growth rate would cause damage to those countries' minimum viable production, a lower positive growth rate may be decided upon after consultation with the exporting country or countries concerned.

3. Should the restraint measures remain in force for further periods, the level for each subsequent period shall not be lower than the level specified for the preceding twelve-month period, increased by six per cent, unless there is further new evidence which demonstrates, in accordance with Annex A, that implementation of the above growth rate would exacerbate the situation of market disruption. In these circumstances, after consultation with the exporting country concerned, and reference to the Textiles Surveillance Body in accordance with the procedures of Article 3 a lower positive growth rate may be applied.

4. In the event any restriction or limitation is established under Article 3 or 4 on a product or products as to which a restriction or limitation had been suppressed in accordance with the provisions of Article 2, such subsequent restriction or limitation shall not be re-established without full consideration of the limits of trade provided for under such suppressed restriction or limitation.

5. Where restraint is exercised for more than one product the participating countries agree that, provided that the total exports subject to restraint do not exceed the aggregate level for all products so restrained (on the basis of a common unit to be determined by the participating countries concerned), the agreed level for any one product may be exceeded by 7 per cent save in exceptionally and sparingly used circumstances where a lower percentage may be justified in which case that lower percentage shall be not less than 5 per cent. Where restraints are established for more years than one, the extent to which the total of the restraint level for one product or product group may, after consultation between the parties concerned, be exceeded in either year of any two subsequent years by carry forward and/or carryover is 10 per cent of which carry forward shall not represent more than 5 per cent.

6. In the application of the restraint levels and growth rates specified in paragraphs 1 to 3 above, full account shall be taken of the provisions of Article 6.

Appendix E
Protocol of Extension, MFA

RESTRICTED
COM.TEX/W/47
14 December 1977
Special Distribution

GENERAL AGREEMENT ON
TARIFFS AND TRADE

Textiles Committee

DRAFT PROTOCOL EXTENDING THE ARRANGEMENT
REGARDING INTERNATIONAL TRADE IN TEXTILES

THE PARTIES to the Arrangement Regarding International Trade in Textiles (hereinafter referred to as "the Arrangement").

ACTING pursuant to paragraph 5 of Article 10 of the Arrangement, and

REAFFIRMING that the terms of the Arrangement regarding the competence of the Textiles Committee and the Textiles Surveillance Body are maintained, and

CONFIRMING the understandings set forth in the Conclusions of the Textiles Committee adopted on ( ) December 1977, copy of which is attached herewith,

HEREBY AGREE as follows:

1. The period of validity of the Arrangement, set out in Article 16, shall be extended for a period of four years until 31 December 1981.

2. This Protocol shall be deposited with the Director-General to the CONTRACTING PARTIES to the GATT. It shall be open for acceptance, by signature or otherwise, by the parties to the Arrangement, by other governments accepting or acceding to the Arrangement pursuant to the provisions of Article 13 thereof and by the European Economic Community.

3. This Protocol shall enter into force on 1 January 1970 for the countries which have accepted it by that date. It shall enter into force for a country which accepts it on a later date as of the date of such acceptance.

Done at Geneva this   day of December one thousand nine hundred and seventy-seven in a single copy in the English, French and Spanish languages, each text being authentic.

Conclusions of the Textiles Committee adopted on   December 1977

1. The participants in the Arrangement exchanged view regarding the future of the Multifibre Arrangement (MFA).

2. It is clear from the annual and major review of the MFA undertaken by the Textiles Committee that certain importing and several exporting countries have encountered practical difficulties in the implementation of the provisions of the MFA. Discussions in this respect covered a wide range of areas of satisfaction as well as dissatisfaction. These difficulties, some of which are of a long-standing nature, affect seriously the trade and economic development of developing countries.

3. Members of the Textiles Committee recognized that there continued to be a tendency for an unsatisfactory situation to exist in world trade in textile products, and that such a situation, if not satisfactorily dealt with, could work to the detriment of countries participating in international trade in textile products, whether as importers or exporters or both. It could adversely affect prospects for international co-operation in the trade field and could have unfortunate repercussions on trade relations in general, and the trade of developing countries in particular.

4. Some participating countries, importing as well as exporting, felt that there was a need for modifications to be made to the text of the MFA. Others were of the opinion that any difficulties that may have arisen were due to problems of implementation, and that the provisions of the MFA are adequate to deal with such difficulties. It was agreed that any serious problems of textile trade should be resolved through consultations and negotiations.

5.1. As regards what was described by one major importing participant in its statement to this Committee as its pressing import problems, the Textiles Committee recognized that such problems should be resolved bilaterally under the provisions of Article 4 or Article 3, paragraphs 3 and 4.

5.2. The Committee noted one major importing participant's statement concerning the basis upon which it intended to achieve its stated objectives by bilateral consultations and negotiations and noted the expression of goodwill and flexibility made by certain exporting participants now predominant in the exporting of textile products of all the three fibres covered by the Arrangement.

5.3. The Committee agreed that, within the framework of the MFA, any such consultations and negotiations should be conducted in a spirit of equity and flexibility with a view to reaching a mutually acceptable solution under Article 4, paragraph 3 of Article 3, paragraphs 3 and 4, which does include the possibility of jointly agreed reasonable departures from particular elements in particular cases.

5.4. It was agreed that any such departures as mentioned in sub-paragraph 3 above would be temporary and that participants concerned shall return in the shortest possible time to the framework of the Arrangement.

5.5. The Committee also urged all participants concerned to move promptly to negotiate mutually acceptable solutions in the spirit of the MFA.

5.6. The Committee affirmed that in seeking such solutions, the interest of the developing countries, new entrants, and small suppliers shall be recognized, and the provisions of Article 1, paragraph 4, would be fully kept in view.

6. The Committee recognized that countries having small markets, an exceptionally high level of imports and a correspondingly low level of domestic production are particularly exposed to the trade problems mentioned in the preceding paragraphs, and that their problems should be resolved in a spirit of equity and flexibility. In the case of those countries, the provisions of Article 1, paragraph 2, should be fully implemented.

7. The Committee reaffirmed that the two organs of the Arrangement, the Textiles Committee and the Textiles Surveillance Body should continue to function effectively in their respective areas of competence.

8. It was reiterated that in the future implementation of the MFA, the special problems of developing countries shall be fully taken into account in a manner consistent with the provisions of the MFA, in particular Articles 1, paragraph 3, and 6 thereof.

9. All participants saw mutual co-operation as the foundation of the Arrangement and as the basis for dealing with problems in a way which would promote the objectives and aims of the MFA. Participants emphasized that the primary aims of the MFA are to ensure the expansion of trade in textile products particularly for the developing countries, and progressively to achieve the reduction of trade barriers and the liberalization of world trade in textile products while, at the same time, avoiding disruptive effects on individual markets and on individual lines of production in both importing and exporting countries. In this context, it was felt that in order to ensure the proper functioning of the MFA, all participants would refrain from taking measures on textiles covered by the MFA outside the provisions therein before exhausting all the relief measures provided in the MFA.

10. Taking into account the evolutionary and cyclical nature of trade in textiles and the importance to both importing and exporting countries of prior resolution of problems in a constructive and equitable manner for the interest of all concerned, and on the basis of the elements mentioned in paragraphs 1 through 9 above, the Textiles Committee considered that the MFA in its present form should be extended for a period of four years subject to confirmation by signature as from 15 December 1977 of a Protocol for this purpose.

Appendix F
Protocol Extending the Arrangement Regarding International Trade in Textiles

THE PARTIES to the Arrangement Regarding International Trade in Textiles (hereinafter referred to as "the Arrangement" or "MFA")

ACTING pursuant to paragraph 5 of Article 10 of the Arrangement, and

REAFFIRMING that the terms of the Arrangement regarding the competence of the Textiles Committee and the Textiles Surveillance Body are maintained, and CONFIRMING the understandings set forth in the Conclusions of the Textiles Committee adopted on 22 December 1981, a copy of which is attached herewith, HEREBY AGREE as follows:

1. The period of validity of the Arrangement set out in Article 16, shall be extended for a period of four years and seven months until 31 July 1986.

2. This Protocol shall be deposited with the Director-General to the CONTRACTING PARTIES to the GATT. It shall be open for acceptance, by signature or otherwise, by the Parties to the Arrangement, by other governments accepting or acceding to the Arrangement pursuant to provisions of Article 13 thereof and by the European Economic Community.

3. This Protocol shall enter into force on 1 January 1982 for the countries which have accepted it by that date. It shall enter into force for a country which accepts it on a later date as of the date of such acceptance.

Done at Geneva this twenty-second day of December, one thousand nine hundred and eighty-one, in a single copy in the English, French and Spanish languages, each text being authentic.

CONCLUSIONS OF THE TEXTILES COMMITTEE ADOPTED ON
22 DECEMBER 1981

1. The participants in the Arrangement exchanged views regarding the future of the Arrangement.

2. All participants saw mutual co-operation as the foundation of the Arrangement and as the basis for dealing with problems in a way which would promote the aims and objectives of the MFA. Participants emphasized that the primary aims of the MFA are to ensure the expansion of trade in textile products, particularly for the developing countries, and progressively to achieve the reduction of trade barriers and the liberalization of world trade in textile products while, at the same time, avoiding disruptive effects in individual markets and on individual lines of production in both importing and exporting countries. In this context, it was reiterated that a principal aim in the implementation of the Arrangement is to further the economic and social development of developing countries and to secure a substantial increase in their export earnings from textile products and to provide scope for a greater share for them in world trade in these products.

3. Members of the Textiles Committee recognized that there continued to be a tendency for an unsatisfactory situation to exist in world trade in textile products, and that such a situation, if not satisfactorily dealt with, could work to the detriment of countries participating in international trade in textile products, whether as importers or exporters or both. This situation could adversely affect prospects for international co-operation in the trade field and could have unfortunate repercussions on trade relations in general, and the trade of developing countries in particular.

4. Attention was drawn to the fact that decline in the rate of growth of per capita consumption in textiles and in clothing is an element which may be relevant to the recurrence or exacerbation of a situation of market disruption. Attention was also drawn to the fact that domestic markets may be affected by elements such as technological changes and changes in consumer preferences. In this connection it was recalled that the appropriate factors for the determination of a situation of market disruption as referred to in the Arrangement are listed in Annex A.

5. It was agreed that any serious problems of textile trade falling within the purview of the Arrangement should be resolved through consultations and negotiations under the relevant provisions thereof.

6. The Committee noted the important role of and the goodwill expressed by certain exporting countries now predominant in the exporting of textile products in all three fibres covered by the Arrangement in finding and contributing to mutually acceptable solutions to particular problems relative to particularly large restraint levels arising out of the application of the Arrangement as extended by the Protocol.

7. The participants recalled that safeguard measures could only be invoked if there existed a situation of market disruption—as defined in Annex A—of real risk thereof. Noting that Article 6 envisages that in the application of such measures developing countries, especially new entrants, small suppliers, and cotton producers shall be given more favourable terms than other countries, the Committee drew particular attention to paragraph 12 below.

8. With respect to the definition of market disruption contained in Annex A of the Arrangement, participants took due note that difficulties had arisen as to its application in practice, leading to misunderstandings between exporting countries and importing participants, which have had an adverse impact on the operation of the Arrangement. Consequently, and with a view to overcoming these difficulties, the participants agreed that the discipline of Annex A and the procedures of Articles 3 and 4 of the Arrangement should be fully respected and that request for action under these Articles shall be accompanied by relevant specific factual information. The participants further agreed that the situation prevailing when such action was requested should be periodically reviewed by the parties concerned, the Textiles Surveillance Body (TSB) being promptly informed of any resulting modifications under the terms of Articles 3, paragraph 9, and/or 4, paragraph 4.

9. It was recalled that in exceptional cases where there is a recurrence or exacerbation of a situation of market disruption as referred to in Annex A, and paragraphs 2 and 3 of Annex B, a lower positive growth rate for a particular product from a particular source may be agreed upon between the parties to a bilateral agreement. It was further agreed that where such agreement has taken into account the growing impact of a heavily utilized quota with a very large restraint level for the product in question from a particular source, accounting for a very large share of the market of the importing country for textiles and clothing, the exporting party to the agreement concerned may agree to any mutually acceptable arrangements with regard to flexibility.

10. The view was expressed that real difficulties may be caused in importing countries by sharp and substantial increases in imports as a result of significant differences between larger restraint levels negotiated in accordance with Annex B on the one hand and actual imports on the other. Where such significant difficulties stem from consistently underutilized larger restraint levels and cause or threaten serious and palpable damage to domestic industry, an exporting participant may agree to mutually satisfactory solutions or arrangements. Such solutions or arrangements shall provide for equitable and quantifiable compensation to the exporting participant to be agreed by both parties concerned.

11. The Committee recognized that countries having small markets, an exceptionally high level of imports and a correspondingly low level of domestic production are particularly exposed to the problems arising from imports causing market disruption as defined in Annex A, and that their problems should be resolved in the spirit of equity and flexibility in order to avoid damage to those countries' minimum viable production of textiles. In the case of those countries, the provisions of Article 1, paragraph 2, and Annex B, paragraph 2, should be fully implemented. The exporting participants may, in the case of countries referred to in this paragraph, agree to any mutually acceptable arrangements with regard to paragraph 5 of Annex B; special consideration in this respect would be given to their concerns regarding the avoidance of damage to these countries' minimum viable production of textiles.

12. The participating countries were conscious of the problems posed by restraints on exports of new entrants and small suppliers, as well as on exports of cotton textiles by cotton producing countries. They reaffirmed their commitment to the letter and intent of Article 6 of the Arrangement and to the effective implementation of this Article to the benefit of those countries. To this end they agreed that:

(a) Restraints on exports from small suppliers and new entrants should normally be avoided. For the purposes of Article 6, paragraph 3, shares in imports of textiles and those in clothing may be considered separately.

(b) Restraints on exports from new entrants and small suppliers should having regard to Article 6, paragraph 2, take due account of the future possibilities for the development of trade and the need to permit commercial quantities of imports.

(c) Exports of cotton textiles from cotton producing exporting countries should be given special consideration. Where restraints are applied, more favourable treatment should be given to these countries in terms of quotas, growth rates and flexibility in view of the importance of such trade to these countries, having due regard to the provisions of Annex B.

(d) The provisions of Annex B relating to exceptional circumstances and cases should be applied sparingly to exports from new entrants, small suppliers and trade in cotton textiles of cotton producing developing countries.

13. The Committee recalled that consideration is to be given to special and differential treatment which should be accorded to trade referred to in Article 6, paragraph 6.

14. Participants agreed to co-operate fully in dealing with problems relating to circumvention of the Arrangement, in the light of the provisions of Article 8 thereof. It was agreed that the appropriate administrative action referred to in Article 8, paragraph 2, should in principle, where evidence is available regarding the country of true origin and the circumstances of circumvention, include adjustment of charges to existing quota to reflect the country of true origin; any such adjustment together with its timing and scope being decided in consultation between the countries concerned, with a view to arriving at a mutually satisfactory solution. If such a solution is not reached any participant involved may refer the matter to the TSB in accordance with the provisions of Article 8, paragraph 2.

15. In pursuance of the objective of trade liberalization embodied in the Arrangement, the Committee reaffirmed the need to monitor adjustment policies and measures and the process of autonomous adjustment in terms of the provisions of Article 1, paragraph 4. To this end, the Committee decided that a Sub-Committee should be established to carry out activities previously performed by the Working Group on Adjustment Measures and to make a periodic review of developments in autonomous adjustment processes and in policies and measures to facilitate adjustment, as well as in production and trade in textiles, on the basis of material and information to be provided by participating countries. The Sub-Committee would report periodically to the Textiles Committee to enable the Committee to fulfill its obligations under Article 10, paragraph 2.

16. Participating countries reaffirmed their commitment to the objectives of the expansion of trade, reduction of barriers to such trade and the progressive liberalization of world trade in textile products, while recog-

nizing that these objectives also depend importantly upon matters outside the scope of the Arrangement, such as the reduction of tariffs.

17. In the context of the phasing out of restraints under the Arrangement, priority attention would be given to sectors of trade, e.g., wool tops, and suppliers for which the Arrangement provides for special and more favourable treatment as referred to in Article 6.

18. The participants reaffirmed the importance of the effective functioning of the two organs of the Arrangement, the Textiles Committee and the TSB, in their respective areas of competence. In this context, the participants emphasized the importance of the responsibilities of the TSB as set forth in Article 11 of the MFA.

19. The participants also reaffirmed that the role of the TSB is to exercise its functions as set out in Article 11 so as to help ensure the effective and equitable operation of the Arrangement and to further its objectives.

20. The Committee recognized the need for close cooperation among participants for the effective discharge of the TSB's responsibilities.

21. The participants also noted that, should any participant or participants be unable to accept the conclusions or recommendations of the Textiles Surveillance Body, or should, following its recommendations, problems continue to exist between the parties, the procedures set forth in Article 1, paragraphs 8, 9, 10 are available.

22. The participants reaffirmed the importance of Article 7 to the effective operation of the Arrangement.

23. It was felt that in order to ensure the proper functioning of the MFA, all participants should refrain from taking measures on textiles covered by the MFA, outside the provisions therein, before exhausting all the relief measures provided in the MFA.

24. Taking into account the evolutionary and cyclical nature of trade in textiles and the importance both to importing and exporting countries of prior resolution of problems in a constructive and equitable manner for the interest of all concerned, and on the basis of the elements mentioned in paragraphs 1 to 23 above, which supersede in their totality those adopted on 14 December 1977, the Textiles Committee considered that the Arrangement in its present form should be extended for a period of four years and seven months, subject to confirmation by signature as from 22 December 1981 of a Protocol for this purpose.

Notes

1. Growth of Protection and International Regimes

1. While the textile and apparel industries are quite distinct, I will use "textile" as shorthand for the two industries except where this would be a misleading term.

2. Mutual control through rules provides a way of overcoming "Prisoner's Dilemma" in international bargaining. For a discussion see Stein (1982).

3. While the rules have been circumvented, most countries still refrain from breaking them outright. Thus the GATT still survives to constrain national actions, in part out of a perception of interdependence by states.

4. See Finlayson and Zacher (1981) for an analytical discussion of the GATT.

5. Reich (1983), p. 783.

6. OECD (1965).

7. GATT (1966).

8. Juvet (1967).

9. Strange (1979).

10. Walters (1983), p. 27.

11. World Bank (1979). For instance, the NICs accounted for 82% of U.S. imports of LDCs clothing and 86% of electrical machinery in 1975. OECD, *Trade by Commodity Imports* (1975).

12. Cowhey and Long (1983).

13. Walters (1983), p. 27. See this article for a good discussion of the steel industry's problems.

14. For a discussion of industrial policy (or the lack thereof) in the United States, see Zysman and Tyson (1983).

15. *The New Republic,* March 28, 1983, pp. 16-21.

16. Gastrell (1897), p. 93.

17. USITC (1981).

18. See Wallerstein (1974) for a discussion of conflict between the Netherlands and the U.K. over markets in textiles and apparel.

19. Davis (1966).

20. In 1690 a 20% duty was imposed on textile and apparel products, and in 1701 they were prohibited under an act entitled "An Act for the more effective employing the Poor by encouraging the Manufactures of this Kingdom." Ibid.

21. With regard to the protectionist action taken by the British restricting the import of textiles from other countries, David argues that "it certainly aided the development of native cotton and silk industries." Ibid.

22. Juvet (1967), p. 540.

23. Gilpin (1975) argues that the U.K.'s hegemonic position was instrumental to its ability to secure an open world trading system. Others (see McKeown [1983] for a recent discussion) are less convinced of the importance of British power in accomplishing these ends.

24. Gastrell (1897), pp. 62, 95-99, 196-200.

25. Juvet (1967), p. 540.

26. Ibid., p. 541.

27. Lynch (1968), p. 43.

28. See Aggarwal with Haggard (1983) for a discussion.

29. Ibid.

30. Minutes of the Foreign Trade Committee, American Cotton Manufacturers Institute, November 18, 1953.

31. Calculations by the author based on Hunsberger (1964), p. 325.

32. *New York Times*, November 1, 1959, and June 1, 1960.

33. Maizels (1963), p. 342.

34. Miles (1976), p. 189.

35. Although this agreement refers to cotton *textiles*, it also includes apparel.

36. See the Appendix for the texts of the STA and LTA.

37. This arrangement, technically known as the Arrangement Regarding International Trade in Textiles, governed trade restrictions on cotton, wool, and manmade fiber-based textiles and apparel. See Appendix for the text of the MFA.

38. The protocol of extension noted that the MFA included the "possibility of jointly agreed reasonable departures from particular elements in particular cases." That is, importing countries were given much more leeway in the bilateral agreements they negotiated without being constrained by the regime. See Appendix for the text of the protocol of extension.

2. Process of International Regime Transformation

1. International law treatments of regimes are not always of much use in political science. While providing a means of grasping the notion of collaborative arrangements among nation-states, legal scholars tend to be concerned with the importance of specific provisions of these arrangements and potential interpretations of accords. By contrast, questions of the conditions under which such international regimes are likely to come into being and their behavioral implications are often slighted.

2. Fellner (1949); Keohane (1982).

3. Keohane and Nye (1977), p. 5 (emphasis in original).

4. Ibid., p. 19.

5. Krasner (1983). This definition was collectively agreed on by the contributors to the volume.

6. Aggarwal and Cahn (1978).

7. Krasner (1983), p. 5.

8. Ibid., p. 3.

9. For an example of a structural approach to regime change, see Krasner (1976) and Keohane (1980, 1982). For cognitive analysis see Haas (1980, 1982) and Young (1980).

10. Keohane (1982), p. 334.

11. See Haas (1980) for a discussion of the interrelationship of goals and knowledge.

12. Meier (1978).

13. One could also argue that the strength of Article 19 (i.e., the need to impose restraints on a most-favored-nation basis) has in fact deterred countries from imposing any restraints whatsoever. To analyze whether or not Article 19 promotes greater liberalism or protectionism, one would have to interview decision makers to assess their calculations in response to a demand for restraints.

14. USITC (January 1978), pp. A-4 through A-20.

15. GATT, "Paper Circulated at the Request of the United States," Com/Tex/W/44 (Restricted, July 24, 1977, p. 2).

16. Some of the bilateral agreements subsequently contained consultation procedures on these products.

17. I start with the assumption that laissez-faire is not proving "successful" and that countries have decided to intervene in the market.

18. Simon's work (1962) on decomposable systems is helpful in understanding the idea of nesting. He argues that if a system is partially decomposable, then the *short-run* behavior of units in a subsystem of the larger system can be predicted by simply focusing on the structure of the subsystem. By contrast, the long-run behavior of units can only be understood if the constraints of the larger system within which the subsystem is located are taken into account. Applying this idea to international politics, if the overall international system is partially decomposable, both subsystem structure and the larger system must be taken into account to predict national behavior.

19. Finlayson and Zacher (1981) identify the norms of GATT as consisting of nondiscrimination, liberalization, reciprocity, development, safeguards, multilateralism, and negotiations led by major suppliers.

20. My analysis in this subsection draws heavily on some of the insight in Keohane (1982).

21. Ibid.

22. See table 4.

23. Hegemonic stability arguments have also associated concentration of capabilities with an open regime. As I have argued, however, it is important to distinguish between the strength and nature of regimes. It is quite possible to have a strong *protectionist* regime as well as a strong open one. For a discussion of hegemonic stability theory, see Kindleberger (1973); Gilpin (1975); Krasner (1976); and Keohane (1980).

24. Organski (1968).

25. The terms "balancing" and "bandwagoning" are taken from Waltz (1979).

26. Waltz has argued that the capabilities of states are based on "how they score on *all* of the following items: size of population and territory, resource endowment, economic capability, military strength, political stability of competence" (1979, p. 131), emphasis in original. Waltz does not formally define the function specifying the interrelationship among the elements leading to power, but appears to weight military capabilities most heavily. Given Waltz's assumption that survival is the key problem states face and his interest in issues of international conflict, his operationalization of capabilities is understandable.

27. See Scherer (1970) for a discussion of oligopsony power and Hirschman (1945) and Strange (1976) for the use of this concept in international political economy.

28. Scherer (1970).

29. Keohane (1980) looks at imports and exports for selected countries and the American share without considering the EEC as a single unit. For my analytical purposes, this categorization is inappropriate since the EEC bargains as a single unit in international trade negotiations. Also, Waltz (1979), on which Keohane's data are based, does not specify whether imports are F.O.B. or C.I.F. This is significant since the U.S. before 1974 was the only major capitalist countries valuing imports on an F.O.B. basis.

30. Kindleberger (1951) discusses the role of liberal ideology in encouraging the movement toward free trade.

31. See McKeown (1983) for a discussion.

32. Hughes (1973) makes a similar argument about the differences faced by developed countries in adjusting to exports from LDCs as compared to exports from other developed countries. While intraindustry or intrafirm trade might ameliorate protectionist impulses, as Helleiner argues based on evidence from the U.S., intrafirm trade is mainly significant in industries with high research and development expenditures. Helleiner (1981, p. 70) finds that in 1977, of total imports from the Third World into the U.S., related party imports accounted for the following percentages: 7.8% in textiles, 11.5% in clothing, 4.4% in footwear, 63.5% in nonelectrical machinery, and 75.2% in electrical machinery (2-digit SITC categories for industry definitions). Lipson (1982) makes a similar argument for intraindustry trade. The future may not be as bleak as crosscutting pressures on firms seeking protection increases. Some evidence for this can be found in the involvement of multinational corporations in African and Latin American countries' textile and apparel industries. While these countries are currently not very important in textile trade, this may change in the future.

33. See Katzenstein (1978) and Krasner (1978) for a discussion of weak and strong states.

34. A "peak" organization is an umbrella association with smaller groupings in a particular sector of industry.

35. I only discuss the domestic structure of the U.S. and the EEC in this section. The cases consider the domestic structure as other actors depending on the period examined. A more detailed discussion of domestic structure in the textile/ apparel issue can be found in Aggarwal with Haggard (1983) for the U.S. and de la Torre (1981) for Europe.

36. More detailed country analyses will be provided in the case studies.

37. The Council of Ministers is composed of the senior representatives of the member states of the EEC.

38. The Article 113 committee is a more specialized body for debating Community trade policy.

39. See Haggard (1983) for a discussion of the political basis of NIC policies. Although Hong Kong is not known for a strong state, the peak business organizations play a key role in policymaking. See the discussion in chap. 3.

40. See Aggarwal with Haggard (1983) for a detailed discussion of the development of protectionist coalitions in the U.S. textile and apparel industries.

41. Holsti (1976).

42. Haas (1980).

43. See George (1979, 1980). I have helped George develop the idea of "process-tracing" discussed in the latter pages.

44. George (1979) identifies four potential problems in the use of comparative case studies: achieving control for comparison purposes, independence of cases, representativeness of cases, and the use of cases for cumulation purposes.

45. One has to be wary of taking interview information at face value. As a result, I cross-checked the information obtained from my interviews with numerous officials and, where possible, sought documentary evidence to assess the quality of my information.

3. Nonexistence

1. Juvet (1967), p. 541. Germany and France experienced destruction of their textile capacity as well, although not to the same extent.

2. Sato (1976), p. 24.

3. In 1953, Japan's textile and apparel exports came to $746 million, while the corresponding figures for the U.S. and U.K. were $539 million and $343 million, respectively. U.N. Statistical Office, *Commodity Trade Statistics* (1953).

4. GATT, *A Study On Cotton Textiles* (1966), p. 121.

5. Minutes of the Foreign Trade Committee, American Cotton Manufacturers Institute, November 18, 1953.

6. Four programs significantly affected textile production in foreign countries: (1) sales and grants of raw materials (cotton) under P.L. 480 and aid through the Commodity Credit Corporation; (2) aid for machinery through the Export-Import Bank, International Cooperation Administration (ICA), and Development Loan Program; (3) procurement of textiles and apparel from foreign countries by the ICA as part of the mutual security program; and (4) technical assistance to the industry under the Mutual Security Act. *Pastore Hearings* (1958), p. 1768.

7. Lynch (1968), p. 55.

8. Ibid., p. 75.

9. The expression "trader's club" is used by Nye (1973).

10. The first U.S.-initiated bilateral agreements have been extensively written about by various scholars. This part of the chapter draws on Lynch (1968), Sato

(1976), and Hunsberger (1964). Much of Lynch's analysis is drawn from Japanese language sources and the *Cotton Trade Journal.* Also, see Aggarwal with Haggard (1983).

11. The industry had negotiated with Japan and concluded an interindustry agreement shortly before World War II. See Lynch (1968), pp. 78-86, for details.

12. This clause allowed industries claiming harm due to tariff reduction to petition for the reinstatement of higher tariffs.

13. *Pastore Hearings* (1958), p. 917.

14. See Dunn (1963).

15. Historically, China had been an important market for Japan. Before World War II, for example, China, Hong Kong, and British India were absorbing 80% of Japanese cotton yarn exports. Furthermore, China was a major recipient of Japanese fabric exports. Lynch (1968), pp. 60-61.

16. *Pastore Hearings* (1958), p. 1820.

17. U.S. *Department of State Bulletin,* June 26, 1953.

18. See discussion below of Japan's problems in entering the GATT.

19. See chap. 4 of this study.

20. See Aggarwal with Haggard (1983) for a discussion of this issue.

21. Dunn (1963).

22. North and Fields (1974). See this article for an excellent discussion of the problems Japan faced both pre- and post-World War II.

23. U.N., *Yearbook of International Trade Statistics,* various issues.

24. See Patterson (1966) for a detailed discussion.

25. Article 35 had originally been advocated by India to allow it to withhold trade concessions from South Africa because of the latter's apartheid policies, see Patterson (1966).

26. Ibid., and JETRO trade statistics, various years.

27. In 1935 total cotton product exports had been almost 462,000 tons. While this dropped to 332,000 tons in 1940, total exports in the postwar period only reached an average of 146,129 tons for the 1950 to 1955 period. Calculated by author from data in Lynch (1968), p. 60, table 1.

28. Ibid., p. 65.

29. *Nihon Keizai Shimbun,* July 14, 1955, cited in Sato (1976), p. 35.

30. *Yomiuri Shimbun,* August 4, 1955; *Nihon Keizai Shimbun,* November 16, 1955, and November 23, 1955, cited in Sato (1976), p. 35.

31. *Pastore Hearings* (1958). This statement was somewhat ironic. As Japanese exports of synthetic fiber-based goods grew in the 1960s, these goods became a more politically charged problem than cotton goods from Japan had ever been.

32. *Department of State Bulletin,* December 26, 1955, cited in Hunsberger (1964), p. 317.

33. Lynch (1968), p. 102.

34. Ibid.

35. Ibid., p. 103.

36. *Cotton Trade Journal,* December 30, 1955, p. 1., quoted in Lynch (1968), p. 105.

37. See Lynch (1968), pp. 103-105.

38. Ibid., pp. 105-106.

39. *Japan Times*, September 7, 1956.

40. *National Federation of Textiles Bulletin*, no. 934 (September 21, 1956): 1-2, quoted in Lynch (1968), p. 106. Emphasis in original.

41. Lynch (1968), p. 107.

42. Department of State Press Release no. 509, September 27, 1956, cited in Hunsberger (1964), p. 319.

43. Curtis (1966), p. 20967.

44. This law was changed in 1958 to allow Congress to override the president's decision with a 2/3 vote. See Goldstein (1981).

45. For a discussion of the escape clause under which the industry was requesting import restraints, see the *Twenty First Annual Report of the President of the United States on the Trade Agreement Program* (1976). For a discussion of the evolution of this clause, see Ris (1977).

46. See *Pastore Hearings* (1961), p. 114, and Aggarwal with Haggard (1983) for a discussion.

47. *Japan Times*, December 23, 1956.

48. Lynch (1968), p. 109. A minor crisis had developed just prior to the announcement of the agreement. The American textile industry discovered the terms of the agreement and put pressure on the government to lower limits on velveteens. The increasingly well-organized textile and apparel industries used their influence in Congress; in response, the administration insisted that the Japanese lower their proposed velveteen exports from 3.5 to 2.5 million sye.

49. For the text of this agreement, see Lynch (1968), pp. 109-113.

50. See Curtis (1966), p. 20967.

51. See Lynch (1968), p. 173.

52. Hunsberger (1964), p. 279.

53. Kindleberger (1964), p. 271.

54. Maizels (1963).

55. Lazar (1975), p. 110.

56. *The Times*, July 16, 1956, p. 7.

57. Cotton Board, *Addresses and Papers* (1958), pp. 51-52, cited in Lazar (1975), p. 118.

58. This agreement was also known as the Imperial Preference System (see chap. 1).

59. Lazar (1956), p. 116.

60. *Hansard*, vol. 590 (June 30, 1958), col. 906.

61. Patterson (1966), p. 276. This agreement allowed various quantitative controls to prevent an outflow of dollars from the U.K. to Japan and to achieve a broad balance of exports and imports between the Sterling Areas and Japan.

62. For the American motivation in doing so and the story of this process, see the excellent account in Patterson (1966).

63. Lazar (1975), p. 145. The remaining discussion in this subsection draws on his account.

64. The prime minister, Sir Anthony Eden, argued that the government is not "prepared at this time to and in existing circumstances, to depart from their long-

established arrangements for duty free entry from the Commonwealth." *Hansard*, May 3, 1955.

65. U.N. Statistical Offices, *Commodity Trade Statistics*, various years.

66. As noted below, the choice was also facilitated by the "precedent" for such an idea set by the Japanese restraint action toward the U.S. market in 1955.

67. In 1956 these three accounted for 30.1% of all British textile and apparel imports. U.N. Statistical Office, *Commodity Trade Statistics, Series D* (1956).

68. *FEER*, various issues.

69. Data from table in *FEER*, August 13, 1959, p. 221, based on data from the U.K. Board of Trade, *Trade and Navigation Accounts*, 1954, 1956, and 1959.

70. Ibid.

71. *FEER*, August 13, 1959, p. 219.

72. Lazar (1976), p. 216.

73. *FEER*, April 10, 1958.

74. *Economist*, April 12, 1958.

75. Ibid., August 13, 1959.

76. *FEER*, August 13, 1959.

77. Ibid.

78. Ibid.

79. Ibid., June 5, 1958, p. 721.

80. Ibid., August 13, 1959.

81. Ibid.

82. Ibid.

83. Lazar (1976), p. 237.

84. *FEER*, November 12, 1959.

85. Ibid., September 3, 1959.

86. *FEER*, August 13, 1959.

87. See Aggarwal with Haggard (1983) for a discussion of the development of a unified textile-apparel coalition in the U.S.

88. The testimony at the hearings was sometimes far-fetched. At the behest of the wool industry, which argued for import restraints to protect the domestic industry, the Office of Civilian and Defense Mobilization testified that "we have estimated that this particular need would approximate between 150 and 200 million blankets." And what was this "particular need"? The Civil and Defense Mobilization office argued that woolen blankets would be necessary to ensure survival in case of nuclear attack. Quoted in the *Pastore Hearings* (1961), p. 215.

89. *Pastore Hearings* (1958), p. 1744.

90. Interview with U.K. official, November 1978.

91. *Pastore Hearings* (1961), p. 266.

92. *U.N. Yearbook of International Trade Statistics* and *Hong Kong Trade Bulletin* (1959).

93. Interview with senior U.S. negotiator.

94. Interview with senior U.S. negotiator.

95. *FEER*, January 22, 1959.

96. Ibid.

97. Ibid.

98. Ibid.
99. Ibid.
100. Ibid., February 12, 1959, p. 222.
101. Interview with high American official.
102. See Lazar (1975), p. 217.
103. *FEER*, September 3, 1959.
104. Ibid., August 13, 1959.
105. *Economic Intelligence Unit*, September 1959, p. 13.
106. *FEER*, January 7, 1960.
107. Ibid.
108. The U.S. used the newly passed Foreign Assets Control Regulation law to restrict some of Hong Kong's exports.
109. *FEER*, February 19, 1959.
110. Ibid., March 27, 1958.
111. Ibid., February 19, 1959.
112. Interview with a negotiator. Also, see *Business Week*, January 16, 1960, p. 70.
113. Interview with a negotiator.
114. *FEER*, February 4, 1960.
115. Ibid., April 2, 1959.
116. Ibid.
117. Ibid., July 30, 1959.
118. *U.S. Imports of Textile Apparel and Related Manufactures and Comparison with U.S. Production and Exports, 1954-1960*, Department of Commerce, Washington, D.C.
119. *FEER*, November 5, 1959.
120. Ibid.
121. Ibid.
122. Ibid.
123. Ibid., June 18, 1959, p. 831, emphasis added.
124. Ibid., July 30, 1959.
125. Ibid., November 5, 1959.
126. Ibid.
127. Ibid. Also see *New York Times*, August 25, 1959, and *Daily News Record*, August 25, 1959.
128. See Curtis (1966), p. 20968. This action supplemented the effort being made by the National Cotton Council to secure restraints for the same reason.
129. Ibid.
130. *FEER*, November 19, 1959.
131. Ibid.
132. *South China Morning Post*, November 18, 1959.
133. *FEER*, November 26, 1959.
134. Ibid.
135. Ibid.
136. Ibid., December 10, 1959.
137. Ibid., January 7, 1960, and *New York Times*, December 29, 1959.

138. *FEER*, January 7, 1960.

139. Ibid.

140. Interview.

141. *FEER*, January 7, 1960.

142. Rapidly growing exports in 1959 encouraged Hong Kong producers to accept orders "beyond their production capacity." Ibid., March 31, 1960.

143. *Hong Kong Trade Statistics* (1961) and Hunsberger (1964), table 9-5, p. 296.

144. See Bhagwati and Srinivasan (1976).

145. *FEER*, March 15, 1962, and March 29, 1962.

146. See British Spinners' and Doublers' Association (1965).

147. See UNCTAD document, TD/20/Suppl. 3, October 12, 1967, for details on the various restraints utilized by the European countries.

4. Creation

1. *New York Times*, November 20, 1959, p. 9.

2. *Pastore Hearings* (1958), p. 1777.

3. Ibid., p. 1845.

4. Ibid., p. 1717.

5. *Daily News Record*, September 5, 1961.

6. *Daily News Record*, December 13, 1961.

7. GATT document, Spec (61) 229, p. 2.

8. *New York Times*, November 20, 1960, p. 9.

9. GATT document, L/1592, p. 5.

10. *New York Times*, June 1, 1960.

11. *Daily News Record*, July 13, 1961.

12. Lawrence Phillips on behalf of the Apparel Industry Committee on Imports, Senate Hearing on the Textile Industry, 1961.

13. GATT document, L/1535, August 24, 1961, p. 3.

14. *Daily News Record*, October 26, 1961.

15. GATT document, Spec (61) 383, December 12, 1961.

16. Ibid., p. 3.

17. Ibid.

18. *Memorandum on the U.K. Cotton Industry for the U.K. Delegation to the Provisional Committee of the GATT, 1961*, cited in Lazar (1975), p. 297.

19. GATT document, L/1535, p. 3.

20. Ibid., p. 4.

21. GATT document, Spec (61) 321, October 25, 1961, p. 3.

22. GATT document, L/3797/Add. 2, p. 70.

23. Aside from the strategic and overall trade dependence on the U.S., the Americans purchased 20% of the EEC's textile and apparel exports. Ibid.

24. GATT document, L/1535, p. 3.

25. Ibid., p. 6.

26. Ibid., p. 7.

27. Ibid., p. 9.

28. GATT document, Spec (61) 229, July 17, 1961.

29. Ibid., p. 2.

30. GATT document, L/1535, August 24, 1961, p. 9.

31. GATT document, L/1592, October 23, 1961, p. 5.

32. Ibid.

33. Ibid., p. 6.

34. Ibid.

35. GATT document, Spec (61) 229, p. 3.

36. Ibid., p. 4 (emphasis added).

37. Ibid.

38. *Daily News Record*, July 10, 1961.

39. Ibid., July 11, 1961.

40. GATT document, L/1535, p. 3.

41. See Aggarwal with Haggard (1983).

42. *Daily News Record*, June 22, 1962.

43. Ibid., July 20, 1961.

44. Ibid., July 24, 1961.

45. Ibid., July 7, 1961. The Trade Agreements Act formed the basis for the Kennedy Round negotiations.

46. Ibid., December 13, 1961.

47. Ibid., February 1, 1962.

48. Ibid.

49. Ibid., December 13, 1961.

50. Ibid., February 1, 1962.

51. Finlayson and Zacher (1981).

52. Finlayson and Zacher develop a similar idea with respect to connections between the anarchic international system and overall trade.

53. STA text, see Appendix. Note that in many ways the STA was a forerunner of the GATT development norm since it only became an important part of the GATT in 1964.

54. See the text of the LTA in the Appendix (emphasis added).

55. LTA text, see Appendix.

56. LTA text, see Appendix.

57. Text of the LTA, Article 2.3 (see Appendix).

58. Ibid., Article 4.

59. See Bardan (1973), Patterson (1966), Curtis and Vastine (1971), and Keesing and Wolf (1980).

60. Bardan (1973).

61. See ibid., and UNCTAD document TD/20/Supp. 3 (1967) for further details.

62. Under the STA, which lasted for only one year, there was basically a standstill on new restraints now consistent with the agreement. But most of the changes in national policies took place under the LTA.

63. UNCTAD document, TD/20/Supp. 3, p. 63.

64. See the Appendix in the LTA. The text of the LTA can be found in the Appendix to this study.

65. UNCTAD document, TD/20/Supp. 3.

66. The fill rate in the U.K. and the U.S. even exceeded 100% in some cases because of overshipping.

5. Maintenance

1. Note that the U.S. had a bilateral arrangement with Italy on cotton velveteen products. But this arrangement was the only exception to the absence of bilateral arrangements between two developed countries (aside from Japan).

2. The U.S. managed to obtain an informal voluntary restraint agreement from Japan on wool suits. In 1961, in response to pressure from an American clothing labor union, Secretary of Labor Arthur Goldberg had discussions with the Japanese ambassador to the U.S., Mr. Asaki. This led to an informal arrangement whereby the Japanese restrained exports of wool suits to the U.S. at a level of 120,000 pieces. In 1966, when the Japanese first violated this agreement, further pressure from the unions led to a new restraint agreement that was arrived at with the help of the secretary of labor, Willard Wirtz. This time, the limit was set at 170,000 until 1968.

3. British Spinners' and Doublers' Association (1965), p. 35.

4. Ibid.

5. The following discussion draws on interviews with some of the participants.

6. Curtis (1966).

7. Ibid., p. 20982.

8. *Daily News Record,* September 30, 1965.

9. Ibid.

10. Ibid., October 21, 1966.

11. *Charlotte Observer,* July 28, 1966.

12. *Daily News Record,* August 31, 1966.

13. See Nye (1973), pp. 334-335.

14. *New York Times,* March 3, 1967.

15. *Daily News Record,* February 15, 1967.

16. Ibid.

17. Ibid.

18. See table 3 for data on textile capabilities.

19. *Economist,* July 16, 1966, p. 284.

20. *Daily News Record,* September 22, 1966.

21. Ibid., September 23, 1966.

22. Ibid., August 31, 1966.

23. See Curtis and Vastine (1971), Evans (1971), and Preeg (1970) for a discussion of the Kennedy Round negotiations and the textile negotiations as a part of these talks.

24. See the text of the LTA in the Appendix.

25. Cot/M/5, p. 12.

26. Ibid., p. 17.

27. Ibid., p. 21.

28. Ibid.

29. Ibid., p. 29

30. Curtis and Vastine (1971), p. 174.

31. *Daily News Record,* January 28, 1966.

32. See Waltz (1979), p. 126, on bandwagoning and balancing behavior by countries.

33. *Daily News Record,* March 30, 1966.

34. Ibid.

35. Ibid., September 19, 1966.

36. Ibid., September 23, 1966.

37. Note that while the U.S. made offers to a number of countries on proposed liberalization measures, it still did not go ahead with liberalization since it wished to use such measures as a bargaining chip to secure renewal of the LTA.

38. Cot/M/7, pp. 12-13.

39. Cot/M/8, p. 3.

40. *Daily News Record,* December 5, 1966, p. 22.

41. *Journal of Commerce,* March 7, 1967, p. 25.

42. The Commission did not represent the EEC members in the textile negotiations. Instead, the Council of Ministers chose a representative.

43. *Journal of Commerce,* March 7, 1967, p. 25.

44. *Daily News Record,* March 23, 1967.

45. Cot/M/8, p. 13.

46. Ibid.

47. *Journal of Commerce,* June 30, 1967, p. 1; Also, Preeg, 1970, p. 21, and Curtis and Vastine (1971), p. 175.

48. See Wyndham-White's statement in Preeg (1970), p. 302, and discussion on p. 231. Also, *New York Times,* June 29, 1967, p. 67.

49. Unilateral actions could be undertaken by the importing country under Article 3 of the LTA to restrict imports if the two parties failed to agree on a bilateral solution. See Bardan (1973), p. 15, for details.

50. For details, see GATT document, L/3797.

51. For example, France had unilaterally restrained imports from a number of Eastern bloc countries.

52. Bardan (1973), p. 19.

53. During the 1960s, clothing trade grew at a rate of 140% as compared to only 30% for fabric and 75% for yarn.

54. The data in this section are drawn from an unpublished study by the Office of Textiles, U.S. Department of Commerce, 1972.

55. At a GATT meeting in October 1969, the American delegate argued that actions to restrict imports by a number of importing countries "have had the effect of channeling exports to the markets of countries that do not have such restrictions." Continuing, he warned: "There are many in the United States who feel that the only viable solution to the textile problems we face should be attained through import quotas enacted in legislation. It has been my Government's view that rather than resort to legislation we should *negotiate* acceptable international arrangements which would establish a reasonable and orderly basis

for the development of the United States textile market and for the continued growth of United States textile imports." Cot/W/118, pp. 3-5 (emphasis added).

56. By 1970 over one quarter of U.S. textile imports came from the EEC. GATT document, L/3797/Add. 2.

57. *Department of State Bulletin,* vol. 65, no. 1674 (July 26, 1971): 94, cited in Sato (1976), p. 66.

58. *Congressional Record,* January 31, 1969, pp. 2328-2329.

59. *Financial Times,* April 8, 1969.

60. Ibid.

61. *Textile World,* December 1969, p. 36.

62. Telegram to Republican members of Congress who supported import control legislation, August 21, 1968. Cited in Brandis (May 1979).

63. *Financial Times,* April 10, 1969.

64. See U.N. document, TD/B/C.2/117/Rev. 1, p. 78, for wool; and GATT document, L/3797/Add. 2, pp. 223-224 and 250-251 for MMF products.

65. This term refers to the export of partially finished goods to low-wage countries where the labor-intensive phase in the production of the goods is completed. Subsequently, for example, these goods are reimported to Germany under special tariff provisions, with duty assessed only on the value added by labor.

66. *Economist,* April 26, 1969.

67. In part, this may account for the Italian agreement to secretly restrict the export of velveteens in the late 1950s. Aside from Japan, this use of restraints against a developed country is unusual since there is an implicit agreement among all textile regime participants that restrictions will not be invoked against other developed countries. See USITC, *The MFA* (1978).

68. *Financial Times.*

69. Ibid., April 18, 1969, p. 16.

70. Textile Council (1969).

71. See Destler et al. (1979) for an extensive discussion of the U.S.-Japanese negotiations of 1969-1971.

72. *Financial Times,* April 8, 1969.

73. Ibid.

74. Ibid., April 17, 1969.

75. Ibid.

76. *Business Week,* April 26, 1969.

77. *Financial Times,* April 26, 1969.

78. Ibid., April 28, 1969.

79. Ibid., April 26, 1969, p. 24.

80. *New York Times,* April 24, 1969.

81. *Financial Times,* April 26, 1969, p. 24.

82. Destler et al. (1979), p. 82.

83. *New York Times,* April 17, 1969.

84. Ibid., April 26, 1969.

85. Interview with an American negotiator; and Destler et al. (1979), p. 101.

86. The reader is referred to Destler et al. (1979) for a discussion of the internal problems that Japanese decision makers encountered, and to Aggarwal with Hag-

gard (1983) for a discussion of U.S. textile and apparel industry pressure in the negotiations.

87. Clothing and textiles accounted for 34% of all value added in manufacturing in 1969, and for 9.1% of all industrial employment. GATT document, L/3797/Add. 1, pp. 82-83.

88. Destler et al. (1979), pp. 84-85.

89. Mills was apparently interested in running for president and wished to secure textile and apparel industry support by demonstrating his willingness to help them.

90. His visit to China on July 15, 1971, without informing the Japanese in advance, also came as a shock to them.

91. In 1970, Malaysia "inadvertently" signed a multifiber agreement with the U.S. on a bilateral basis. This did not have much impact on the negotiations with Japan and other Far East Asian countries in terms of setting a precedent, however. (Interview with a top U.S. textile negotiator.)

92. *Daily News Record,* October 18, 1971.

93. See table 6.

94. *Daily News Record,* October 19, 1971.

95. *Wall Street Journal,* October 18, 1971.

96. The GATT Working Party included most countries involved with textile trade. GATT document, L/3716/Rev. 1.

97. Interview with an American negotiator.

98. Interview with an American negotiator.

99. *Textile Asia,* April 1973, p. 69.

100. Interview with an American negotiator.

101. Minutes of the Foreign Trade Committee of the ATMI, 1973.

102. Ibid.

103. Ibid., November 1973.

104. Rather than an "impartial body," the American proposal merely read: "International surveillance would be carried out by a broadly representative Sub Committee of the Textiles Committee." Com/Tex/W/27, GATT document.

105. Interview with an American negotiator.

106. Ibid.

107. *Textile Asia,* August 1973, p. 11.

108. Interview with an American negotiator.

109. See the data in chap. 2 on imports by the EEC and the U.S.

110. *Textile Asia,* December 1973.

111. Ibid., February 1973, p. 63.

112. Interview with an American negotiator.

113. *Textile Asia,* May 1973, p. 80.

114. Ibid., February 1973; *Textile Month,* April 1973.

115. *Textile Asia,* May 1973.

116. "Soft" in the sense that the U.K. had few import controls on man-made fiber and wool-based imports. *Textile Month,* April 1973, p. 32.

117. *Textile Asia,* August 1973, p. 62.

118. Interview with an American negotiator.

119. Destler et al. (1979), pp. 316-317.
120. *Daily News Record,* January 12, 1973.
121. Ibid., June 27, 1973.
122. *Textile Asia,* May 1973.
123. Interview with an American negotiator.
124. GATT document, Com/Tex/W/23.
125. *Textile Asia,* May 1973.
126. Ibid.
127. Ibid.
128. Ibid.
129. Interview with an American negotiator.
130. Ibid.
131. *Textile Asia,* October 1973.
132. Ibid., April 1974. In fact, shortly after the conclusion of the MFA, in bilateral U.S.-Hong Kong talks, it was reported: "Both want a strong and effective TSB to supervise the MTA's working" (ibid., p. 10). By contrast, the French wished to have the chairmanship of the TSB rotated—a desire that prompted the same trade journal to comment that this would "certainly make the body impotent."
133. *Daily News Record,* June 27, 1973.
134. Ibid.
135. The U.S. procedure for imposing restrictions involved a long and drawn-out process that could be challenged by importers. See Aggarwal (1982) for a discussion.
136. *Textile Asia,* April 1973.
137. Interview with an American negotiator.
138. In the MFA renegotiations in 1977, the EEC got what it was unable to obtain in 1974 on this issue.
139. *Textile Asia,* August 1975, p. 11.
140. Ibid., October 1973, p. 11.
141. Ibid., p. 6.
142. See MFA test in the Appendix.
143. Ibid.
144. Ibid.
145. Ibid.
146. Ibid.
147. Ibid.
148. Ibid.
149. Ibid.
150. Ibid.
151. Com/Tex/SB/196.
152. See table 8.
153. The United States had followed the latter procedure and granted higher levels of access as an incentive for the LDCs to sign on quickly.
154. See *The EEC and the Textile Arrangements* (n.d.), Brussels.
155. *Textile Asia,* June 1974.

156. *Europe*, no. 290 (January 7, 1976).

157. Ibid., and *The Guardian*, January 6, 1976.

158. Telex, *Europe*.

159. *The EEC and the Textile Arrangements*, n.d.

160. Com/Tex/SB/196.

161. See Com/Tex/SB/196 for details of the actions of all countries from January 1, 1974, to September 30, 1976.

6. Destruction

1. See table 3.

2. Note that this may have been done for tactical reasons since they knew that the EEC had been making loud noises about its dissatisfaction with the first MFA and wished to have major changes in the arrangement. Under these circumstances, an extension without changes was probably the best the LDCs could hope for.

3. Interview with American official.

4. Interview with American official.

5. Com/Tex/W/50.

6. Minutes of the Foreign Trade Committee, ATMI, May 18, 1976.

7. One can see the ATMI position as "fallforward" as they actually wished to see more severe restrictions. They had decided to seek a simple extension of the MFA since they did not expect to be able to pursue a more restrictionist course.

8. Minutes of the Foreign Trade Committee, ATMI, May 18, 1976.

9. Ibid., March 10, 1977.

10. Interview with U.S. textile negotiator.

11. Interview with U.S. negotiator.

12. Europe Information, *The EEC and the Textile Arrangements* (n.d.), p. 3.

13. *Europe*, External Relations.

14. Com/Tex/W/39, pp. 16-17.

15. This type of export performance buildup had been used successfully by Japan in television trade as well.

16. *Textile Asia*, May 1978.

17. In 1976, Japan ran a $4.2 million deficit in textile and apparel trade with South Korea. U.N. Statistical Office, *Commodity Trade Statistics* (1976).

18. Interview with Japanese official.

19. *Textile Asia*, May 1978.

20. Ibid.

21. Interview with Japanese official.

22. *Textile Asia*, February 1977.

23. Ibid., 1977.

24. Com/Tex/W/39, p. 20.

25. This statement must be partially qualified since some of these highly competitive countries were becoming less competitive in some products as wages rose. Ironically, large quotas protected these countries from newly emerging suppliers with even lower wages.

26. Interview with Pakistani official.

27. Interview with an LDC delegate.

28. *Europe*, January 26, 1977, p. 9.

29. Ibid.

30. Interview with an American negotiator.

31. Ibid.

32. Ibid.

33. Ibid.

34. Ibid.

35. Article 19 allows countries to restrict exports from other countries if there is a threat of "market disruption." The significance of this threat is that it had been implicitly understood that countries would not resort to the GATT possibilities for restrictions in textile and apparel trade (since the MFA was supposed to govern national action in this issue area). Another significant implication of the French threat was the violation of the understanding among EEC countries that Article 19 would only be invoked by the Community—and not by individual member states.

36. *Europe.*

37. Ibid.

38. Ibid.

39. Com/Tex/W/50.

40. *Europe.*

41. Ibid.

42. Ibid.

43. Ibid.

44. Com/Tex/W/50, p. 18.

45. Ibid.

46. Ibid.

47. See the case against the Committee on the Implementation of Textile Agreements brought by the Consumers Union. As one American negotiator later remarked, "the EEC probably wanted even more severe restrictions (such as rollbacks) than were allowed under Article 4 of the MFA. (Interview with an American official.)

48. Com/Tex/W/50, p. 48.

49. *Europe.*

50. Com/Tex/W/50, p. 11. Emphasis added.

51. *Textile Asia*, September 1977. Emphasis added.

52. The key paragraph of the American proposal stated: "The Committee noted one major importing participant's statement concerning the basis upon which it intended to achieve its stated objectives by bilateral negotiations and noted the expression of goodwill and flexibility made by certain exporting participants. The Committee urged that within the framework of the MFA any such consultations and negotiations should be conducted in a spirit of equity and flexibility with a view to reaching a mutually acceptable solution under Article 4.3 or Article 3, paragraphs 3 and 4, which does include the possibility of jointly agreed reasonable departures from particular elements in particular cases." Com/Tex/W/44, p. 2, GATT Restricted coument.

53. Com/Tex/W/50, GATT Restricted document.

54. Ibid., p. 54.

55. Ibid., p. 56.

56. Ibid.

57. *Textile Asia*, August 1977.

58. Ibid., September 1977.

59. Ibid.

60. Ibid.

61. Ibid.

62. *Europe*, no. 2283 (September 9, 1977).

63. For example, it wished to have an annual growth for cotton yarns of 0%; the EEC Commission suggested 1.2%. The net result was a compromise of 0.6%—halfway between the U.K.'s and the EEC's suggestions. This type of bargaining went on for a number of other products.

64. Based on Europe Information, *The European Commission and the Textile Arrangements*, pp. 29-30, and *Europe*, various issues of press release series.

65. The first group consisted of products such as cotton yarn, knitted shirts, trousers, etc. The growth rates of quotas for these products ranged from a low of 0.3% for cotton yarn to 4.1% for cardigans and pullovers. The second group consisted of products with an import to consumption ratio over 20%. Here rates ranged from 4% to 6%. Four other groups with varying growth rates were also developed with the objective being to maintain the overall 6% growth rate in import quotas mandated by the MFA. (*The European Community and the Textile Arrangements* [n.d.], p. 40.)

66. Once again, this varies according to the sensitivity of particular products. For example, the basket extractor rates for "political products" was 0.2% of total imports from outside the EEC, for Group II products, between 1% and 1.5%, and for other groups, 3% to 5%. This sytem allowed the EEC to rapidly restrict imports when they rose above a certain percentage—without having to formally negotiate quota levels for every product.

67. *Textile Asia*, November 1977.

68. The four countries were Singapore, the Philippines, Macao, and Thailand.

69. *Textile Asia*, December 1977, p. 11.

70. *Europe*, no. 2322 (November 5, 1977).

71. Interview.

72. Interview.

73. *Europe*, no. 458 (November 1977).

74. *Textile Asia*, December 1977, p. 16.

75. Ibid.

76. Interview.

77. Ibid.

78. *Wall Street Journal*, November 11, 1977.

79. *Textile Asia*, January 1978, p. 15.

80. *Wall Street Journal*, November 11, 1977.

81. *Textile Asia*, December 1977, p. 10.

82. Ibid., reported that by November, "only 10 of the 34 textile exporting countries were reported to have completed their negotiations with the EEC."

83. See ibid., August 1977, for a detailed discussion of the bilateral with Hong Kong. Some interpret the MFA to allow no growth in quotas in the first year of the negotiations; thus, the U.S.-Hong Kong agreement can be seen to be consistent with the MFA's provisions.

84. Interview.

85. Com/Tex/W/50.

86. Com/Tex/W/50, p. 61. Emphasis in original.

87. *Textile Asia*, January 1978.

88. Com/Tex/W/50.

89. Interview with Canadian negotiator.

90. Interview with American delegate.

91. See discussion below.

92. Europe Information, *The EEC and the Textile Arrangements* (n.d.), p. 31.

93. Com/Tex/W/50, p. 64.

94. Minutes of the Foreign Trade Committee of the ATMI, April 28, 1978.

95. *Washington Post*, June 30, 1978.

96. Ibid.

97. One former high-level U.S. government official argued in an interview that the industries' complaints about possible tariff reductions were simply a bluff to encourage the government to renegotiate the bilateral accords.

98. *Memorandum of Disapproval*, The White House, November 11, 1978. The industries were unhappy with "surges" in imports, that is, a situation wherein exporting countries would ship much more in one year in a particular category than they did in the previous year in response to market conditions. They were able to do this because of the swing carry over/carry forward provisions in the bilateral agreements—flexibility provisions that were in accord with the MFA.

99. This bill was needed to give the president authority to waive countervailing duties on subsidized exports from the EEC until the negotiations on a new subsidy code were concluded. See the *Washington Post*, February 16, 1979, for discussion of the industries' efforts.

100. This clause stated that in the event the MFA was not renewed, tariffs would be restored to their level prior to the Tokyo Round cuts. More important, the White Paper promised that if the MFA was not renewed, "legislative remedies will be proposed to allow the President authority to unilaterally control imports of textile and apparel products." *Administration Textile Program*, p. 3.

101. While the industry would have preferred stricter limits on growth per se (consistent with their demands for the last 25 years), in the end this was rejected because of counterpressure from more liberal agencies in the U.S. government. (Based on an interview with a former American official.)

102. In actual fact, Canada had not "departed" from the text of the MFA (as interpreted by the TSB later on) but had merely mentioned the Protocol of renewal in its agreement with the Philippines. Com/Tex/SB/443, p. 3, July 1, 1979.

103. Interview with a TSB member.

104. *Financial Times*, July 1979.

105. Com/Tex/SB/446.

106. Ibid., SB/610.

107. See MFA text in Appendix of this study.

108. Com/Tex/SB/610, p. 49.

109. Ibid., p. 61.

110. Ibid.

111. Ibid., p. 59.

112. This clause allowed deviations in growth from 6% when a country's production had been so reduced as to endanger the future of the industry. By informal understanding, only the Nordics were allowed to use this provision.

113. Com/Tex/SB/610, p. 50.

114. See Com/Tex/17 for the debate between LDCs and DCs. Also, see Keesing and Wolf (1980) for the effect on trade of the 1977 MFA renewal.

115. Keesing and Wolf (1980), pp. 87-88.

116. This section draws heavily on Aggarwal (1983).

117. The exception was a slight gain in the U.S. textile balance. See table 11.

118. In 1979 the U.S. imported $810 million worth of textiles from the LDCs and $4,341 million in apparel (exports were $1,043 million and $435 million, respectively). In the EEC, the corresponding import figures were $4,076 million for textiles and $6,266 million for apparel (exports were $3,304 million and $1,117 million, respectively). GATT document, Com/Tex/W/78, September 1980, pp. 1, 3, 5, 7.

119. The Big Three countries are Hong Kong, South Korea, and Taiwan. Together they accounted for 62% of all U.S. apparel imports in 1980. U.N. Statistical Office, *International Trade Statistics, Series D.*

120. U.S. Position Paper for the GATT Textile Committee Meeting, 14 July 1981, by Peter Murphy, USTR.

121. Ibid., p. 3.

122. Interview with U.S. government officials.

123. July U.S. Position Paper (emphasis added).

124. Ibid.

125. Interview with U.S. government officials, December 1981, Washington, D.C.

126. *Daily News Record,* May 4, 1981.

127. This section allowed the U.S. to unilaterally restrict imports from countries not willing to agree to restraints. The U.S. government could only do this, however, if a multilateral accord was in existence.

128. July U.S. Position Paper.

129. Ibid. (emphasis added).

130. Interview.

131. Statement of George Vargish on behalf of the U.S. Apparel Council before Oversight Hearings of the Trade Subcommittee, The House Committee on Ways and Means, July 21, 1980.

132. *Daily News Record,* April 6, 1981.

133. Letter from Ronald Reagan to Strom Thurmond, September 3, 1980. Keying the import growth rate to the domestic market's growth would freeze the importers' proportion of the American domestic market.

134. The White Paper called for renegotiation of bilaterals with the Big Three

exporters—Hong Kong, South Korea, and Taiwan—to decrease the swing and flexibility available to them.

135. Letter from Congressional Textile Caucus, U.S. House of Representatives, to Ambassador William E. Brock, III, United States Trade Representative, May 22, 1981.

136. *Daily News Record*, October 2, 1981.

137. Of course, the MFA violated in part the norm of nondiscrimination by allowing restraints against LDCs without similar restraints on developed countries. Yet, even though such discrimination was permitted, no discrimination was allowed against *particular* LDCs. Bilateral accords unregulated by the MFA would, however, allow for this possibility.

138. July U.S. Position Paper.

139. See table 2.

140. *Europe*, May 8, 1981.

141. Ibid., no. 3180 (July 16, 1981).

142. *Financial Times*, July 14, 1981.

143. *Textile Asia*, January 1981.

144. *Financial Times*, July 14, 1981, p. 18.

145. *Textile Month*, July 1981.

146. *Daily News Record*, June 25, 1981.

147. Ibid., July 6, 1981.

148. *Textile Asia*, August 1981.

149. *The Wall Street Journal*, July 10, 1981.

150. Interview.

151. "Aide memoire of the Bogota Meeting of Textile Exporting Countries," held November 3-6, 1980, confidential document.

152. Ibid.

153. Ibid. As we shall see later in the negotiations, however, an adviser to the ASEAN countries argued in favor of ambiguity to prevent a highly protectionist accord.

154. Interview.

155. *Daily News Record*, November 3, 1981.

156. Com/Tex/W/85, December 9, 1980.

157. When Peter Murphy visited ASEAN countries in 1981, he reported that they saw it "in their interest to keep the agreement intact." Since they were "residual suppliers," most of them would be less competitive under market conditions than with the MFA.

158. Com/Tex/20, February 13, 1981.

159. Ibid.

160. Ibid., May 8, 1981.

161. The Scandinavians had inserted this clause in the MFA as a way of protecting their industry, arguing there was a limit to which their textile and apparel industries could be reduced given strategic considerations.

162. See Com/Tex/24, September 8, 1981, for a discussion.

163. *Textile Asia*, June 1981.

164. *Europe*, no. 3180 (July 16, 1981).

165. Ibid.

166. The proposal noted: "The protocol in Annex I is an initial proposal. We do not expect, or for that matter, want, acceptance of this protocol for it would permit rollbacks in levels of trade, due to the maintenance of reasonable departures language. Optically, however, it is helpful in our ability to manage industry pressures and at the same time it may encourage certain exporters to put forward a pragmatic counter-proposal." July U.S. Position Paper.

167. *Daily News Records*, July 14, 1981.

168. Interview.

169. *Daily News Record*, September 10, 1981. Interview.

170. *Daily News Record*, September 22, 1981.

171. Ibid., September 28, 1981.

172. Ibid., September 25, 1981.

173. Confidential memo made available by a consultant to ASEAN, October 9, 1981.

174. *Europe*, no. 820 (November 10, 1981).

175. An internal ceiling differs from an external ceiling in that the latter would have to be agreed to by exporting countries. Under the MFA, this would probably be illegal. When the British tried to justify their global ceiling in 1966 under the predecessor to the MFA, the LTA, the Textiles Committee ruled this was not permitted under the regime's rules.

176. *Europe*, External Relations, no. 829 (December 12, 1981).

177. Interview. As many of the LDCs saw it, "If the M-FA isn't renewed the only course left would be to regulate trade on a country by country basis. Because of its enormous size as a buyer, the EEC would carry much greater bargaining power in negotiations for such separate accords than it does in an international forum, where it is one group among nearly 100 participating countries (*Daily News Record*, November 3, 1981).

178. Interview.

179. *Daily News Record*, December 14, 1981.

180. Interviews.

181. MFA Protocol, GATT document, December 23, 1981.

182. Ibid.

7. Conclusion

1. Gibson (1960), pp. 141-142.

2. George (1981), p. 18.

3. A very simple example will illustrate how a particular variable can be sufficient without being necessary. If one is trying to explain how a light is turned off, knowing that there is a switch may be sufficient condition to explain the outcome. Yet there are other ways in which one can turn off a light; obviously if the electricity fails or, more mundanely, if someone breaks the bulb, then the same outcome will be realized. While we immediately see the sufficient condition in this case, establishing what is necessary requires more knowledge of the operation of the system.

4. Barry Sullivan, "Down with Protectionism," *Euromoney*, October 1983, p. 42.

5. See *Manual for Textile Negotiators*, UNCTAD document, MD/TX/1, Geneva, July 1982. For a theoretical analysis of bargaining strategies for the weak, see Aggarwal and Allan (1983).

6. See Aggarwal with Haggard (1983).

7. My doctoral student, Ronald Gutfleish, is currently preparing a study on the comparative politics of protection. I am indebted to him for his help in developing the ideas in this section.

8. Curtis and Vastine (1971).

9. Ibid., p. 154.

10. Borrus (1983), p. 84. The next paragraph draws heavily on this article.

11. *The Economist*, December 31, 1977, in Borrus (1983).

12. Reich (1983).

13. *Wall Street Journal*, October 22, 1982.

14. Ibid., January 28, 1983.

15. Brazil's exports to the U.S. increased almost eightfold, South Korea's quadrupled, and LDCs in general tripled their exports in the five-year period from 1975 to 1980. American imports during this period increased by 73%, while the Japanese, whose exports were restricted, increased their exports by 43%. Data from U.N. *Trade Commodity Statistics, Series D*, various years.

16. Author's calculations based on Cowhey and Long (1983).

17. For further discussion, see Krasner (1979).

18. *Washington Post*, September 12, 1984.

Glossary

Basket category. A category for the items not assigned to specific categories in a group. The quota allocated to the basket is the residual square yard amount of a group ceiling not accounted for by the specific category limits in that group.

Basket extractor mechanism. Extracting a specific textile or apparel product from a "basket" category and assigning a specific quota for the extracted article.

Bilateral. A written agreement governing apparel and textile trade between the United States and another country. Currently, the United States has 22 bilateral agreements, 20 of which were negotiated under the MFA. Agreements with Taiwan and China exist pursuant to the provisions of Section 204 of the Agricultural Act of 1956; they are similar to those under the MFA despite the fact that these two countries are not signatories thereto.

Called category. A category on which the U.S. government requests or calls for consultation when imports are approaching a certain limit or consultation level.

Category. An apparel/textile product or aggregation of similar products for import-control purposes. There are several thousand apparel and textile products into 104 categories—39 for cotton, 24 for wool, and 41 for man-made fibers.

The numbering system of the categories designates both the fiber content and the product. All categories numbered 300-369 are cotton; 400-469 are wool; and 600-669 are man-made fibers. The first digit indicates fiber content and the second two digits, the product line. Category 635, for example, is women's and children's man-made fiber coats. The fiber of chief value in the garment generally determines its fiber classification.

Consultation levels—designated. A designated consultation level (DCL) is a more flexible import control than specific ceilings or limits; DCLs are usually somewhat above existing levels of trade and once reached cannot be exceeded unless the United States agrees to further shipments. They normally apply to categories in which trade is not as great as those for which specific limits are set and are determined annually through the consultation procedure with each bilateral country with which they exist.

Consultation levels—minimum. A minimum consultation level (MCL) is the level up to which any country may ship in any category before the United States will request consultations for controlling imports in that category. MCLs apply to all categories that do not have specific ceilings or designated consultation levels. Unlike the DCL, the MCL may be the same for all categories within a group. Generally, the level is 1 million sye for categories covering textiles and textile articles (except apparel) of cotton and man-made fibers; 700,000 sye for categories covering apparel of cotton and man-made fibers; and 100,000 sye for categories covering wool textiles and textile articles.

Embargo. A prohibition on the imports of additional articles in a category beyond a certain limit or restraint level. If exported to the United States in an amount over the limit, the articles are held in a bonded warehouse until agreement on disposal has been reached.

Export authorizations (EAs). Authorization given by the exporting country's government to an exporter to ship a stated amount of articles in a category to the importing country. EAs are issued by the countries using the system for categories not under specific limits. Under this system, the United States may request that the exporting country cease issuing EAs for any category in which imports are increasing rapidly. The United States may then negotiate a specific limit for the category.

Export control system. A stipulation in the bilateral agreement that the exporting country will administer an export control system. Exports are allocated to exporters by the government of the exporting country. The importing country's government also monitors to assure compliance with the import limits set forth in the agreement. The countries which provide for export control systems in their bilateral agreements with the United States are Hong Kong, India, Malaysia, Singapore, Taiwan, and Thailand.

Flexibility. Provisions in a bilateral agreement for increases or decreases in import restraint levels or limits through use of carry over, carry forward, or swing. Flexibility provisions apply only to specific import limits set forth in the bilateral agreements. This can include transfer from natural to man-made fibers or vice versa and from one product group to another.

Carry over. Use in the present bilateral agreement of an unused portion of an import limit for a category from the corresponding category of the previous year up to a certain percentage increase specified in the agreement.

Carry forward. Use for a category in the present bilateral agreement year of a portion of the next year's limit for a corresponding category up to a certain percentage increase specified in the agreement. The amount "borrowed" must be deducted from the category's restraint level in the following year. Most bilateral agreements provide that carry over and carry forward cannot exceed 11 percent of the receiving category's quota and that no more than 7 percent can come from carry forward.

General imports. Imports that have arrived in the United States regardless of whether they have entered for immediate consumption or are being held in a Customs bonded warehouse to be subsequently withdrawn for consumption. General import data are used for monitoring purposes under the MFA.

Globalization. A term used to describe a method of controlling imports of textiles and textile products by an overall limit for each category and apportioning a certain percentage of the total to each country under the MFA.

Imports for consumption. Imports that have entered the U.S. stream of commerce. This includes imports entering directly into consumption and imports withdrawn from U.S. bonded warehouses for consumption.

"India" or "Philippines" items. Textiles and textile articles made in India or the Republic of the Philippines which are considered traditional products of these countries. The items are cut, sewn, or otherwise fabricated by hand in cottage industries and are not subject to limits if properly certified by the exporting country.

Limit (aggregate). A limit or ceiling on the total amount of cotton, wool, and man-made fiber textiles and textile articles which a country agrees not to exceed in its exports to the United States in a given year. The unit of measurement is square yard equivalent, obtained by converting the units of each category to sye by specified conversion factors.

Limit (group). A group limit is a subdivision of the aggregate limit. In many U.S. bilateral agreements, there are three groups. The total of the group limit equals the aggregate ceiling. Each group is defined in each agreement and usually includes a large number of categories. For example, a group may include (1) all apparel of cotton and man-made fibers or (2) yarns, fabrics, made-up goods (except apparel) and miscellaneous textile products of cotton and man-made fibers. The group limits are measured in square yard equivalents.

Limit (specific). The limit set on the amount of imports which may enter the United States in a specific category in a designated 12-month period. This limit is subject to change according to the flexibility provisions in the bilateral agreement.

Market disruption. The definition of market disruption is set out in Annex A of the MFA and is found in the Appendix. Article 3 of the MFA provides, in part, that if importing countries feel that imports of a textile product not under restraint are causing market disruption, they may seek consultations with the exporting country with a view to removing such disruption.

Shortfall. The unused portion or the amount of imports which falls short of or is below the restraint level for an aggregate, group, or category ceiling or limit. An agreement may specify that the shortfall must be used in the same category as the one in which it occurred.

Signatories to the MFA. Countries which accepted the MFA, which ends 31 December 1981, include Argentina, Austria, Bangladesh, Bolivia, Brazil, Canada, Colombia, Czechoslovakia, Dominican Republic, European Economic Community, Egypt, El Salvador, Finland, Ghana, Guatemala, Haiti, Hungary, India, Indonesia, Israel, Jamaica, Japan, Republic of Korea, Malaysia, Mexico, Pakistan, Peru, Philippines, Poland, Portugal for Macao, Romania, Singapore, Sri Lanka, Sweden, Switzerland, Thailand, Trinidad and Tobago, Turkey, United Kingdom for Hong Kong, United States, Uruguay, and Yugoslavia.

Square yard equivalent. The square yard equivalent of imports of apparel and textile articles. It is an overall measure of trade in physical terms. With the exception of fabric, all apparel and textile products are assigned a conversion factor that converts units into sye. A dozen men's and boys' woven shirts represents 24 sye. Square yard equivalents are an essential measure because limits within bilaterals are set in sye.

Surge. A large increase in imports from one year to the next. This may occur when a quota is underfilled one year and filled the next. The full quota may be augmented by a normal growth factor and carry over. Surges are closely monitored on items that have high import penetration and/or high volume.

Swing. The use of a portion of an unfilled limit for a category to increase the restraint limit of another category up to a certain percentage (usually 7%).

Transshipment. The exportation of goods from one country which are, in fact, the product of another country.

Visa and certification system. A certification by the exporting country's government that the articles originated or were produced in that country.

White Paper. The Carter administration's apparel/textile trade program made public on 15 February 1979.

Source: USITC, 1981.

References

The references consist of three sections: books and articles, a list of individuals whom I interviewed, and a list of newspapers and periodicals.

Books and articles listed are only those works cited in the study. Naturally, numerous other works not cited here provided background for either the theory or the empirical research.

Over a three-year period (1978-1981), I interviewed over 125 individuals in seven countries. In many cases, the same people were interviewed three or four times. Although open-ended, interviews were structured to gauge the degree to which decision makers perceived international structural and other factors as an influence on their behavior. Statements were almost always cross-checked with published and unpublished material as well as with other individuals. The list of individuals is categorized by country or association. The position indicated is either the last position of the individual related to textile and apparel trade or the current position.

Numerous newspapers and periodicals were consulted over a thirty-year time span. These are listed in the final section but are not specifically referenced by date.

A number of documents of an internal nature were made available to me by various individuals. These were used for background and to provide leads for purposes of interviewing individuals about specific events. By agreement with those individuals, these are not cited. In all cases, the information was verified with other publicly available sources and interviews.

BOOKS AND ARTICLES

Aggarwal, Vinod. "The U.S. Textile Policy." In *Manual for Textile Negotiators.* UNCTAD Doc. MD/TX/1. Geneva. July 1982.

———. "The Unraveling of the Multi-Fiber Arrangement, 1981: An Examination of International Regime Change," *International Organization* 37 (Autumn 1983).

Aggarwal, Vinod, and Pierre Allan. "Evolution in Bargaining Theories: Toward an Integrated Approach to Explain Strategies of the Weak." Paper presented at the American Political Science Association Meeting. Chicago. September 1983.

Aggarwal, Vinod, and Linda Cahn. "The Political Foundations and Implications of Trade Controls: A Conceptual Framework." Paper presented at the Peace Science Society International (Western Section) Conference. Stanford University. February 1978.

Aggarwal, Vinod, with Stephan Haggard. "The Domestic and International Politics of Protection in the U.S. Textile and Apparel Industries." In *American Industry in International Competition.* Ed. John Zysman and Laura Tyson. Ithaca: Cornell University Press, 1983.

ATMI. Minutes of the Foreign Trade Committee of the American Textile Manufacturers Institute. Various.

Bardan, Benjamin. "The Cotton Textile Agreement, 1962-1972," *Journal of World Trade Law* (1973): 8-35.

Bhagwati, Jagdish, and T. N. Srinivasan. *Journal of International Economics* 6 (1976): 317-336.

Blake, David, and Robert Walters. *The Politics of Global Economic Relations.* 2d ed. Englewood Cliffs, N. J.: Prentice-Hall, 1983.

Borrus, Michael. "Slow Growth and Competitive Erosion in the U.S. Steel Industry." In *American Industry in International Competition.* Ed. John Zysman and Laura Tyson. Ithaca: Cornell University Press, 1983.

Brandis, R. Buford. "A Short History of U.S. Textile Import Quotas." American Textile Manufacturers Institute. Washington, D.C., 1979.

British Spinners' and Doublers' Association. "International Trade in Cotton Textiles." Manchester, November 1965. Unpublished document.

Cowhey, Peter, and Edward Long. "Testing Theories of Regime Change: Hegemonic Decline or Surplus Capacity?" *International Organization* 37 (Spring 1983).

Curtis, Thomas. Congressional Record Testimony (1966).

Curtis, Thomas, and John Vastine. *The Kennedy Round and the Future of American Trade.* New York: Praeger, 1971.

Davis, Ralph. "The Rise of Protection in England, 1689-1786," *The Economic History Review* 19 (August 1966).

Destler, I. M., Haruhiro Fukui, and Hideo Sato. *The Textile Wrangle.* Ithaca: Cornell University Press, 1979.

Donaldson, John. *International Economic Relations: A Treatise on World Economy and World Politics.* New York: Longmans, 1928.

Dunn, Frederick. *Peacemaking and the Settlement with Japan.* Princeton: Princeton University Press, 1963.

Europe. Press releases issued by the Agence Presse de Informacion. Paris and Brussels. Various issues.

Europe Information. *The European Community and the Textile Arrangements.* Brussels: Commission of the European Communities, n.d.

Evans, John. *The Kennedy Round in American Trade Policy: The Twilight of the GATT?* Cambridge, Mass.: Harvard University Press, 1971.

Fellner, William. *Competition Among the Few.* New York: Alfred A. Knopf, 1949.

Finlayson, J., and Mark Zacher. "The GATT and the Regulation of Trade Barriers: Regime Dynamics and Effects," *International Organization* 35 (1981).

Gastrell, William. *Our Trade in the World in Relation to Foreign Competition 1885-1895.* London: Chapman, 1897.

GATT. Documents, Series Com/Tex/SB, Com/Tex/W, Cot/W, Cot/M, Tex/ W, Com/Tex, L/, Spec. Various issues (1959-1981).

———. *International Trade.* Various issues.

———. *A Study of Cotton Textiles.* Geneva, 1966.

George, Alexander. "Research Proposal: Case Studies and Theory Development in Political Science." MS. Stanford University, October 1981.

———. "Case Studies and Theory Development: The Method of Structured Focussed Comparison." In *Diplomacy: New Approaches in History, Theory, and Policy.* Ed. Paul Gordon. New York: Free Press, 1979.

———. "The Causal Nexus Between Cognitive Beliefs and Decision-making Behavior: The Operational Code Belief System." In *Psychological Models in International Politics.* Ed. L. Falkowski. Boulder: Westview Press, 1980.

Gibson, Q. *The Logic of Social Enquiry.* London: Routledge & Kegan Paul, 1960.

Gilpin, Robert. *U.S. Power and the Multinational Corporation.* New York: Basic Books, 1975.

Goldstein, Judith. "The State, Industrial Interests and Foreign Economic Policy: American Commerical Policy in the Postwar Period." Presented at the National Science Foundation Conference on the Politics and Economics of Trade Policy. Minneapolis. October 1981.

Haas, Ernst. "Why Collaborate? Issue Linkage and International Regimes," *World Politics* 32 (April 1980): 357-405.

———. "Words Can Hurt You, Or Who Said What to Whom About Regimes," *International Organization* (Spring 1982).

Haggard, Stephan. "Pathways from the Periphery: The Newly Industrializing Countries in the International System." Ph.D. diss. University of California, Berkeley, 1983.

Helleiner, Gerard. *Intra-Firm Trade and the Developing Countries.* New York: St. Martin's Press, 1981.

Hirschman, Albert. *National Power and the Structure of Foreign Trade.* Berkeley: University of California Press, 1945.

Hong Kong. *Trade Statistics.* Various issues.

———. *Trade Bulletins.* Various issues.

Hughes, Helen, ed. *Prospects for Partnership: Industrialization and Trade Policies in the 1980s.* Baltimore: Johns Hopkins University Press, 1973.

Hunsberger, Warren. *Japan and the United States in World Trade.* New York: Harper and Row, 1964.

Juvet, Jean-Luis. "The Cotton Industry and World Trade," *Journal of World Trade Law* (September/October 1967): 540-563.

Katzenstein, Peter, ed. *Between Power and Plenty.* Madison: University of Wisconsin, 1978.

Keesing, Donald, and Martin Wolf. *Textile Quotas Against Developing Countries.* Trade Policy Research Centre. London, 1980.

Keohane, Robert. "The Theory of Hegemonic Stability and Changes in International Economic Regimes, 1967-1977." In *Change in the International System.* Ed. Ole Holsti, Randolph Siverson, and Alexander George. Boulder: Westview Press, 1980.

———. "The Demand for International Regimes," *International Organization* 36 (Spring 1982).

Keohane, Robert, and Joseph Nye. *Power and Interdependence.* Boston: Little, Brown, 1977.

Kindleberger, Charles. "Group Behavior and International Trade," *Journal of Political Economy* 59 (1951).

———. *The World in Depression, 1929-39.* Berkeley, Los Angeles, London: University of California Press, 1973.

Krasner, Stephen. *Defending the National Interest.* Princeton: Princeton University Press, 1978.

———. "State Power and the Structure of International Trade," *World Politics* 28 (April 1976): 317-347.

———. "The Tokyo Round: Particularistic Interests and Prospects for Stability in the Global Trading System," *International Studies Quarterly* 23 (December 1979): 491-531.

———. "Introduction: International Regimes and Structural Constraints," *International Organization* 36 (Spring 1982).

Lazar, Harvey. *Politics and Public Policy in the Lancashire Textile Industry.* Ph.D. diss. University of London, 1975.

Lipson, Charles. "The Transformation of Trade: The Sources and Effects of Regime Change," *International Organization* 36 (Spring 1982).

Lynch, John. *Towards an Orderly Market: An Intensive Study of Japan's Voluntary Quota In Cotton Textile Exports.* Tokyo: Sophia University Press, 1968.

McKeown, Timothy. "Tariffs and Hegemonic Stability Theory," *International Organization* 37 (Winter 1983).

Maizels, Alfred. *Industrial Growth and World Trade.* Cambridge: Cambridge University Press for the National Institute for Economic and Social Research, 1963.

Meier, Gerald. "Economic Aspects of Orderly Marketing Agreements." Paper presented at the American Society of International Law Panel (April 1978).

Miles, Caroline. "Protection and Adjustment Problems of the UK Textile Industry." In *Protection and Subsidies in Britain and Germany.* Ed. W. M. Corden and G. Fels. Boulder: Westview Press, 1976.

North, Robert, and Linda Fields. "Trade as an Influence in the International Politics of Japan: A Comparison of Pre-War and Post-War Patterns." MS. Stanford University (December 1974).

Nye, Joseph. "UNCTAD: Poor Nation's Pressure Group." In *The Anatomy of Influence: Decision Making in International Organization.* Ed. Robert Cox and Harold Jacobson. New Haven: Yale University Press, 1973.

OECD. *Modern Cotton Industry.* Paris, 1965.

Organski, A. F. K. *World Politics.* New York: A. Knopf, 1968.

Patterson, Gardner. *Discrimination in International Trade: The Policy Issues, 1945-1965.* Princeton: Princeton University Press, 1966.

Preeg, Ernest. *Traders and Diplomats: An Analysis of the Kennedy Round Negotiations under the General Agreement on Tariffs and Trade.* Washington, D.C.: The Brookings Institution, 1970.

Reich, Robert. "Beyond Free Trade," *Foreign Affairs* 61 (Spring 1983): 773-804.

Ris, Williams. "Escape Clause Relief Under the Trade Act of 1974: New Standards, Same Results," *Columbia Journal of Transnational Law* (1977).

Sato, Hideo. *The Crisis of an Alliance: The Politics of US-Japanese Textile Trade, 1969-1971.* Ph.D. diss. University of Chicago, 1979.

Scherer, F. *Industrial Market Structure and Performance.* Chicago: Rand McNally, 1970.

Simon, Herbert. "The Architecture of Complexity." Proceedings of the American Philosophical Society (December 1962).

Stein, Arthur. "Coordination and Collaboration: Regimes in an Anarchic World," *International Organization* 36 (Spring 1982): 299-324.

Strange, Susan. "The Study of Transnational Relations," *International Affairs* (July 1976): 333-345.

———. "The Management of Surplus Capacity: How Does Theory Stand Up to Protectionism, Seventies Style?" *International Organization* 33 (Summer 1979): 303-334.

Sullivan, Barry. "Down with Protectionism," *Euromoney* (October 1983).

Textile Council. *Cotton and Allied Textiles.* Manchester, 1969.

de la Torre, Jose. "Public Intervention in the European Clothing Industries," *Journal of World Trade* 15 (March-April 1981).

United Kingdom Board of Trade. *Trade and Navigations Acts.* London, 1954, 1956, 1959.

UNCTAD. Document Series TD. Various issues.

———. Manual for Textile Negotiators. Doc. MD/TX/1. Geneva (July 1982).

United Nations *Yearbook of International Trade Statistics.* New York: United Nations Statistics Office. Various years.

———. *U.N. Commodity Trade Statistics, Series D.* New York: United Nations Statistics Office. Various years.

United States Department of Commerce. *Commodity Exports by Country* and *Imports of Merchandise for Consumption.* Washington, D.C.

———. *U.S. Imports of Textiles, Apparel and Related Manufactures and Comparison with U.S. Production and Exports, 1954-1960.* Washington, D.C.

United States. *Department of State Bulletin.* Various issues.

———. *Twenty First Annual Report of the President of the U.S. in the Trade*

Agreements Programs. Washington, D.C.: GPO, 1976.

United States Senate. *Problems of the Domestic Textile Industry.* Committee On Interstate and Foreign Commerce, 1959-1963.

USITC. *The History and Current Status of the Multifiber Arrangement.* Publication 850 (January 1978).

――――. *The Multifiber Arrangement, 1973-1980.* Publication 1130 (March 1981).

Wallerstein, Immanuel. *The Modern World System: Capitalist Agriculture and the Origins of the World Economy in the Sixteenth Century.* New York: Academic Press, 1974.

Walters, Robert. "America's Declining Industrial Competitiveness: Protectionism, the Marketplace, and the State," *PS* 16 (Winter 1983): 25-33.

Waltz, Kenneth. *Theory of International Politics.* Reading: Addison Wesley, 1979.

White House. *Memorandum of Disapproval.* Washington, D.C.: Office of the White House Press Secretary (November 1978).

――――. *Administration Textile Program.* Washington, D.C.: Office of the White House Press Secretary (March 1979).

Young, Oran. "International Regimes: Problems of Concept Formation," *World Politics* (April 1980): 331-356.

Zysman, John, and Laura Tyson, eds. *American Industry in International Competition.* Ithaca: Cornell University Press, 1983.

INTERVIEWS

UNITED STATES

Bale, Harvey. U.S. Delegation to the Multilateral Trade Negotiations.

Bennett, James. Office of Textiles, Department of Commerce.

Blackman, Herbert. Associate Deputy Under Secretary of Labor for International Affairs.

Brandis, Buford. Director, International Divison, American Textile Manufacturers Institute.

Brew, William. Assistant Chief, Textile Division, Department of State.

Dabney, Henrietta. Amalgamated Clothing and Textile Workers Union.

Daniels, Michael. Attorney and Partner in Daniels, Houlihan & Palmeter (law firm representing numerous LDCs).

Garel, Arthur. Director, Office of Textiles, Department of Commerce.

Jackson, Mattie. Vice President and Manager of San Francisco Joint Board, International Ladies Garment Workers Union.

Jurich, Anthony. Former Chief Textile Negotiator (MFA negotiations).

Kearns, Henry. Former Assistant Secretary of State and President, Import-Export Bank.

Kramer, Irving. Assistant Director, International Commodities Division, Department of Labor.

Lamar, Harold. Chief Assistant to the Chairman, Subcommittee on Trade of the Committee on House, Ways, and Means, U.S. House of Representatives.

Levin, Ronald. Director, International Agreements and Monitoring Division, Office of Textiles, Department of Commerce.

Martello, Philip. Commodity Industry Analyst, International Trade Commission.

Nehmer, Stanley. Former Deputy Assistant Secretary of Resources, Department of Commerce. President, Economic Consulting Services, Inc. (consultant to textile and apparel groups).

Phelan, Harry. Former Director, Office of Textiles, Department of State, and U.S. representative to the Textiles Surveillance Body (TSB).

Priestland, Carl. Economist, American Apparel Manufacturers Association.

Smith, Michael. Deputy Special Trade Representative and Former Chief Textile Negotiator (first MFA renewal, 1977).

St. John, John. Chief, Textiles Division, Department of State.

Tagliani, William. Office of Textiles, Department of State.

Taylor, John. Textile, Leather Products, and Apparel Division, International Trade Commission.

Trezise, Philip. Former Assistant Secretary of State for Economic Affairs.

UNITED KINGDOM

Burns, K. F. X. Counselor, Deputy Permanent Representative, U.K. Mission to the U.N.

Cable, Vincent. Overseas Development Institute.

Callan, Roger. Chemical and Textile Division, Department of Industry.

Corran, Hugh. Imperial Chemical Industries.

Crompton, D. Chemical and Textiles Division, Department of Industry.

Douglas, Stuart. Director, Man-Made Fibers Federation.

Eely, Jane. BCICE (clothing association).

Ford John. Senior Marketing Manager, Shirley Institute.

Godden, A. J. Chief Economist, Imperial Chemical Industries.

Irvin, Joe. Trade Union Congress.

Kinchen, Richard. Foreign and Commonwealth Office.

Longworth, John. Textile Support Campaign and Oldham and District Textile Employers' Association.

Love, E. L. The Textile Institute.

McCluney, Ian. Foreign and Commonwealth Office.

McMillan, Neal. Department of Trade.

Murray, A. W. Department of Trade.

Purvis, Colin. Deputy Director, British Textile Confederation.

Rothwell, Sidney. Director (Commercial), British Textile Employers' Association.

Roberson, Barbara. Trade Policy Research Centre.

Skelton, D. H. Secretary, British Importers' Confederation.

Smallbone, Teresa. Consumers' Association.

Spencer-Phillips, Jean. Government Relations, Courtaulds Limited.

Thompson, Brian. National Economic Development Organization.

France

Brender, Anton. CEPII (research institute).
Champigneulles, Claude. French Mission to the EEC.
DeBandt, Jacques. University of Nanterre. (Consultant to the EEC.)
De Guerre, Patrick. Subdireccion Textile du Ministere de l'Industrie.
Leurent, Jean-Noel. Director of Marketing, Rhone-Poulenc.
Leflon, Michel. Commercial Attaché in Geneva.
Rousseau, M. UIL.
Scialom, Michel. Ministere de l'Economie.
Stoffaes, Christian. Centre d'Etudes et de Prevision, Ministere de l'Industrie.

Italy

Bedin, Dott. FULTA (labor organization).
Berrini, G. Snia Viscosa.
Capuani, Paolo. GEPI (state-owned enterprise).
Castagno, M. Commercio Estero.
Collasanti, Dott. Associazione de Fibre Chimiche.
Cosentino, Dott. Ministero dell' Industria.
Cuatruci, Dott. FILTEA (labor organization).
Galdi, Federico. Vice Minister, Commercio Estero.
Giardino, Sig. FILTEA (labor organization).
Mascolini, M. Ministero dell' Industria.
Merola, Dott. Partecipazione Statali.
Moro, Roberto. Federtessile (pan-textile association).
Pizzini, F. Christian Democratic Party.
Rosio, Dott. Ministero dell' Industria.
Rossi, Dott. Confindustria (pan-industrialist organization).
Sardi, Giovanni. Representative to the EEC.
Torotora, Beniamino. TESCON (state-owned enterprise in textiles and apparel).
Vitali, Ing. Ministero dell' Industria.

West Germany

Berzau, Heinz. Bundesministerium für Wirtschaft.
Gass, Ms. Gesamttextil. (Employers' Textile Organization.)
Hirth, Dr. Industrie Vereinigung Chemiefasen, Frankfurt.
Kroner, Dr. Industrie Vereinigung Chemiefasen.
Lange, Mr. German Delegation to the GATT.
Rothenbucher, Nicholas. Delegate to the EEC.

EEC

Beck, John. EEC Representative to the TSB.
Coker, John. Principal Administrator, DG 3, Directorate-General for Industrial Affairs and the Internal Market.

Hall, A. John. DG 3.
Heisler, Peter. DG 1, Directorate-General for External Relations.
LeBail-Elles, François. Office of the Special Trade Representative, DG 1.
Tran Van Thinh. Former Chief Textile Negotiator (MFA renewal) and Special Representative, Geneva.

INTERNATIONAL ORGANIZATIONS (INCLUDING INDUSTRY ASSOCIATIONS)

Abbas, S. Manufactures Division, UNCTAD.
Bagchi, Mr. GATT Consultant on Textiles.
Bonus, Jacques. CIRFS (International Rayon and Synthetic Fibres Committee).
Davies, Robin. Counselor, Assistant to the Chairman, TSB.
Depooter, Mr. AEIH (pan-European clothing association).
Martins, Mr. Comitextil (pan-European textile association).
Gibbs, J. Murray. UNCTAD.
Salib, Michele. GATT.
Sampson, Gary. Manufactures Division, UNCTAD.
Tullock, Peter. GATT.
Tumlir, Jan. Director, Trade Intelligence Division, GATT.
Wolf, Martin. World Bank.

OTHER COUNTRIES

Alvarez, Eric. Mexican delegate (Geneva Mission).
Das, B. L. Resident Representative of India to UNCTAD and GATT.
Dassen, Marie. Sri Lanka Delegate (Geneva Mission).
Hall, Roderick. Minister (Commercial), Australian Permanent Mission to the U.N.
Hamid, Mohammed. Pakistan's Economic Counselor, Geneva.
Jayanama, Voraputh. Thailand's Representative to the TSB.
Kim, Shi-Hyung. Attaché, Permanent Mission to International Organizations and Korea's Representative to the TSB.
Kujirai, Koichi. Counselor, Japanese Delegation and Representative to the TSB.
Martin, Robert. Economic Counselor and Canadian Representative to the TSB.
Patek, Stanislaus. Swedish Delegate to the TSB.
Suarez, J. Colombian Delegate and Representative to the TSB.
Tsao, Peter. Chief Hong Kong Delegate to the U.N. and Textile Negotiator.
Wise, Peter. Hong Kong Delegate to Mission in London.
Yamada, Hiroshi. Japanese Delegation to the OECD.

NEWSPAPERS AND PERIODICALS

Business Week
Charlotte Observer
Daily News Record (Fairchild Publications)
The Economist (London)

Economic Intelligence Unit
Far Eastern Economic Review
Far Eastern Economic Review Yearbook
Financial Times
Fortune
The Guardian
Japan Times
Journal of Commerce
Los Angeles Times
The New Republic
New York Times
South China Morning Post (Hong Kong)
Textile Asia
Textile Month
Textile World
The Times
Wall Street Journal
Washington Post

Index

Designer: UC Press Staff
Compositor: Janet Sheila Brown
Printer: Braun-Brumfield
Binder: Braun-Brumfield
Text: 10/12 Paladium
Display: Paladium